INDIFFERENCE AND REPETITION

Indifference and Repetition; or, Modern Freedom and Its Discontents

Frank Ruda

TRANSLATED BY HEATHER H. YEUNG

FORDHAM UNIVERSITY PRESS   NEW YORK   2024

This book was originally published in German as Frank Ruda, *Indifferenz und Wiederholung: Freiheit in der Moderne* by Konstanz University Press, 2018.

Fordham University Press has no responsibility for the persistence or accuracy of URLs for external or third-party Internet websites referred to in this publication and does not guarantee that any content on such websites is, or will remain, accurate or appropriate.

Fordham University Press also publishes its books in a variety of electronic formats. Some content that appears in print may not be available in electronic books.

Visit us online at www.fordhampress.com.

Library of Congress Cataloging-in-Publication Data available online at https://catalog.loc.gov.

Printed in the United States of America

26 25 24   5 4 3 2 1

First edition

Contents

Foreword

Frank Ruda's Philosophical Oeuvre

Alain Badiou

To understand the place and significance of Frank Ruda's writings, it is, I believe, necessary to have present in mind a synthetic vision of "classical" philosophy, which was born just after the scientific discoveries of the sixteenth century and which continues its course today.

We are able to distinguish in the "occidental" history of this philosophy, as well as in history tout court, three grand creative orientations that are symbolically aligned with three proper names and with three languages from the moment on when "philosophy" ceased to speak Latin, as it did in the phase that was dominated by the Christian predication. In France and largely in French: Descartes. In Great Britain: Hume. In Germany: Kant. The first orientation proposes an integral rational affirmation, which was supported by the spectacular renaissance of mathematics and science in general. The second opposes the "dogmatism" of the first with a sort of rationalized skeptical caution, a manifest impossibility for the human being to reach some dogmatic certitude, which concerns being qua being as well as the universe. The third responds to the second as well as to the first by distinguishing the knowledge of what appears to us in lived experience from the pretension to know anything "absolutely," but also by salvaging the link of thought to the absolute in the register of moral action and its imperatives.

My friend Frank Ruda is German, and I am French. Our speculative routes are marked by our origins: I claim for myself explicitly the mathematized rationalism of Descartes, just as Frank moves in a subtle way in the thicket of German philosophy that begins with Kant.

It is this movement whose origin and subtlety I want to describe, not in detail (since the whole world reads the works of Frank Ruda), but only very briefly.

The claim that thought cannot access the Absolute through means of a strictly scientific type, like axioms, theorems, demonstrations and experiences, for Frank, distances thought from all scientific positivism and thus from the Cartesian ambience. But that thought can however move itself *in the Absolute* is, if one can say so, absolutely possible, without its having to necessarily pass through science and also without its needing to take recourse to morality and the gaze of God.

This is why I can speak of a dialectical internationalism of Frank Ruda. One can identify him neither with French Cartesianism, to which he affirmatively opposes some accents of Hume's relativism, nor with Kant's morality, to which he will oppose some parts of Cartesian absolutism. Finally, in all three cases, he concedes and refuses: Hume is somewhat right against Descartes, Descartes is somewhat right against Kant, and Kant, in the end, is largely right against the other two to the degree to which he is also wrong.

One will ask: How is this possible? Well, to do this, Frank invents a new reading of a fourth villain, who is no one else than Hegel.

To understand this tour de force, one must see clearly that the question that Frank finally poses at his triple origin (Descartes, Hume, Kant) is all at once the question of the Absolute. The classical question in this matter is very clear: Through which paths must thought pass to at least "touch" the absolute? Descartes answers according to the mathematic model: through an irrefutable proof of the existence of God. Kant answers: through the indisputable existence of the moral imperative. Hume answers: through a belief without any warranty.

This brings us to the very heart of Frank Ruda's theoretical choice: All three pose the question badly. Why? Because all three declare that philosophy is a conquest—difficult, laborious, even impossible, or chosen in the void—of the Absolute. They define philosophy as the mental path of thought toward the Absolute, as examination of material possibilities, as statement of success or failure of the road thus traced. Yet—and this is Frank Ruda's *coup de force*— *one must think that the Absolute is not the laborious result of the philosophical path, but that it is its initial condition.*

A sentence, a single sentence of another towering German, namely Hegel, Frank's true absolute master, serves then as a compass for a march which moves in some sense backward: *"The absolute is with us all along."*

Everything then changes: One must be able to think under the guarantee of the initial absoluteness. Thus, philosophy can unfold itself according to a sort of immanent historicity, as it does for Hegel in *The Phenomenology of Spirit*, or according to a strict conceptual sequence, as it does in the *Logic*. In truth, under the law of an Absolute present from the beginning, the rigor of these liaisons covers the necessity of the history of thought as well as that of its final organization. This is how Hegel summarizes it in his glorious affirmation: "The becoming is the being-there of the concept."

It is this Hegel, with the certainty which is given by the originary presence of the Absolute and the adventure that is to constantly remain on the path of its final appearance, which governs the dense, affirmative, suddenly poetic style of the admirable oeuvre of my friend Frank Ruda—this thinker of the today—in all its details, under the sign of the captivating form of the "always already there."

Preface to the English Edition: Freedom as Slavery

"Freedom—but for which class and for what purpose?"
        —V. I. LENIN, *SEVENTH ALL-RUSSIA CONGRESS OF SOVIETS*

When work stops, freedom begins. Or, when work seems to stop, a period seems to begin which we identify with freedom. This time is when we do whatever we want, enjoy whatever and however we please, and use our bodies as we like. When we make this move from the working week to leisure time it is, as Silvia Federici argued in 1975, as if we move from culture back to nature, yet at the same time it is not. Since the nature to which we seem to return to is always already a cultural one. It is, more precisely, a nature produced and organized by culture. But because such a nature nevertheless appears as if in the time when we are "off" work, in the time where we just are how we "naturally" are, this very time is also marked and determined by the pleasure in naked bodies and in sex, viz., the stripping off to a naturist state, and finding all the pleasure that the workday does not allow. In this way, sex appears to be culturally placed as the opposite or as the other of work; when work is done (for now), there is sex. And thus it is sex that appears to open up a space of freedom, of free self-expression, of liberation (from labor);[1] "a space of freedom in which we can presumably be our true selves."[2] Everything is rationalized during the working week, and then there is the time and the space for release; a time and space that seems unregulated, that is not rationally organized and can therefore even seem to engage with the irrational—for who could explain what turns us on and why—and this is the time and space of sex.

Since we are never really moving out of culture, the space and time of sexual nature and freedom we are engaging in is unavoidably culturally framed.

Even when (and this is Federici's argument) we are supposed to be fully (re-duced to just being) our bodies over the weekend and after labor time, nota-bly during "love-making time,"[3] this time itself is at least doubly (culturally) conditioned and (pre)determined. It is therefore not and can never be free, even though it may seem so. Why? First, because it is determined in its function. It is supposed to provide release from the strict regime of labor. What is supposed to happen in the time off labor is therefore predetermined and not free: It is the time to reproduce labor. This functional determination is thus what frames it. Second, even though this is supposed to be an unregulated time and there-fore "free time," *when* it is going to take place and when it is going to end is entirely prescribed, and in this sense, it can never be anything but a "paren-thesis."[4] Such a prescription is derived from and ordained by the existing re-gime of work. Thus, the entire constitution of that which is supposed to be free of the time of labor and its constraints does not depend on itself but is in fact constrained by the very thing it appears to be demarcated from. So, sex is not the paradigm of freedom, since such a freedom is not a freedom as such; rather, it is functionally and temporally determined and framed.

From this diagnosis—that whoever is supposed to be free is not really free, because its function is determined from the outside and its temporal occurrence and framing is derived from the dominant form of organizing labor—Federici infers a peculiar antagonism, its manifestation and its form: that for some what defines free time, the time *off* labor, is the time when others have to work. So, such "free" time, the time of pleasure, is also the time when others have to give pleasure (and have to enjoy it—it is their "duty to please").[5] The latter's work is reproductive and is thereby placed in the service of the reproduction of the laboring powers of the former. This apparent condition is one which can appear as "a schizophrenic condition"[6] because we are dealing with a temporal realm that is supposedly free but which in its entire constitution is structurally unfree, and whose organization is both alleviated and seemingly dissolved by splitting the realm into two. In the time *off* work, only some do not work. Others do. Those who do, those who exist in *this* time *of* work, are expected to and tasked with providing release for those who have stopped working (but note that even for those who have stopped working this pause is temporary—they will return to the time of work after the time off work ends). And so even if the time off work is the time of intimacy and sex, and this is the paradigm of free self-expression, for some this time is the time of work—it is labor time.

For Federici, in the middle of the 1970s, this was a crucial implication of the organizational device that is the bourgeois family, and was seen most clearly in the reproductive duty that women were—structurally—obliged to fulfill. In

Federici's sense, then, sex is work (and in its fullest sense is work only for women), and "sexual work" (endorsed by a rigidly imposed heterosexual-reproductive framework) "is still one of the main occupations of women and prostitution underlines every sexual encounter."[7] Thus Federici affords us a perspective which complicates and works against the background of the famous claim about the bourgeois family made by Marx and Engels in the *Communist Manifesto*; that the bourgeois family was never per se obverse to prostitution but rather not only tolerated it but in fact encouraged its reproduction, since it "has reduced the family relation to a mere money relation."[8] There is something prostitutional about the various ways in which capitalist societies organize intimacy which one may describe as the constitution of a "pornographic age"[9] in which "women's work and women's labor are buried deeply in the heart of the capitalist social and economic structure."[10]

Reproductive labor is, after its exhaustion or its unavoidable death, the labor of reconstituting this labor power by offering release through another embodiment of labor power (a child). But for Federici such labor is invisible and gendered: "those who carry out the invisible labor of reproduction to keep the body and soul together, raise the young, nurse infants, give birth to future generations"[11]—women—are invisible not in general but *as workers*. It would be a hard case to make that this has generally disappeared from contemporary societies, but certainly in the 1970s as Federici is writing, we are confronted with a situation where labor is performed and structurally invisibilized as the very labor that it is. According to a standard Marxian account[12] this is rather obvious in its invisibility—that is, if we understand the wage expressed as the collection of commodities (food, rent, cigarettes, etc.) that are needed within a particular (and historically specific) society to reproduce the labor power of the worker, so the reproductive labor done by women is part of this very commodity-collection. Her work is invisibly paid (and accounted) for, without even being properly acknowledged (and visibly paid for [individually]). Reproductive labor, even though it is absolutely crucial—so crucial that Federici and others claim that "reproduction precedes social production"[13]—is only indirectly waged and therefore is paid for in a way that reinforces existing social antagonisms and hierarchies. This manifests itself in the antagonism of free versus labor time, structuring the realm that is supposed to be outside of work, and vice versa, since the free time *off* labor, the time of freedom, is structurally not only *not* really free, it is also the time when only some can feel free (or, really, when some can have the illusion, despite their existing unfreedom, of feeling free), because they nevertheless structurally rely on the others who are forced—and repeatedly initiated such that they learn—to (like) do(ing) the very invisible unfree labor upon which their feeling of freedom rests.[14]

   Thus, even after the abolishment of slavery and the (moral) condemnation of prostitution, capitalism from this perspective is a system in which wage slavery relies on a generalized and invisibilized structural prostitution; wage slavery is upheld on the backs of "female domestic slavery."[15] Capitalist political economy is, according to this perspective, ultimately less about free exchange and trade, but rather, for the majority of people, about a peculiar non-choice between (wage-)slavery and (unwaged-)slavery. It is a structural slavery of different modalities, a form of anonymous domination that produces peculiar slaves without (direct) owners—even as there is present quite clearly an ownership relationship in many sexual and personal relationships. But is bourgeois society, modern capitalism that abolishes and overcomes feudal structures (arising from a crisis of the feudal system), not born from a claim to freedom? Born, more precisely, from a revolution that claimed equality, liberty, and solidarity for all?

In 2008, two hundred years after the official abolition of the slave trade, Angela Davis gave a lecture at the Metropolitan State College in Denver, during so-called Black History Month (an institution she problematized as having become "an occasion to generate profit,"[16] where people are asked to celebrate it by buying—in Davis's example—Walmart products). This lecture was titled "The Meaning of Freedom." Her opening observation is that everyone is so relieved about the official abolition of slavery that they seek to forget about it altogether, seek to treat it as if it were "a kind of nightmare," so that "we try not to think about it except in abstract terms, and we assume that it will go away."[17] But here a problem shows its truly nightmarish face, and this problem becomes very quickly twofold: if we consider the declaration of slavery to be a thing of the past and abolished, and observe that this allows everyone the relief that there is no longer any—legal(ized)—form of slavery, and then, following the not unsurprising claim that if one can abolish slavery "simply by proclamation, a few words here, any by a clause in the Constitution,"[18] it is then somewhat surprising to find that this proclamation never articulates and explains what in its view constitutes slavery. This is one side of the problem. That without clear definition, any abolishment of "slavery" can therefore without any problem be in line with the ongoing existence of de facto slavery. For how is it possible to abolish something if "we don't even clearly know what was supposed to be abolished?"[19] How is it possible to abolish something that remains not even ill-defined but instead structurally undefined?
   This first side of the problem demonstrates the ease of the unthinking maintenance of a position where one (nominally) abolishes without (really) abolishing.[20] This can mean just abolishing the use of a certain term and word but not changing the practice or the thing the word concerns or signifies at

all. It can mean just to displace or rename. The abolition of slavery *by word* can therefore and without any problem come with, for example, what Federici refers to as domestic slavery *by deed*. But because this latter type of slavery is neither defined nor addressed as what it is, it does not come under the terms of the slavery that must be abolished. We thus encounter a practice in which one acts if one is agreeing with the fact that there is a problem and it needs fixing; but fixing it means to make the (perception of the) problem go away. It means to invisibilize the very thing that one seeks to make disappear, because, in this way, it seems to have disappeared. Making invisible and making inexistent, or abolition, thereby become synonyms. Yet—of course—they are not. This is why, surprisingly again, after the abolition of slavery, there continue to exist—depending on one's definition—forms of slavery. Since people still buy and sell other people's time, or, through the selling of (life-)time which is embodied by a person or worker, buy and sell other people (tout court). But one still acts knowing that there is slavery, yet as if one does not really believe there were slavery. One such example here, raised by Davis, is that of the player trade in sports. Are those people (athletes) not treated as if they were property? And, following this, what "about coerced labor?"[21] So, and this is the question Davis asks, why is it that we assume that slavery no longer exists even if there is still, quite visibly, coerced labor everywhere; and even when people are still treated as if they are property, and maybe even as if they are chattel (belonging to and sold by such and such a team, for example)? Sometimes a liberation from slavery allows the continuation of invisible (but structural) organizations of slavery on another level.

Following this, the other side of the problem is that structures of "enslavement . . . were translated into the terms of freedom—slavery translated into the terms of freedom."[22] It is not only unclear what we mean by slavery—a thing that is supposed to be abolished—but it is also unclear what is meant by freedom.[23] Davis, because of this very reason, problematizes the existence of prisons: They can only operate in the way they officially operate if they only imprison free people, but, strangely, most of the people they imprison are from socioeconomic backgrounds that rather harshly seem to limit their freedom.[24] So, what if in this and other occasions freedom threatens to become no more than a new name for slavery?[25] Davis indicates precisely this, remarking that "if slavery was declared dead, it was simultaneously reincarnated through new institutions, new practices, new ideologies."[26] Or again differently: "It's not democracy, it's capitalism, or it's a democracy that uses capitalism as its model, that sees the free market as the paradigm for freedom and that sees competition as the paradigm for freedom."[27] "Freedom" is unfreedom. To recast the old phrase: first time as (visible) slavery, second time as (invisible) slavery . . .

In 1919, Lenin noted that under present economic and political—that is, capitalist—conditions, it is important to refrain from using the word "freedom."[28] The reason for Lenin's claim was mainly ideological and directly concerns the second nature that is generated from our everyday practices. The more the signifier "freedom" is used under unfree conditions, the more deceptive it becomes. The more we get used to referring to ourselves as free beings, the more we believe, under conditions that are those of unfreedom, that we are truly free. There is an inverted Pascalian dimension to freedom under conditions of unfreedom: it is no longer a "kneel down and you will (start to) believe!"; it is a "believe (you are free) and you will kneel down (while not noticing that you are kneeling)!" For Lenin, this was the result of the practice of (over)use of specific signifiers that, through such practice, generate a disorienting effect and deceptive impact. Potentially all signifiers can produce such an effect, but (for Lenin) it was mostly those signifiers that suggest a kind of orientation (in a "for or against x" way),[29] whose orientation therefore precisely means that, through wrong use or overuse, they can disorient. When signifiers of disorientation become pertinent and dominant, disorientation becomes the principle of subjectivization; it is only, ultimately, disorientation that is subjectivized; the principle of subjectivization thus blocks what it was supposed to initiate in the process of initiation.[30] I am disoriented when I understand myself to be free and when I feel free when I am not. For example, when I am Google-searching things as I please, and even when I am undoubtedly knowledgeable of my being de facto surveilled in this practice, I feel as if I can *freely* Google-search things, can feel (perhaps even feel furtively) that no one is watching my moves. This is an embodiment of disorientation. Signifiers of disorientation can generate a peculiar, notably practical suspension of the very knowledge one has about the constitutive features and coordinates of one's practice and the world. Signifiers of disorientation are signifiers that condense the practice of fetishistic disavowal whose formula is, famously, that we know but nevertheless believe what we know not to be the case.[31] We can know that we are not free and nevertheless believe we are free.

For Lenin, this disorientation is a specific effect generated by modern capitalism after it has entered the phase in which it is organized in the form of "bourgeois democracy," because in this phase it "promises equality and liberty," but, in his writings of 1919, "in fact, not a single bourgeois republic, not even the most advanced one, has given the feminine half of the human race either full legal equality with men or freedom from guardianship and oppression of men."[32] Even though with the French bourgeois revolution the grand ideals of liberty, equality, and solidarity were officially declared, in practice they were always given a specific twist, a twist away from the ideals themselves in the

name of these ideals.[33] Lenin here repeats a critical insight already formulated by Hegel, and then by Marx. Marx and Engels had famously argued
that the bourgeoisie, in the aftermath of its revolutionary overcoming, in dis-
charging the feudal structures replaced "the numberless indefeasible chartered
freedoms" with "that single, unconscionable freedom—Free Trade."[34] Indeed,
bourgeois society is all about freedom, but it is not always immediately clear
what sort of freedom it is all about actually, nor is the definition of this sort of
freedom made explicit. This was precisely why Marx and Engels were able to
infer that when the bourgeoisie identifies the politics of the communist party
with the "abolition of individuality and freedom,"[35] they were (in a sense) right:
"The abolition of bourgeois individuality, bourgeois independence, and bourgeois freedom is undoubtedly aimed at."[36] The reason for this is simple:
bourgeois individuality—as, in the twentieth century, Adorno and critical theory will tirelessly point out—is neither really nor in any form the realization of
free individuality. Rather, it is a formal, enormously constrained, demand to
"be individual! (Re)Invent yourself (constantly)! Be an original!" And this demand, being placed on everyone, which is to say that everyone is similarly constrained vis-à-vis what it means to be free, not only makes everyone the same
(kind of individual) but also has direct implications for the idea of freedom
itself. Bourgeois independence is not real independence, because even the
bourgeoisie fully depend on money to be what they are (a fact that became
blatantly obvious during the last financial crisis, when everyone was able to
see that even the former haute-bourgeoisie had ultimately turned out to be a
"salaried bourgeoisie")[37] and can also always just lose their means (and thus
their class position). Bourgeois freedom is not real freedom; rather, it is a
signifier (of so-called freedom) which leads to a misunderstanding of the basic coordinates of our material and sociopolitical existence, and to the resultant (disorientation in the) idea of freedom protecting actual practices of
unfreedom: "Bourgeois democracy is [a] democracy of pompous phrases, sol-
emn words, exuberant promises and the high-sounding slogans of freedom
and equality. . . . It screens the nonfreedom and inferiority of women, the
nonfreedom and inferiority of the toilers and exploited."[38]

Freedom can function as a screen by the means of which we shield ourselves from the actual unfreedom that is otherwise visible everywhere in the
world. It is thus, paradoxically, freedom, or "freedom," that becomes a defense
mechanism against unfreedom. This does not simply mean, however, that we
solely misdescribe the real world of unfreedom when we look at it through the
lens of "freedom" (and "equality"), it also means that we can mis-identify and
experience our own nonfreedom as freedom. Not only objective structures but
also ways of subjectivation are affected by this logic. Freedom as unfreedom

becomes a form of subjectivity (beyond but also in the role of the housewife), thus becoming a tool to endorse unfreedom.

How is this possible? Casting an interesting new light on the often-praised increased sales of books on stoic ethics during the pandemic of the recent years, returning to Hegel helps. Did people really strive for philosophy more than before? Hegel would disagree. He described stoicism as a peculiar (reactionary) ideology of freedom. Stoicism (this is part of his argument in the *Phenomenology of Spirit*) was *inter alia* introduced into the world to make those who are not free—for example because they are the bondsman whose time and actions are determined by others—feel free while nonetheless continuing to serve their masters. How does this work? The impression is given (to the bondsman) that not only are they free when they do not work (and are not under the control, command, and domination of their lords), but are also free during that very work, because they could always also *not* work. The fact that they work is a "free" choice. This assumption—"freedom" of the inner life even when in external domination—thereby serves to produce an even more effective servant. What stoicism brought into the world, then, is the assumption that we have freedom as our possession no matter what our external life is really like. Stoicism thereby operates as a slave ideology of freedom.[39] Why? Because the bondsman, the servant, the slave, will work even more efficiently and never seek to rebel if and when one can make them feel free even (and, perhaps, particularly) when they are not. The slave who is made to feel free in slavery is the most efficient slave, is the slave who misidentifies as not being a slave.

Bourgeois society was therefore described by Marx, not accidentally, as a society that implements both structurally and within its working members a system of universalized "wage-slavery" in which all wage laborers are effectively (Hegelian) bondsman—made to feel free even as they sell their labor power on the market. This is not only the case because personal domination was replaced with structural and impersonal forms of domination[40] (I do not need to be whipped to be forced to work as the threat of not being able to pay my rent or for food, or even not being able to afford a holiday, might already suffice) but also because if I am free to sell my labor power for a certain period of time (usually all the time of the working day), someone else is "free" to buy it. Freedom is thus the conceptual territory which allows for a peculiar asymmetrical exchange of those who are legally considered to be equal (in and due to their freedom). This is constitutive for the legal framework of bourgeois society (that manifests in the employment contract).[41] Such freedom disguises the antagonism between wage slave and (temporal) slave owner. For Marx, then, "freedom" is described as a crucial component of the functioning and dynamics of capital.

In *Capital* Marx notes, not without irony, that within the "Eden" that is the legal framework on which capitalist forms of production rely, "[t]here alone rule Freedom, Equality, Property and Bentham."[42] Freedom, here, is part of a series of signifiers, and it gains its consistency through the addition of a term of a fundamentally different quality: Jeremy Bentham, the utilitarian philosopher. It is on Bentham's name, used as a signifier, that the consistency of the series hinges and concludes, and through which use each of the other terms in the series is redefined. "Freedom" then does not only mean that the exchange between two equals, laborer and capitalist, is determined by their equally free wills, but that it generates the effect that their free will is determined by that which "Bentham" stands for: pure self-interest. Pure self-interest, under the name of Bentham, is what holds the exchange together. And strangely, even as this is transparent to everyone, as Adorno remarked some time ago, we all "desire a deception which is nonetheless transparent to [us]"[43] We know this is not freedom, but this knowledge is blocked from becoming practically effective. "Freedom" may be a deception, as Adorno, fully in line with Lenin, claims, but it is nevertheless desired, even when and even though it is identified as deception. Suspending one, knowledge of freedom as deception, how is it possible to act?[44] What do we need turn freedom into so that it is something we can nevertheless believe in, even though we know it is not freedom?

The answer to these questions offered by the present book is that we will have to turn "freedom" into a natural capacity that we possess no matter what. It is the assumption of the present book that there is a problematic metaphysics of freedom, and this is a constitutive part of a specific "ideology of freedom" which makes freedom into a natural possession of human beings while at the same time creating an understanding not only of freedom, but also of the world and our actions within it, that serves the very obverse of freedom. Such an understanding of freedom as natural possession—freedom in the form of an inalienable capacity—is a naturalization of freedom. Such naturalization of freedom is often identified with the way in which we express ourselves in and through our bodies. But the problem with identifying freedom paradigmatically with the expression of one's (bodily) identity—even though it can certainly be highly significant to be recognized in one's identity[45]—is that it endorses the view that our bodies and the languages with which we articulate ourselves already entail all (material and corporeal) elements to realize our freedoms. Freedom then is bodily or articulatory freedom. It becomes freedom of (self-)expression and (bodily) self-determination.

The present book is not critical of self-expression or ideas of self-determination per se, but it does offer a critique of the process whereby these are turned into the paradigm of freedom and grounded in an understanding of freedom as a given capacity. The claim, which this book does not unfold but will allow its readers to anticipate as its conceptual consequence, is that our identity and our freedom do not preexist in our bodies and in their expression in our natural language. It is hetero-determination that is more essential for an understanding of freedom than auto-determination, as freedom does not begin with what is given and already part of or a potential of our life-form; freedom is itself not a given either; freedom, rather, begins with an addendum to the bio-materialist givenness (of bodies and languages),[46] an addendum that adds to what is (notably bodies and languages).

What you will find in the following book is neither a theory nor a philosophy of freedom, but rather a critical account of how we cannot (and therefore should not) conceive of freedom; that we should not conceive of freedom as a capacity that we possess. How to overcome this conception is what another book articulates—*Abolishing Freedom*[47]—in which I demonstrate that overcoming what I term "the ideology of freedom," or "the myth of the givenness of freedom," leads us to see the emancipatory uses of fatalism, providence, and determinism—not as theological but ultimately and fundamentally as rationalist, materialist, and dialectical concepts. The basis for understanding the argument of *Abolishing Freedom*—and one should read in the title its Davis-esque[48] abolitionist overtones—is unfolded in the present book. This is to say, if we want to understand what modern (and maybe all) philosophy as critique of ideology is up against, the present book—*Indifference and Repetition*—attempts to provide an answer.

The problem that immediately poses itself—and what this book goes on to describe in terms of a mythic conception of freedom—is linked to a historical form of organizing the collective life on this planet, namely capitalism. Capitalism is an immense organization of indifference, and this has an impact on what we make of freedom within it.[49] It relies on organizing the difference(s) between things and people in such a way that they become indifferent to—and exchangeable for—one another, so that nothing makes (a) difference—not even nothing or nothingness or the vanity of its own unfolding. And since capitalism is not a local phenomenon, it confronts us with a process of indifferentiation on a global scale. The present book—and its systematic sequel, *Abolishing Freedom*—differently from the assumption of (some) proponents of critical theory or other theoretical traditions, does not argue that against the dominant form of indifferentiation one needs to emphasize difference and that which is not-identical. Rather, the orientational guideline of the present book is that one has to oppose the dominant form of organizing indifference with another type of indifference. That, we might say, one has to become indifferent to even the predominant form that is (freedom as) indifference.

The main argument of the present book takes the line that, exactly during the time when the world and all life on it was replaced, reframed, and exchanged for the "world market," which has "given a cosmopolitan character to production and consumption in every country,"[50] modern philosophy identifies the possibility of misunderstanding what freedom is and what the detrimental effects may be. It has done so because, from this moment on, the needs and demands of one country could not be conceived of without the productions of other countries;[51] the world(-market) of capitalism is per se internationalist.[52] And thus we encounter an internationalism of indifference, one that is indifferent toward all specificity and singularity. In this process, the disregard for cultural specificity is part of its own operation— and it often manifests by not changing cultural specificities at all, but by silently and nevertheless integrating them into a global capitalist framework— which is why it has no problem whatsoever with the strongest claim to identity or identitarianism. The present book, then, is concerned with the issues this creates for the predominant understanding of freedom as perceived and critiqued by modern philosophy. Thereby, even if articulated from the perspective of a series of European thinkers, the book rests on the assumption that the problem it addresses—notably problematic because ideological understandings of freedom—is a global one or, put differently, it believes that it contributes to the understanding of a problem of global significance. The problem here is how freedom can become a tool of enslavement, and how to understand this operation precisely.

If we are in a situation where there is actual slavery—as in the parts of the world where there is more slavery now than ever before in the history of mankind—the problem is obviously a different one. Sometimes, and obviously, the claim to freedom does not obfuscate freedom, it is indeed a claim for liberation. But with capitalism—as the present book shows—such a liberatory claim in fact is frequently not one, and this then becomes a disorienting problem for theories of liberation. The present book addresses the mechanisms in which freedom—and not slavery—becomes an instrument of oppression as thematized from within the (dominant) history of modern philosophy, for understanding the problem is rather important if one seeks to overcome it. The main trait of this problem consists in the naturalization and substantializing of "freedom" into something that we have, into a possession. But it also comes with the implication that any possession can be (and often has to be) invested. Such an idea has a calming and assuring effect: If you always already have freedom, you may need to defend it, but you do not need to strive for it. Freedom is, in this sense, paradoxically the only possession, even of the slave. This is the "ideology of freedom."[53]

Following this, this possession takes a specific form, the form of being a "capacity." Why? Because a capacity can be actualized but already has an actuality, even when not actualized (we are able to eat, even when we are not eating, for example). To take freedom to be a capacity means to assume that there is an actuality of freedom before the becoming actual of freedom—an actuality of a potential, of a possibility. This is what I term the "ideology of the possible"—but who could have anything against possibilities? I argue that the possible is a disorienting category, because it is constitutive of a problematic understanding of freedom.

The outcome of this peculiar conglomerate is that the most fundamental version of freedom as capacity that we have in our possession is identified with a freedom of choice: the freedom to choose X or non-X. This is what the philosophical tradition referred to as *liberum arbitrium*. I am and remain free, even if I do not realize freedom. . . . My rather profane argument is that one should always remember (and one can still learn this from Hegel) that not-realized freedom is not(-realized) freedom. The history of modern rationalist philosophy frequently attacked the idea that freedom is an always already given, natural capacity, as what I will call *ontic indifference*. Ontic indifference manifests in a certain mode, and this mode manifests in how we understand (what we take to be our) freedom. We naturalize freedom (and with it the world in which it manifests). This has detrimental consequences not only for freedom but also for our understanding of ourselves.

The present book thus seeks to join forces with Federici and attempts to find the invisible form(s) of slavery inscribed in what appears to be the space of freedom. It does so by indicating how certain understandings of freedom have an ideological impact, which prevents actual freedom, and it demonstrates this by indicating how freedom therefore becomes directly compatible with domination (or slavery). The present book also agrees with Davis and Federici that through such a demonstration we can understand the organization of freedom under capitalism as a particularly perfidious form of oppression, notably one that we do not even recognize as such. What enables the present book to endorse these claims is the assumption—that it will seek to substantiate—that modern philosophy since its conception was ultimately a form of ideology critique, notably a critique of an ideology of freedom which takes freedom to be a natural given in the form of a capacity. This is not simply an individual misunderstanding of freedom but one that is unavoidably mediated by modern society—a claim that becomes fully apparent in the accounts of problematic understandings of freedom formulated by Hegel and by Marx.

The present book thus seeks to reconstruct and prepare tools for an ideology critique of freedom as instrument of domination by drawing on the history of modern philosophy—the latter therefore is transformed into an armory which will contribute to breaking the cozily optimistic assumption that, even if we have nothing, we at least have the freedom to change things—if we could just get ourselves around to changing things. It is metaphysically optimistic—which is to say: wrong—to assume that freedom is always already there and just awaits activation. Such an optimism is similar to believing that the present state of things will bring about the potentials by means of which it can happily be overcome and transformed into something new and better. Any such model of critique or assumption of change invests exactly what should be the outcome and therein mirrors the movement of capital(ism). It revolutionizes everything in order to never change anything.

If freedom is not—and maybe never will be—something we have or possess, it might make sense to stop imagining we have what we do not—even though it may hurt, as losing what one does not have could thereby contribute to gaining what one never possesses. Sometimes it is important to see the minimal difference by means of which a third option appears. In one of the greatest books about ending things, Samuel Beckett's *Unnamable*, one can read: "I see nothing. It's because there is nothing, or it's because I have no eyes, or both, that makes three possibilities to choose from."[54] Sometimes the problem does not lie in not being able to solve a problem, but in seeing that the problem is in how we perceive the problem—as it blinds us for our own involvement with what is problematic. Politically, although this is only a first step, one should opt for Beckett's third option. It is what *Indifference and Repetition* and *Abolishing Freedom* argue for. Such an option is certainly not (yet) emancipation. But it does help avoid seeing what is not there with eyes one has only ever imagined. It could prove a valid starting point for thinking politics (differently).

Abbreviations

CDD   John Cottingham. *A Descartes Dictionary*. Cambridge: Cambridge University Press, 1993.

CMS   Rebecca Comay. *Mourning Sickness: Hegel and the French Revolution*. Stanford, CA: Stanford University Press, 2011.

DCB   René Descartes. "Letters." In *The Philosophical Writings of Descartes: The Correspondence*, vol. 3. Translated by John Cottingham. Cambridge: Cambridge University Press, 1991.

DDM   René Descartes. "Discourse on the Method." In *The Philosophical Writings of Descartes*, vol. 1. Translated by Robert Stoothof. Cambridge: Cambridge University Press, 1985.

DMP   René Descartes. "Meditations on First Philosophy." In *The Philosophical Writings of Descartes*, vol. 2. Translated by John Cottingham. Cambridge: Cambridge University Press, 1984.

DPP   René Descartes. "Principles of Philosophy." In *The Philosophical Writings of Descartes*, vol. 1. Translated by John Cottingham. Cambridge: Cambridge University Press, 1985.

GLD   Pierre Guenancia. *Lire Descartes*. Paris: Folio, 2010.

HDFS   G. W. F. Hegel. *The Difference between Fichte's and Schelling's System of Philosophy*. Translated by H. S. Harris and Walter Cerf. Albany: SUNY Press, 1977.

HEL1   G. W. F. Hegel. *The Encyclopedia Logic. Part I of the*
        Encyclopedia of the Philosophical Sciences with the *Zusätze*.
        Translated by T. F. Geraets, W. A. Suchting, and H. S. Harris.
        Indianapolis: Hackett, 1991.

HLPHR I G. W. F. Hegel. *Lectures on the Philosophy of Religion*, vol. 1:
        Introduction and the Concept of Religion. Berkeley: University of
        California Press, 1984.

HOAD   Max Horkheimer and Theodor W. Adorno. "Diskussion über
        Theorie und Praxis." In Max Horkheimer, *Gesammelte
        Schriften*, vol. 19: *Nachträge, Verzeichnisse und Register*, 32–74.
        Edited by Gunzelin Schmidt Noerr. Berlin, Fischer 1989.

HPCR   G. W. F. Hegel. "The Positivity of the Christian Religion." In
        On Christianity: Early Theological Writings, 67–182. Translated
        by T. M. Knox. New York: Harper Books, 1948.

HPR   G. W. F. Hegel. *Outlines of the Philosophy of Right*. Translated
        by Stephen Houlgate. Oxford: Oxford University Press, 2008.

HPS   G. W. F. Hegel. *Phenomenology of Spirit*. Translated by A. V.
        Miller. Oxford University Press, 1977.

HRSP   G. W. F. Hegel, "On the Relationship of Skepticism to Philosophy,
        Exposition of its Different Modifications and Comparison of the
        Latest Form with the Ancient One." In *Between Kant and Hegel:
        Texts in the Development of Post-Kantian Idealism*, 311–362.
        Translated by H. S. Harris. Indianapolis: Hackett, 2000.

HSL   G. W. F. Hegel. *The Science of Logic*. Translated by George di
        Giovanni. Cambridge: Cambridge University Press, 2010.

KAP   Immanuel Kant. "Anthropology from a Pragmatic Point of
        View" (1798). In *The Cambridge Edition of the Works of
        Immanuel Kant. Anthropology, History, and Education*, 227–429.
        Translated by Robert B. Louden. Cambridge: Cambridge
        University Press, 2007.

KCPR   Immanuel Kant. *Critique of Pure Reason*. Translated by Paul
        Guyer and Allen W. Wood. Cambridge: Cambridge University
        Press, 1998.

KCPrR   Immanuel Kant. *Critique of Practical Reason* (1788). In *The
        Cambridge Edition of the Works of Immanuel Kant: Practical
        Philosophy*, 133–272. Translated by Mary J. Gregor. Cambridge:
        Cambridge University Press, 1996.

KGMM   Immanuel Kant. *Groundwork of the Metaphysics of Morals* (1785). In *The Cambridge Edition of the Works of Immanuel Kant: Practical Philosophy*, 37–108. Translated by Mary J. Gregor. Cambridge: Cambridge University Press, 1996.

KRBR   Immanuel Kant. *Religion within the Boundaries of Mere Reason*. In *The Cambridge Edition of the Works of Immanuel Kant: Religion and Rational Theology*, 39–216. Translated by George di Giovanni. Cambridge: Cambridge University Press, 1996.

MECW   Karl Marx and Friedrich Engels. *Collected Works*. London: Lawrence and Wishart, 1980.

NP   Antonio Negri. *Political Descartes: Reason, Ideology, and the Bourgeois Project*. London: Verso, 2007.

SAWH   Carl Christian Erhard Schmid. *Adiaphora wissenschaftlich und historisch untersucht*. Leipzig, 1809.

SCF   Jean-Paul Sartre. "Cartesian Freedom." In *Literary and Philosophical Essays*. Translated by Annette Michelson. New York: Collier Books, 1962.

ZLN   Slavoj Žižek. *Less Than Nothing: Hegel and the Shadow of Dialectical Materialism*. London: Verso, 2012.

INDIFFERENCE AND REPETITION

Introduction

Indifference and the History of Philosophical Rationalism

Incomprehensible stupefaction of the people of our time! . . . They sacrifice everything, truth, virtue, and even life. . . . Nothing is more absurd than indifference. . . . Nothing is darker than indifference.

> —F. R. DE LAMENNAIS, *ESSAI SUR L'INDIFFÉRENCE*
> *EN MATIÈRE DE RELIGION*

. . . mere dulling and ignorance and indifference (i.e., the oblivion of being everywhere).

> —MARTIN HEIDEGGER, *ZU ERNST JÜNGER,*
> IN *GESAMTAUSGABE. IV. ABTEILUNG:*
> *HINWEISE UND AUFZEICHNUNGEN*

. . . mere agreement, on the level of an increasing indifference to all essential decisions . . .

> —MARTIN HEIDEGGER, *PONDERINGS VII–XI,*
> *BLACK NOTEBOOKS 1938–1939*

Between 1942 and 1948, Martin Heidegger wrote in his notorious, much-discussed black notebooks: "The validity [*Geltung*] of the same [*Gleichen*] promotes indifference [*Gleichgültigkeit*]. The indifferent moves in between everything. It eats away one's own [*das Eigene*]. It suffocates inclination's loveliness [*das Holde*]. It yields the discouraged [*das Mutlose*]. It buries all the sources that are about to well up [*die im Anlaß quillen*]."[1] The indifferent moves in between everything, producing despondency. The courage that is lost is the courage to feel any sort of inclination. The state of being discouraged

1

manifests as lack: the lack of inclination for a direction, of taking a position, of the courage to decide in favor of something (or of anything). Such indifference hinders any form of inclination or propensity toward anything, and obscures all possibilities of novelty; it seems that nothing can be new. Indifference thus nips in the bud real transformation; it allows for everything to become identical, or to be and stay ever the same. Indifference is that in which everything is problematically equalized.

However one might evaluate Heidegger's black notebook remarks in the political context of their time or with regard to his own engagement with National Socialism,[2] in the passage above the insight brought forth is one that is essential for Heidegger's *philosophical* thought and which, furthermore, is one that he takes to be essential for contemporary philosophical thought in general. For Heidegger here, indifference and callousness are symptomatic expressions of the fact that the difference between being and beings (*Sein und Seiendem*) has been forgotten. The universal "indifference between the ontical [*sic*] and the ontological"[3] is one whose origin point Heidegger traces back to Plato's thought, Plato, with whom the *aletheia* came under the yoke of the idea. Such an oblivion of difference, which is seen to have its origin in Plato, achieves its modern worsening in Descartes[4] and is (for Heidegger) grounded in the essence of the representative and formative, the *zu- und vorstellende*: the universally equalizing and omni-rationalizing technology that Heidegger calls the enframing (*Gestell*).[5] Ultimately, the enframing generates such a form of indifference and equivalence that all possibility, even the possibility of a memory of difference, is obliviated. Thus the predominant understanding of what appears as rationalism is precisely that which allows for a universalized "planetary indifference."[6] This in turn makes true thinking impossible, thereby also rendering impossible any real action. In this way, humanity is cheated out of any understanding of its own being and with that, is cheated out of any understanding of what freedom could mean.

The effects produced by this technological equalization—this de- as well as in-differentiation—are superimposed in an obfuscating and obscuring fashion upon what the Greeks called *physis*, or nature. They cause the loss of any real sense or meaning (or sense of meaning), because there is meaning and sense only where there are differences. And they ultimately destroy the very space in which human beings might even possibly realize their projects—viz., their freedom—the world. Such equivalence of everything existing, because it is simultaneously a uniformity and a conformity, makes everything the same in so dumb and dull a manner that even any idea of real change is forestalled. And if everything perishes in and through such leveling egalitarianism without difference, then freedom is lost, and consequently history, the thinking of history, and the history of thinking are, likewise, lost.

As is well known, the general name that Heidegger assigns to the above-described phenomenon is nihilism. Heidegger's nihilism effectuates, to use a rather Kantian or Hegelian vocabulary, the predominance of an all-measuring, all-surveying, and all-calibrating understanding over reason and actual thought. In a passage from his lectures in *The Fundamental Concepts of Metaphysics* he expresses this as follows:

> And yet—the *most profound indifference* and indifference of ordinary understanding does not lie in that undifferentiated comportment toward various beings, within which ordinary understanding is able to manage and find its way through. The enormity of that indifference pertaining to ordinary understanding is that such understanding fails to hear the being of beings and is able to acquaint itself only with beings.[7]

For Heidegger, the most profound indifference lies in the oblivion of the distinction between being and beings. The immense vulgarity of this forgetting consists of the way in which both become so indifferent, so equivalent, that ultimately only one of them (viz., only *beings*) counts. Being, thereby, is understood merely as another of these beings (e.g., as the highest being). Such indifference installs and erects itself under the supremacy of an understanding that is oblivious of difference—a sort of "thinking" that knows only one type of difference, namely that between beings, and therefore does not have any actual concept of difference—and does so under a predominance of non-thinking, as there is no thinking without difference. In such conditions ultimately even the thesis about indifference becomes an indifferent thesis, a thesis that does not introduce any difference, a thesis that is thus meaningless, since meaning in general is grounded in and upon difference. In this way, and at this point, as Heidegger will even infer, philosophy encounters its own performance limit. The only act that remains for philosophy is that it must do everything in its power to make the admonishment and reminiscence of the poets heard. But even in this amplificatory gesture philosophy remains peculiarly impotent and powerless, since if one forgets the difference between being and beings, and consequently forgets even the meaning of meaning and the sense of sense, the sayings of the poets appear meaningless, and philosophy, which points out these sayings to everyone, is reduced to appearing as if a useless esotericism.

This, then, is nihilism.

Such nihilism brings with it a fundamental indifference whose effect is that even the meaning of the philosophical diagnosis that nihilism reigns in this world loses its meaning and becomes unintelligible. This is not only the reason for the limitation of the effects of the philosophical discourse but also actually makes nihilism in its proper sense into what it is in the first place. The disregard of philosophical thinking—even when it does not attempt to assert itself but only indicates that we have to think differently about thinking to be thinking at all and therefore have to listen to the poets—becomes the fundamental symptom of nihilism. Heidegger's nihilism is precisely, then, a reign of indifference and equivalence that does not want and cannot know anything of or about itself and that permanently misunderstands itself; assuming philosophy just exaggerates all this, we assume we will make it eventually and things are not that bleak after all ("don't worry—things are going to be okay . . .").

In and through nihilism what is lost is not only thought, since there is no thought without difference, but also freedom, since freedom is, as Heidegger notes, "not the conduct [*Betreiben*] of the individual, not arbitrariness, not choice, not decision, not the indifference of the yes or no."[8] Nihilism abolishes freedom because it deteriorates it into an individual matter, into mere arbitrariness and choice. Nihilism is the end of the freedom that no one recognizes as such, an end no one can see or wants to believe in. The nihilistic understanding of freedom is expressed paradigmatically in the fact that freedom is taken to be the business of the individual and is thus identified with and as the individual's capacity to choose, select, opt for this or that. Such a "freedom" of choosing is a capacity with which all individuals are supposed to be endowed. In this interpretation of freedom as arbitrary capacity to choose, freedom itself becomes indifferent, because it implies an indifference of affirmation and negation. An indifferent *yes or no* clings to the merely objective givenness, to what seems objectively prescribed. An indifferent *yes or no* adheres to what is merely given, to what is preexisting objectively. We thus forget true difference. This is a freedom that does not have any relation to real difference, that does not make any actual difference anymore. It is a freedom that becomes an indifferent arbitrary choice, turning into a freedom without meaning, a meaningless freedom.

To understand freedom as indifference in this sense is an effect and a product of the indifference at the ground of and as essence of nihilism.[9] There is in such a nihilism (which does not recognize itself as such and which can thus only misrecognize itself) a "freedom" that is none, even as it takes itself to be freedom. If one assumes that freedom is the freedom to choose, one commits one of the most "fundamental errors"[10] that has ever been committed. In this way, the facultative, free-to-choose subject has obliterated for itself the possibility of recognizing even the erroneousness of its own error. It is precisely such a self-misrecognizing error that is an expression and a symptom of the nihilism, which, beginning with Plato, spread, ever-growing and ever-proliferating, over the planet. Not only is the difference between being and beings forgotten, but what is forgotten also and in addition is the truth of being and of freedom. It has been forgotten what the truth of freedom, true freedom, freedom in truth are, and thereby also what the being of truth and the truth of being is.

One forgets without knowing that one forgets when one believes that there is nothing except and beyond knowledge. This is to say that knowledge is essentially oblivious, since for Heidegger knowledge is indifferent to truth because it only knows objects (of knowledge). But truth cannot be conceived of in this objective and objectifying manner. Truth, if it is the truth of being—and thus not of objective relations—is in this sense not an indifferent object among others, but rather, and necessarily, it introduces a difference. Truth makes and marks a difference to knowledge.

Assuming the indifference of nihilism even toward itself, then, it becomes obvious how thought and consequently freedom can be dragged into the swamp of indifference. Heidegger notes in relation to this that indifference (different from what it is and becomes in the nihilistic framework) "does not occur a constitutivum of *libertas*, but only qua creatura [insofar as it is part of a creature]; the indifferentia is to be conceived as *deficiens* [as deficiency]. Indifference is not inherent in freedom, although it occurs in acting."[11] Indifference is freedom's deficiency. This can yield far-reaching effects: If freedom is taken to be arbitrariness or ability-to-choose, and thus is taken to be indifference, indifference thus becomes freedom-of-choice. What is in fact a deficiency and lack of freedom is turned into a constitutive moment of freedom. The essence of the deficiency (of freedom) is realized as deficiency of the essence (of freedom which is understood as indifferent capacity to choose). We thereby attribute to freedom that which does not belong to it. Heidegger captures an effect of such problematic attributions (with regard to man's own self-understanding and in relation to the resultant comprehension of freedom) in a drastic formulation: He points out that here man would "sink" even "lower than the animal."[12] Through nihilistic indifference and by understanding freedom as indifferent capacity to choose, human beings can lose, or sink below, their humanity, regressing in very peculiar ways. There are thus, for Heidegger, understandings of freedom that can lead to such regression that human beings may act and behave not only as if they were animals but also as if they were even less than that. This is a further nihilistic product of nihilism and indifference.

The present book takes up Heidegger's diagnosis of indifference and takes it seriously. It examines the problematic and catastrophic effects that indifference and equivalence have in relation to the concept and the actuality of freedom. At the same time, this book is neither Heideggerian in its orientation nor in its reasoning, marked as it is by a series of points that fundamentally differ from Heidegger's framing of the indifference-diagnosis. Of these points, there are six worth noting here:

First, the present book does not understand indifference and equivalence as a symptom of a decay that begins with Plato and intensifies up to the present day. Rather, by emphasizing that it was not Heidegger who first identified indifference as a fundamental problem, and that it had already been identified as a problem before, notably at the beginning of modern philosophy, the present book will indicate that freedom as capacity is a problem that modern philosophy seeks to resolve. It will thereby demonstrate that this problem appears as a specifically modern problem in philosophy, and it appears as a problem that is intimately linked with the very constitution and self-understanding of what makes *modern* philosophy.

Second, the present book will show how indifference names the product of a peculiar misunderstanding much more than it does a problem of the oblivion of being. This misunderstanding does not concern being in difference to beings, or the obliteration of their distinction, but rather it directly and essentially concerns the conception, concept, and understanding of freedom. It is therefore not the case that nihilism leads to an understanding of freedom as freedom of choice, but rather that understanding freedom as freedom of choice leads to a peculiar nihilism. The present book treats and deals with a problem—and it only points to how this problem can be overcome or sublated in passing[13]—and so, in this sense, it presents a philosophical problem-history in which the problem that is examined is not that of the forgetting of being, but rather that of a misunderstanding, which nevertheless did not yield less problematic consequences than those depicted by Heidegger.

Third, Heidegger's thesis that human beings can behave as if they are less than animals will also need to be modified. In the reconstructed positions from the history of philosophy herein, the present book will show how one frequently encounters the thesis that even though human beings are not animals, they can act and behave as if they were mere animals. It will render intelligible and plausible how such a regression is possible—that is to say what its conceptual preconditions are—and why such a possible regression is grounded in a misconception of freedom.

This is realized in the present book, *fourth*, by affirmatively turning toward the history of modern philosophical rationalism, rather than, as Heidegger did, critically turning against it. It will be shown in what follows that it is precisely modern philosophical rationalism which detects and identifies indifference as a fundamental problem of understanding freedom (in modernity), and provides us with complex diagnoses vis-à-vis its origin and the possibilities of its overcoming.

Thus, *fifth* (and again in difference to Heidegger), the present book does not make a plea for the return to or reactivation of the forgotten or pre-philosophical poetic roots of the philosophical thought of the Greeks (or of their contemporary representatives). Rather, by its conviction and in its orientation, it defends a modern philosophical rationalism decidedly linked to the names of Descartes, Kant, Hegel, and Marx. The argument is not to dream up alter-modernities, or attempt to finally become premodern again, but to endorse the rationalist tradition that stands in the heart of modern thought, even if it is not only modern, but has originated earlier. The modernity of modernity is linked precisely to the accounting for the rationality of even that which seems to escape the rational framework, the rationality of the irrational.

As will be shown, it is exactly the rationalist tradition embodied by Descartes, Kant, Hegel, and Marx which repeatedly demonstrates that one not only has to think reason and unreason, but that one must also think the rationality of irrationality and unfold a rationalism of the irrational that has both problematic and productive sides. Accordingly, it is not rationalist thought which brought an oblivion of difference and a misconception of freedom and indifference over humanity; rather, this very rationalist tradition was constantly engaged in unraveling, criticizing, and overcoming the problematic conceptions of freedom that lead to the nihilism Heidegger diagnosed.

This implies, *sixth*, that the present book does not share Heidegger's assumption that philosophy (specifically rationalist philosophy) has nothing to say about the problem of indifference, nor that philosophy is a constitutive component of the problem of indifference, nor that it can only turn to the recalling and admonishing discourse of the poets. Rather what you are about to read is a fundamental and thorough defense of modern rationalist philosophy articulated against the background of its own history. This defense will demonstrate precisely how it is that such a rationalist philosophy—rationalist thought—is needed to think freedom in its most problematic but also most true conception.

Subsequently, the central diagnosis that will be derived and elaborated out of the history of modern philosophical rationalism is the following: The identification of freedom with the freedom of choice identifies freedom with a givenness and more specifically with the givenness of a capacity. A far-reaching implication of this diagnosis is, in a slightly different rendering, that freedom is taken to be a given if one speaks of it in terms of a capacity, and so, if one assumes that freedom is a capacity, one assumes that one has freedom or, more generally, that freedom is possible at all. It is exactly this identification of freedom with the form of capacity to which the rationalist tradition assigns the name indifference. *Indifference is problematic*—this is the diagnosis to be elaborated—*because it results from a determination and comprehension of freedom that relies on a mythical assumption of givenness.*[14] The assumption of freedom as given capacity is mythical not only because it assumes that certain beings—human beings—are always already free, but because it also always already pre- and co-determines, through this assumption, at least implicitly, what freedom is. Freedom thereby becomes the freedom to decide within the framework of a given set of possibilities. In this way freedom is fundamentally determined as freedom of choice, as the possibility to choose within a framework of possibilities.

Modern philosophical rationalism, as reconstructed in the present book, is directed against the diverse versions and varieties of this *myth of the givenness of freedom* (as capacity).[15] It is precisely this modern philosophical rationalism which is directed against such mythical assumption of givenness, because such an assumption is mythical rather than rational. Such an assumption (because it is mythical) can also be classified as an essentially premodern assumption. The philosophy of modern rationalism takes its form and shape from its repeated and persistent critique and from the expulsion of mythical structures of premodern spirit (that constantly threaten to return) from the spirit of freedom. The struggle of reason against mythicality (even its own) thereby becomes the struggle of modernity to be fully modern.

In the present book this idea will be formulated in such a way that it will be demonstrated how modern philosophy, and perhaps philosophy *tout court* because it is critique of ideology, is the critique of the myth of the givenness of freedom.[16] This means that philosophy undertakes the critique of a certain ideology of freedom, or a critique of freedom as ideology. We will see that exactly this mode of critique promotes the development of the philosophy of rationalism and ensures its persistent systematic continuation. In the background of the following investigations is the insight that, despite all explanations of the end of ideology, despite all insistence that certain problems would simply have to be solved in a rational manner (with the adjournment of all ideologies), a reconstruction of the history of parts of modern rationalist philosophy can demonstrate that ideology—and specifically the ideology of freedom or freedom as ideology (culminating in the assumption of freedom as a given)—has the unwavering tendency to return again, even against improved and more rational insight.[17]

Even though Spinoza will not play a role in and for the following reflections, a pointed remark by Louis Althusser on the former's *Ethics* is instructive here in order to orient the reader. Althusser once presented the *Ethics* (and more precisely, its last book) as the first theory of ideology in the history of philosophy—the theory of ideology *avant la lettre*.[18] It deserves this distinguished title because Althusser saw in it for the first time a formulation of the thought that a problematic (or false) representation (or idea) of reality does not simply dissolve and disappear even after its falseness has been recognized. For example, I perceive the sun as a small yellow ball in the sky whose size corresponds to that of my hand because I can, from my perspective, cover it with my hand. But then, after this immediate observation, I establish a scientific understanding of the sun, the physical relations between the sun and earth, and related matters, so that I no longer build on my immediate, sensuous cognition but rather on a scientifically grounded knowledge; then the presumption can be made that all the impressions and convictions I formerly had will disappear. But Althusser argues that Spinoza was the first to prove that this is precisely not the case. Although we gain a more precise knowledge about the relations between ourselves, the sun, and the earth, if we were to step outside after our "research" we would still see the sun exactly as we saw it previously: as a small, yellow, warm-looking ball that we could cover with our hand.[19]

The *Ethics* thus shows how and why false representations of reality can remain in place unimpeded, how and why false representations are (co-)constitutive of reality as such. In Althusser's reading, Spinoza thematizes in the *Ethics* the (at least potential) practical ineffectiveness and powerlessness of knowledge and cognition against false representations and ideas, from which, even by identifying them as false, we cannot directly liberate ourselves. We may very well know that something is true, but nevertheless we do not believe what we know in full, and we can continue to believe in what we know not to be true. This does not concern a form of subjective akrasia or weakness of will ('I know very well that I should (not) do X, but I just cannot (right now) resist') but rather concerns a far more fundamental problem, one that raises the question of the practical consequences of knowledge and cognition in general. More precisely, it concerns the question of how a knowledge that we have can become practically effective in general, namely, in and for our actions. The difficulties that this question brings with it are difficulties that lie at the heart (of the concept) of ideology.

This can be formulated in more general terms: Ideology does not disappear with the insight that it is ideology. Ideology persists and returns, even after the "end of ideology."[20] This insight, here only briefly formulated with reference to Spinoza, thereby differing from what Althusser assumed, is present throughout the history of the philosophy of modern rationalism and in its critique of ideology, even though it is not always explicitly so. Since this philosophy is a critique of ideology, it repeatedly confronts its task of always needing to reconfigure what is conceptually at stake with the ideology of freedom and with freedom as ideology. Modern rationalist philosophy continuously *remembers* the insight that a false understanding of freedom is not simply to be pushed out of the world qua cognition (precisely because it is practically effective). It seems to be always *repeating* its own founding gesture—which resides in the critique of the ideology of freedom—in order *to work through*, in different ways, the presently available forms in which one can effectively accomplish any critique of ideology at all.

As the present book goes on to demonstrate at greater length, modern rationalist philosophy performs this self-historicizing, singularizing, formal maneuver because it always and repeatedly attempts to maintain, and indeed must attempt to maintain, the modernity of the modern age. This is an attempt to be modern in the fullest sense of the term,[21] for the ideological-mythical structure of the premodern spirit constantly threatens to return from and within the spirit of freedom. The reason for this, as will be shown, is that the ideological-mythical structure does not simply belong to the "historical" epoch of the premodern age, but rather to a premodern age that is only "discovered," or even invented, with and within the modern age itself (and is embodied in premodern and mythical ideas of "modernity" as well as in the modern idea of premodernity). Thus, a misunderstanding of freedom that is the result of a problematic regression from modernity to something that does not exist before the act of regression and is therefore peculiarly coextensive with it ("it" being both modernity and the acts of regression it produces) is brought to our attention. In this sense, it will also be shown that certain modifications of the ideology of freedom are first brought forth by the critique of that very ideology of freedom.

We will encounter the problems related to freedom as that luminous ideal that we simply have in our possession. The ideology of freedom and the myth of its givenness constantly threaten to return. In a certain sense, they always already have returned, and it is crucial to constantly reassert freedom as well as modernity, to reassert freedom of (and in) the modern age as well as the modernity of freedom, against this threatened return. This dynamic describes neither a modern conservatism (as if modernity would be fundamentally conservative) nor a tendency to a permanent self-revolutionizing. Rather, the dynamic situates modernity as fundamentally connected to the concept of repetition, and to the repetition of its own founding act. In this respect, modernity is not an incomplete but a fundamentally insecure project. One could perhaps even venture that it is an Idea, an *Idea-ology* that it is crucial to affirm *repeatedly*, persistently.

The following elaborations reconstruct one of the fundamental philosophical diagnoses of modernity in its different articulations and realizations by

returning to a select group of thinkers from the tradition of modern philosophical rationalism. Each turns around what we may call, with a modifying reference to Heidegger, *ontic indifference* (i.e., the interpretation of freedom as a
given capacity to choose). Each raises the question what effects are generated
by understanding freedom as a given indifferent capacity, and how it comes
about. And so the following investigations commence with the thinker who is
classically identified with the beginning of modern philosophy: Descartes. They
proceed to the commencement of German Idealism, with Kant (and one of
his pupils, Carl Christian Erhard Schmid). They reach their culmination
through an engagement with the thinker who is taken to be the last thinker of
the German Idealist tradition: Hegel.[22] The book concludes with a cartogra-
phy of the persistence of indifference problems after Hegel, and delineates how
indifference is (and this, of course, is the thesis of Marx) directly linked to the
organization of modern (capitalist) society.

This book is about indifference and repetition; about the repeated diagnoses and analyses of ontic indifference.[23] As we will see, there is more than a
merely external—because a rather dialectical—relationship between the two.
So after (reading) the present book it will be indispensable to supplement the
conceptual-historical and diagnostic part of this study with two further parts.
First, within the horizon of philosophical rationalism, a conceptual strategy for
overcoming ontic indifference will consist of inferring and then thinking *ontological indifference*. The step from ontic to ontological difference is not accomplished in the present book, but rather, it is taken in a systematic second step (and
it means to assume that things are already and irretrievably lost and that this is
what constitutes the assumption of an unavoidable fatalism, the reasons for which
will already be graspable in what you are about to read).[24] This second step will
have to be followed by a third, which consists of an account of the precise modalities in which one actually does what one actually cannot do (this is what it
means to subjectivize fatalism and which will be called "courage"). Withal, this
will allow for the formulation of a different concept(ion) of freedom.[25]

The project begun in the present book thus concerns a systematic examination of the *ontic-ontological indifference* that presents us with the task of
conceptualizing a precondition for a nonmythical concept of freedom. The
insight of the necessity of a dialectical transition from ontic to ontological
indifference, and the step from the ideology of freedom to the precondition of
an Idea-ology of freedom, can be attained only by traversing the (first) problematic understanding of freedom. In keeping with one of Hegel's mantras,
the path to truth begins not with positing or postulating something true but
rather with working out what is false, an insight if it is true, that presents us
with the first true insight.

Now, to end this introduction and to begin the present book properly: About one hundred years before Heidegger's elaborations on nihilistic indifference, Hugues Félicité Robert de Lamennais, a thinker almost unknown outside France and almost entirely forgotten even within it, published multiple volumes that addressed and defined indifference (particularly indifference to questions of religion and belief) as an "endemic symptom of modernity."[26] All this, eventually, would be collected in three volumes under the grand title *Essay on Indifference in Matters of Religion* (v. 1, 1817, vv. 2–3, 1818–1824). Some hundred and fifty years later, in 1965, Jacques Lacan mentions Lamennais's corpus in one of his public lectures and therein raises the following provocation: "[W]ho among you will write an essay worthy of Lamennais in political matter?"[27] Almost sixty years after Lacan voiced this publicly, the present book attempts to give an answer, which is concerned rather with the broadly practical rather than singularly political matters of indifference. But the task now has been taken up.

1
Descartes and the Transcendental of All My Future Errors

[A]ll really profound thinkers, however different in their other views may have been, were in agreement . . . in rejecting the *liberum arbitrium*.

—ARTHUR SCHOPENHAUER, *PRIZE ESSAY ON THE FREEDOM OF THE WILL,*
IN *THE TWO FUNDAMENTAL PROBLEMS OF ETHICS*

The displacement of the distribution of forces in favour of satisfaction may have the dreaded final outcome of paralyzing the will of the ego, which in every decision it has to make is almost as strongly impelled from the one as from the other [side].

—SIGMUND FREUD, *INHIBITIONS, SYMPTOMS AND ANXIETY*

You may be unfree, if you wish. . . .

—RENÉ DESCARTES, "AUTHOR'S REPLIES TO THE FIFTH SET OF
OBJECTIONS," IN *THE PHILOSOPHICAL WRITINGS OF DESCARTES*

Humans and Animals: A Detour via Kant

Human beings are animals. For centuries, this has been assumed, contended, and disputed. But human beings are not only animals. This, for quite as many centuries, has been assumed, contended, and disputed.[1] Human beings are at the same time like animals, yet also different from animals. Human beings are therefore particular, singular animals. One way of explaining this idea is to suggest that human beings are animals that are equipped with a unique quality, animals with a surplus—social animals for Aristotle (animals + sociality), dangerous animals for Hobbes (animals + egotism and aggressivity), and so on—and because of this surplus, human-beings-as-animals transgress the mere realm of animal existence.[2]

In what follows I will develop a view on the relation between human beings and animals, and I will do this by thinking through the relation of human action and animal behavior. This will lead me to a discussion of a remarkable reflection on this relation that can be found in Descartes. But to make this step intelligible, a short anticipatory detour through Kant is instructive.

In his *Critique of Judgment*, Kant characterizes human beings in a way that initially seems to fall in the above-mentioned category (animals + surplus): Human beings are animals, but they are the only animals that are able to find something to be beautiful. But with this characterization (humans are those animals that possess the ability to adjudge something to be beautiful) Kant turns the question around. The question is no longer *What are human beings?* But *How does one determine those beings that can judge something to be beautiful?* Following this reversal, the answer is *they are human beings.* So, what then constitutes these beings that are able to find something or judge something to be beautiful? Kant answers that beauty has purport "for beings at the same time animal and rational (but not merely for rational beings—as spirits for example—but only for them as both [*zugleich*] animal and rational)."[3] Human beings are at the same time *zugleich* animals and not animals. And so it is precisely this "at the same time," this "*zugleich*," that turns humankind into a peculiar species of its own.[4]

For Kant, the surplus is linked to the fact that human beings are rational creatures. But the rationality to which he refers is not only a criterion of demarcation which is externally added to an animal being that enables us to then distinguish between man and animal, but it is also bound to an adequate explication of the "at the same time" that makes humans into humans. This is why in his theory of judgment on the beautiful Kant develops a form of judgment that is distinct from the form that pertains to judgments of reason and to judgments on the agreeable. As their name indicates, conceptual judgments of reason use and are related to a given concept; they are, for example, related to what is good. Conceptual judgments are therefore constituted in such a way that they are more than just subjective, since concepts have an objective value. And it is precisely due to their objective constitution that they are of a universal nature; they hold true for all rational beings.

For Kant, though, there are also judgments on the agreeable. These sit in contrast to objective judgments. These are subjective judgments. They are thus merely particular and never (or only ever accidentally) universal. If, for example, I like taking baths, it may be that I find others that feel like me about baths and bathing. But there is no systematic force that would force my judgment to universalize itself. This is why it can happen, quite arbitrarily, that I remain all alone and by myself with my judgment. Universality is thus not included in the judgment's form. What Kant addresses vis-à-vis the judgment on the agreeable is the question of how a judgment can be merely particular and subjective. He goes on to call such judgments pathological judgments: judgments that have the form of judgments but which nevertheless at the same time do not have the form of (proper, objective) judgments. Kant, here, might be reformulated as follows: Judgments on the agreeable are judgments that are similar to judgments animals would (potentially) articulate (even if they cannot/do not). This is why Kant can state that "agreeableness is a significant factor even with animals devoid of reason; beauty has purport and significance only for human beings."[5]

Judgments on the agreeable are judgments that human beings make in such a way that they do not judge as human beings but as animals, that is as starting from and grounded in their pathological constitution. Judgments made in this moment are akin to how unreasonable animals also (would) judge. This peculiar form of judging is different from the forms of judgment that are purely conceptual, as such forms of judgment can also be performed by spirits (that is, by purely intellectual entities without worldly embodiment). If a human judges in a purely conceptual manner, she judges in a way that is proximate to spirit. If a human judges in a purely pathological manner, she judges in a way that is proximate to animals. Human beings only then judge as human beings if they judge as spirits that are *at the same time* animals and as animals that are *at the same time* spirits. And these simultaneous forms of judgment happen when human beings judge beauty. So, if judgments on the agreeable are subjective private judgments without universal dimension, and if conceptual judgments are objective judgments without particularity, it is, precisely, Kant's aim in his theory of judgments on beauty to link universality and particularity as well as subjectivity and objectivity.[6] He believes that one judges in an authentically human way when one judges something that is pleasurable for oneself under the conditions that this pleasure is more than a private pleasure and more than particular(ized) pleasure. Judgment only becomes genuinely human when human beings judge in a way that is at once subjective rather than conceptual, and at the same time not simply particular, namely, not merely pathological.

This brief passage through the *Critique of Judgment*'s forms of judgment is instructive as an entry point to what will follow because it enables us to clarify a diagnosis of the human being that is found repeatedly in decisive moments of pre- as well as post-Kantian philosophy. The diagnosis goes as follows: Human beings are at the same time animals and this "at the same time" does not simply make it possible for human beings to be different from merely rational beings, the "at the same time" also opens up the possibility for human beings to act and behave as if they were only animals even though they are not mere animals.

What will now be developed works toward an understanding of the ways in which this diagnosis can be comprehended, and how it can contribute to how we can account for the fact that such a peculiar regress can occur. If human beings are animals that are able to behave as if they were mere animals even though they are more than mere animals, the plausibility and senses of the idea of such a regress must be placed under question. For human beings only behave as if they were animals, animals who lack something, and this lack is that which the whole of modern rationalist philosophy has taken to be the decisive feature of humanity's essence: freedom. Thus, the question I will address in the following is: How can it happen that human beings judge and act as if they were animals? How can it happen that those beings of whom one assumes a state of freedom act as if they are not free? The discussion begins with Descartes, since he was the first modern thinker to lay a cornerstone for an understanding of the thesis that human beings are beings that can (potentially) act freely but can also (potentially) act in such a way that they regress from the realm of freedom to that of animal behavior. Descartes reserves a categorical place for the mode of human activity that is indistinguishable from animal behavior. Descartes refers to this peculiar regress as indifference, and it is to this regress so named that (via Sartre, now) we will turn.

Freedom or/of Indifference: Sartre's Problem

In 1947 Sartre published an article examining the concept of freedom in Descartes. For Sartre, Descartes's thought stands at the origin of a long series of (French) thinkers who conceive of freedom as freedom of thought and judgment, but who, therefore, are unable to comprehend freedom as situation-specific, as freedom which is experienced, creative, lived, and practiced. Sartre's reading of Descartes's concept of freedom also sees that such a freedom signifies independence but not creation. Thus, freedom in Descartes is initially a negative freedom: "a simple negative power, that of saying *no* to whatever is not true."[7]

For Sartre, such a determination of freedom refers to a decision made. And, more precisely, the decision to reject whatever is false. But any such decision must always conceptually contain the implication of the ability to say no or yes; yes or no to truth and to falsehood; no decision without a yes or a no. To say no to falsehood in this way is not only a (one-sided) act of negative freedom but also includes reference to the other side of the decision. In it—even in Descartes—there is "a positive and constructive freedom";[8] in each no is concealed a logically implied yes, even if this yes never becomes explicit.[9] In sum, the no to falsehood relies on a yes to truth; there can be no no without the background of a yes. In this way, the concept of freedom for Sartre always implies the task not only to cognize something true—for this a no on its own could achieve—but also "to cause a truth to exist in the world."[10] Without such causation, without becoming existent, without realization, freedom is not truly (comprehended) freedom. Freedom is an active and activated choosing.

Descartes elaborates systematically on how to conceive of the no of freedom and of its consequences (of which the paradigm is the infamous Cartesian doubt that says no to all certainties), and arrives at what Sartre calls "freedom of indifference,"[11] that is, the combination of the doubt and the no of freedom (or, the freedom of the no). Indifference, then, is to free oneself from all necessities and all givens and to make oneself independent of all objective determinations. The freedom of the no and the no of freedom is a making-oneself-indifferent against objectivity. But the freedom of indifference can only be a part of freedom. Freedom *tout court* would be a freedom that does not only make itself free (from all possible determinations), but it also actively *makes* freedom. There is no freedom of the no without a freedom of the yes. It is against this background that, for Sartre, problems with Descartes emerge.

Is Descartes's doubt not exactly the methodically and consistently conducted freedom of indifference that exposes what lies at its ground and must therefore be a freedom of affirmation, an affirmation of freedom (of the "I think")? Why is it that Sartre develops a problem with Descartes here? Sartre's problem arises precisely where he has to account for the fact that for Descartes indifference is a problem of freedom, even a depletion and privation of freedom, even as Descartes conceives of the freedom of indifference as a component of freedom. Since, as Sartre rightly puts it, Descartes "goes so far as to deny the freedom of indifference or rather so far as to make it the lowest degree of freedom."[12] And from this point onward things get more complicated.

Descartes seems to be the thinker of the freedom of indifference (viz., of doubt). But, and this is Sartre's critical intuition, he insufficiently emphasizes the practical and the creative that is the constitutively positive side of freedom: Doubt is not affirmation. Yet at the same time Descartes himself explicitly rejects the freedom of indifference, adjudging it the lowest degree of freedom, that is, a privation of freedom. Freedom as indifference is never truly freedom. So it seems as if Descartes makes precisely the claim that Sartre contends that he does not make but should have made. Here one can get a clearer view of the proper problematicity of the problem. Descartes claims that, first, freedom of indifference is not really freedom (doubt is the path to freedom but not yet freedom) and therefore there may be in his thought, second, no other than the insufficiency Sartre demands to be addressed. However, this means that, third, Descartes neither assumes that freedom is a freedom of the no nor that it is indifference, and so, fourth, a mirror-inverted problem arises, namely that another aspect of freedom disappears—the freedom of the no that is ultimately no real freedom—and for Sartre freedom must consist in the *yes and no*, it cannot be freedom without both sides. In Descartes it seems that there is either only a freedom of the no, which knows no freedom of the yes, or only a freedom of the yes which, paradoxically, negates the no as component of freedom. "Thus, Descartes constantly wavers between the identification of freedom with the negativity or negation of being—which would be the freedom of indifference—and the conception of free will as simple negation of negation,"[13] that is as affirmation. Descartes vacillates. And he vacillates between the yes and the no of freedom.

How to explain this? First, such a fundamental equivocation implies that it is not possible to talk about only *one* form of freedom in Descartes. Rather, it is only possible to speak of freedom in Descartes with recourse to a discussion of at least two forms, even if it remains to be seen how to conceive of and relate these forms. And these two distinct forms in Descartes seem to be different from what Sartre suggested when he made critical recourse to the classical distinction of negative and positive freedom, since eventually the negative and positive forms of freedom are for Sartre two content-related components of only *one* form of freedom.[14] Sartre's critical engagement with Descartes produces the result that in Descartes one neither finds *one* form of freedom nor are the components of freedom conceived in a *uniform* manner. Rather, at least in Sartre's reconstruction, the form of freedom as well as its components seem to multiply in quite a peculiar way. Why? Because there is on the one side the freedom of indifference (the freedom of the no) that is doubt, but there is at the same time an indifference in freedom, which is what is conceived by Descartes as the lowest degree of freedom and therefore as almost different from freedom. On the one side, doubt as the paradigm of the freedom of indifference is negative, but there is also a determination of indifference which almost separates it from freedom. On the other side it seems there is an instance of the creative freedom that Sartre thought was missing in Descartes, which is nonetheless part of the freedom of indifference (and this is an indifference that one must conceptualize as differing from what Descartes classifies as the privation of freedom). And so the following questions can be raised: Is there nevertheless an indifference in Descartes where Sartre did not locate it? Is there another kind of indifference (different from the no of freedom) than the one that Sartre did see? How can it be that one form of indifference is problematic and the other is not? Does indifference split into two?

Reading Sartre's reading generates an odd result. It seems that there is no unified indifference in Descartes, which is to say that there is neither a unified freedom of the no nor, more generally, a unified and/or stable form of freedom. But can there be a unified and nonproblematic form of freedom? As a result of Sartre's reading, what seems to exist in Descartes is a no of freedom without a yes and a yes of freedom without a no, or, a problematic and a nonproblematic indifference. The separation of content-related determinations of freedom leads to a separation within the form of the concept of freedom, and this in turn leads to a separation of the (previous) content-related components of freedom. The consequence of Sartre's analysis is a reading of Descartes which shows him to have bound the concept of freedom to a yes and a no, even as this yes and no shows itself precisely in such a way that the yes excludes the no and the no excludes the yes so that that each time the other side seems to disappear. This is irritating and peculiar—and not only for Sartre—and what it ultimately shows is that it is weirdly difficult to determine what the Cartesian concept of freedom is. This peculiar difficulty is not only because the movement of splitting freedom (yes and no are falling apart) and the making of distinct sides of freedom (in each yes as well as in each no the yes *or* no split is repeated) dis-unifies freedom, but also because it makes intelligible that there is a freedom which can itself be directed in multiple ways against (the realization of) freedom. Thus a freedom whose realization does not know freedom any longer but which must nonetheless be thought, on some level, as a realization of freedom is formed.

If, even in a highly speculative way, we were to attempt to draft an answer to Sartre's criticism of the Cartesian concept of freedom, it could begin with the emphasis that there is a problematic reifying tendency within Sartre's critique itself. If one assumes freedom is the givenness of a yes and no (and therefore assumes that both stand in a relation of dependence to each another), one must also assume that freedom *is* the capacity to say yes or no (even if one assumes that the "yes" constantly primes the "no"). If freedom is the permanent givenness of the choice of a "yes or no" this means that freedom is ultimately always the capacity to say yes *and* no. Which then determines the "yes *and* no" as the structure of freedom (of any concrete yes or no decision). There is thus no primal "yes" grounding all decisions, rather there is a "yes and no" at the ground of freedom. Such freedom is the capacity to judge freely and thus to realize freedom. But such a freedom is therefore not yes or no, but yes *and* no. For Sartre, this means that freedom is a capacity,[15] and this capacity is that of human beings to say yes or no, and is one therefore to which one in turn cannot say yes or no, because any no is already a realization of (and thus already a yes to) freedom.[16] Thus is man doomed to freedom. And this free-doom is (for Sartre) what makes it a (Sartrean) capacity—a capacity humans cannot not realize. The structure of this capacity is that of indifference: the givenness of a "yes and no" that primes any (determinate) "yes or no" choice. There is—there must be—always a choice.

Concerning the Cartesian concept of freedom, the passage that most irri-tated Sartre into commentary can be found in the fourth meditation of the *Meditations on First Philosophy*—the passage on the foundations of philoso-phy.[17] The fourth meditation deals with the concepts of truth and falsity, that is, with the comprehension of that which is true and with that which is an er-ror, a fallacy. That truth and falsity are systematically linked to the concept of freedom means that, for Descartes, only those beings that can be called free are responsible for that which one calls true and false; if humans are beings that can be called free, then it must hold that they are responsible for their own errors. Which is to say that one cannot blame God for human error. In this way, Descartes aims to determine a concept of freedom which is linked to the concept of truth, and which is thus, albeit in a derivative way, linked to the con-cept of error. Or, more precisely, he aims to determine that the former (truth) must prove derivable from the latter (error). Through this move, all conceptual deductions of true and false judgments which stem from the concept of God will become more complicated, if not downright impossible.[18] But to under-stand adequately the locus and precise nature of Descartes's argument against indifference, it is important to sketch the exact systematic place of these reflec-tions in the *Meditations* as a whole.

After having registered and charted all the areas of possible doubt in the first meditation,[19] after having demonstrated the difference between body and spirit in the second meditation, and after he believed to have developed a concept of and proof of the existence of God in the third meditation, the fourth meditation opens a different field. "In the Fourth Meditation it is proved that everything that we clearly and distinctly perceive is true, and I also explain what the nature of falsity consists in."[20] In this fourth meditation, where freedom both in the form of and also as indifference is criticized, Descartes also clarifies why and how we as humans can err, misjudge, and go wrong. It stands to reason to connect these two aspects: Freedom of and as indifference is criticized because freedom of and as indifference is a false understanding of freedom.

Error about Error and the Cartesian Conflict of Faculties

A short reconstruction of the argumentative course of the first three meditations (indeed, this is something Descartes also allows himself at the beginning
of the fourth meditation) helps to clarify the above ideas and their intercon-
nection. The fourth meditation commences with a reminder that a deficient
being is (among other things) deficient because it is "at the same time" body
and spirit. A being that is body *and* spirit can doubt. It can doubt because
it, itself, generated the experience of the possibility of its own erring, because it,
itself, made the very experience that it is "a thing that is incomplete and dependent."[21] And the thing to be further determined is this thing, in incompletion and dependency, that doubts, for it is a thing that can err and that *knows*
that it can err.

As Descartes demonstrates, it is not only the knowledge about the possibility of error that enables the possibility of doubt, it is also what forms the foundation for generating a concept of error. As soon as a particular experience of
error leads me to want to understand what has befallen me, this leads me to
articulate the concept of error. If I then understand it adequately, I see that
each error is an expression of a lack. And so in this way the concept of lack
results from the concept of error. Not only this, but the former can also be
applied to itself. One can thereby generate a further conceptual inference: The
concept of error enables one to derive the concept of lack; the concept of lack
enables one (through self-application) to derive the thought that there can also
be a lack of lack; this lack of lack, then, is perfection. Descartes's name for
this lack of lack is God.[22] Following this, the fourth meditation attempts to
show that the final thought arrived at (God) cannot be false, "for in every case
of trickery or deception some imperfection is to be found; and although the
ability to deceive appears to be an indication of cleverness or power, the will
to deceive is undoubtedly evidence of malice or weakness, and so cannot ap-
ply to God."[23] Here, then, to think God means to think in a necessarily true
manner the absence of falsity and error and the sources of falsity and error.

If we think God as that which is free from the source of error, then it cannot simply be a false notion to identify God with inerrancy (or, with lack of
lack) precisely because through the experience of error we are necessarily led
to the thought of an absence of falsity, that is, God. If we think God in such a
way we thus cannot think something false. Truth or falsity here name both
the form and the content of the thought, for if we think God as that which
lacks lack, we are led, necessarily, to think something true. And so God cannot and will never deceive us if we think God. To think God, because we need
to think her when we have erred and adequately comprehended what it means

to commit an error necessarily implies to think the absence of the cause of falsity. This cannot be a formal falsity.[24]

Up to and with the fourth meditation, if what Descartes has demonstrated (or at least what he believes he has shown) is that there is error, and how through an adequate understanding of the formal and conceptual implication of the concept of error we get from error to truth, he has not yet achieved an explanation as to why there is error in the first place. The existence of error is known. What is also known is what consequences may be drawn from it (the two names of these consequences are ultimately the "*cogito*" and "God"). But what is insufficiently understood is how error becomes error. Descartes has explained the existence and the being of falsity but has not yet addressed its becoming and origin.

How, then, to comprehend the cause of error(s) for Descartes? One answer might read as follows: "Error is not a pure negation, but rather a privation or lack of some knowledge which somehow should be in me."[25] Error is a privative form of cognition, judgment, action, and so on, which is a way of saying that error is lack. Where does this privation come from? It depends "on two concurrent causes, namely on the faculty of knowledge, which is in me, and on the faculty of choice or freedom of the will; that is, they depend on both the intellect and the will simultaneously."[26] Error is the result of a dualism (quite a surprising thesis from a thinker so often criticized for his dualism). Error results from an "at the same time"; from the simultaneity of intellect and will, of knowledge and freedom of choice. Emerging when knowledge and freedom enter into conflict, error is therefore constitutively linked to the concept of freedom. One way of understanding this is to infer from it that there is error when we misunderstand the cognition of freedom (even if we do this out of freedom), that, conceptually, error must be an error of cognition because it emerges from freedom. The mistake lies in an erroneous understanding of freedom. Freedom, thereby, seems to enable not only the making of mistakes but also the making of mistakes in relation to freedom itself.

In the customary understanding of the first meditation, Descartes states that every error originates in the senses and that humans can make mistakes precisely because they are not only rational and spiritual but are *at the same time* embodied (that is bodily) and sensuous (thus also animal beings), and so the fact that the fourth meditation gives rise to the above thesis on freedom and error may come as rather a surprise. Traditionally, one might be tempted to think that error results for Descartes from the composition of body and spirit, of understanding and pathological inclinations.[27] But Descartes's thesis in the *Meditations* is that error does not result from the composition of body and spirit; rather, it describes a form of spiritual fallacy, which has something to do with the difference and the relation between spirit and body. This is because the fallacy of spirit concerns the locus of the sources of error; with the fallacy of spirit what is at stake is also an erroneous understanding of fallacy. In a second rendering, the thesis is also, and for additional reasons, surprising. Why? because it means that error and fallacy not only designate an error regarding some external object, but also a self-misunderstanding. So error, not simply based on external causes (for example, in God or in the body, both of which are exterior to spirit or the faculty of judgment) may in general be grounded in the fact that free beings misunderstand themselves. So, one kind of fallacy (or at least one kind) is a mistaken understanding of what freedom is, and if this is as such, then the basic form of fallacy still remains unexamined. This is a third surprise, because this also implies that at least one component of error, perhaps even an essential component, consists in making a mistake about what it means to make a mistake, in erring about what it is to err. Error is not only an erroneous judgment about an object, it is also self-misunderstanding. So there is not only error but, even worse than that, there is error about error.[28] And such error about error must necessarily be spiritual error. This cannot be grounded in our bodily constitution. Thus we are led to the questions: How does error become error for Descartes if it cannot simply be a consequence of the bodily constitution of a spiritual being? How might we understand the peculiar conflict between knowledge and will that forms the ground of error? And it is with these questions that we finally draw nearer to the precise passage that so irritated Sartre in his reading of Descartes.

But first, a little more context. Descartes continues, clarifying that error cannot only be an error of the intellect, since "all the intellect does is to enable me to perceive which are subjects for possible judgments; and when regarded strictly in this light, it turns out to contain no error in the proper sense of that term."[29] The argument is along the following lines: If I have the idea of something, then, since I have this idea, I can judge it. So, even though I may lack some ideas, this does not change anything regarding the fact that the intellect cannot make an error when it judges those ideas that are present within it, however scant. If it judges, for example, that the idea of X is within it, this judgment is necessarily true because it actually finds this idea of X within itself; this very judgment would have been otherwise impossible. The immanence of the intellect is due to this tautology without error. Descartes, moving on from the intellect to the will, continues thus:

> Besides, I cannot complain that the will or freedom of choice which I received from God is not sufficiently extensive or perfect, since I know by experience that it is not restricted in any way. Indeed, I think it is

very noteworthy that there is nothing else in me which is so perfect
and so great that the possibility of a further increase in its perfection
or greatness is beyond my understanding. . . . It is only the will, or
freedom of choice, which I experience within me to be so great that
the idea of any greater faculty is beyond my grasp; so much so that it is
above all in virtue of the will that I understand myself to bear in some
way the image and likeness of God.[30]

The will that is in God is not freer than the will that is in man. Human as
well as divine freedom is formally limitless. Human beings are able to will what
they want without any inherent limitation to this willing. In precisely this respect, the human "free will" is formally equal to the will of God, which means
it also must be as perfect as the latter. The form of the human will is thus as
fundamentally indeterminate as that of the divine will. If the will is what is
most like God in man, since God cannot will anything wrong, error cannot
as such lie in the infinite freedom of the will. This is why in freedom as such
there is no error.

How, then, does error emerge when it does not find its ground in the intellect as such nor in the free will as such, as neither have any internal problem
of erring? Descartes's response to this is to indicate a problem that arises from
the bringing together of the intellect and the will, and it is with this problem
that Descartes, highlighting a peculiar conflict between two as such infallible
faculties, designates the concept of indifference. Thus, finally, we reach the
specific "Sartre-passage" of the fourth meditation. Descartes claims:

In order to be free, there is no need for me to be inclined both ways;
on the contrary, the more I incline in one direction—either because
I clearly understand that reasons of truth and goodness point that way,
or because of a divinely produced disposition of my inmost thoughts—
the freer is my choice. . . . [T]he indifference I feel when there is no
reason pushing me in one direction rather than another is the lowest
grade of freedom; it is evidence not of any perfection of freedom, but
rather of a defect in knowledge or a kind of negation.[31]

Descartes is unambiguous: Freedom is one-sidedness. Freedom means to
decide. Freedom is inclination, partiality, partisanship. One-sidedness does not
in any way limit the freedom of the will; it is, rather, the genuine expression
of the will.[32] Freedom rests in the decision for one of two sides. In Descartes
freedom is only conceivable as realization of freedom, which is precisely the
point with which Sartre found fault. Such a conception of freedom is, in contrast to Sartre's, positive rather than negative, and it involves, as in Rousseau,

a certain kind of coercion,[33] a kind of Lutheran "I could not but"[34] in its doing (or our doing of it). For Descartes the mode of a "I could-not-(do-otherwise)-but" is where freedom is realized, and whether this "could-not-but" originates from an insight into truth or from the structure of my thought plays no decisive role. Rather, freedom is either decisive resolve because of an insight or because of an inevitable decision, but it is in all cases a decision. If freedom is so formed, it must be at the same time indifferent toward all the other possibilities it may also have realized. So realized freedom is indifferent toward other possibilities of realizing freedom.

Sartre's problem occurs here: If freedom for Descartes consists in deciding for one side and therefore in becoming indifferent toward any other possibilities of realizing freedom, how can he at the same time understand indifference, namely, freedom of choice as the lowest degree, as the zero point of freedom, as lack? How is it possible to bring together these two things without vacillation or conceptual vagueness?[35] How does freedom relate to indifference, and what, precisely, is the relationship of freedom and indifference to the concept of error?

Indifference I: Theoretical Error and Practical Indecision

To answer these questions it is necessary give a more precise explanation of the above cited passage. Initially, Descartes introduces indifference as the lowest degree of freedom ("if I am indifferent then I am the least free"). This is the case because indifference is an expression of an absence of inclination and of partiality; it is an absence of both decision and of good reasons for any decision. And freedom, in contrast, consists precisely in decision-making, partisanship, and partiality. Thus for Descartes indifference is the result of a lack of cognition and knowledge,[36] where knowledge in the face of options or a choice necessarily means deciding for and having an inclination for one of the options or choosing one of the sides ("I am least free when I do not do what constitutes freedom, namely that I cannot decide for one of the options given"). Indifference names a state of the subject for whom both sides of a decision are equally plausible, equally valid, and where, without difference, they are equivalent.[37] Indifference thus names a subjective state in which the subject is undecided as to how it decides (where to decide is to judge and choose) because the choice or object it is confronted with presents what appears to be two indifferently and equally valid sides. In Descartes the state named indifference is a concatenation of subjective indecision, which results from the (objective) equal validity of the possibilities with which we are confronted.

On the one hand, indifference names a state of the subject or subjective state—a subjective state of sensation ("the indifference I feel . . .").[38] Indifference describes the absence of inclination toward any decision-making direction, a fundamental indecisiveness on the part of the subject with regard to the possibilities of the choice with which they are confronted. By mobilizing this side of the concept of indifference as subjective, Descartes criticizes the prevailing understanding of freedom as *liberum arbitrium indifferentiae*, as capacity to be able to freely and groundlessly choose opposed options in any given moment:[39] "For if I always saw clearly what was true and good, I should never have to deliberate about the right judgement or choice; in that case, although I should be wholly free, it would be impossible for me ever to be in a state of indifference."[40] In the Middle Ages, for example, William of Ockham classified a non-causal (that is contingent) two-sided (that is indeterminate) capacity of the will, a capacity to indifferently will x and non-x, namely, a capacity to choose without causal necessity as *liberum arbitrium indifferentiae*.[41] Descartes's critique of indifference via the critique of *liberum arbitrium indifferentiae* is therefore a part of his explicitly modern understanding of freedom, and this shows in addition that the classification of indifference as the lowest degree of freedom, and the critique of the identification of freedom with an indifferent capacity shows that—similar to what Hegel will develop in the *Phenomenology of Spirit*—certain states of consciousness, for example the lack of knowledge and indecisiveness, can correlate with certain positions within the history of philosophy.[42]

As it lies in distinction to the medieval determination of freedom, the problem that Descartes articulates with the concept of indifference has a direct relationship to what in Cartesian times appears as Aristotelianism.[43] Why? Because behind this category and through the concept of capacity a specific type of determining freedom appears, which has the tendency to lead to theoretical as well as practical problems.[44] More precisely: The problematic trait of the conception and articulation of freedom as *libertas indifferentiae* lies in the identification of freedom with an indubitably given capacity of indifferent choice. It is precisely this identification which Descartes determines as a problem in his concept of indifference.[45] To this, we need to add that the Cartesian concept of indifference not only describes the identification of freedom with an indeterminately given capacity to choose contingently: Indifference has another side, namely, an objective one.[46]

The subjective side of the indifference problem, the *libertas indifferentiae*, is problematic because it characterizes freedom as a *form before its realization*. It describes freedom as a capacity that is supposed to have an actuality before it is itself actualized, which is the same as saying that it describes freedom's actuality before freedom becomes actual freedom. In this way freedom becomes a givenness that, even though not yet realized, is nonetheless supposed to be real. Descartes's problem with this determination is that indifference as a description of the actuality of the capacity of freedom before its actualization only captures freedom conceptually as indeterminacy (this is the *how*, the *mode* of this freedom) and in subjective practical matters as indecision. This critique is convincing under the condition that one determines freedom as Descartes has done, namely as decision, resolve, inclination, and so on. But it is important not to equate the indecision that shines through the subjective side of the concept of indifference with a complete misunderstanding of freedom. Since although, as Descartes points out in the passage cited above, indifference is the lowest degree of freedom, it is not an overall negation of freedom. Indifference is not bondage and unfreedom. This means that indifference—freedom as already realized in the form of capacity and thus interpreted as *libertas indifferentiae*—becomes problematic precisely when at the same time it is assumed that the possibility to choose (some things) arbitrarily is already the highest degree of freedom.

As we have seen above, this critique can of course be opened up to include references to different positions in the history of philosophy. Therefore, the problem with regard to the concept of freedom does not consist in the assumption that indifference is freedom. Rather it consists in the assumption that indifference (freedom as conceived of in the form of a given capacity to choose) is the highest and most essential form of freedom. The problem thus lies in the identification of freedom with an indeterminate capacity of choice, with freedom of choice and the identification of freedom of choice with the highest degree of freedom,[47] since indifference—that is, freedom before its actualization—is, even though this seems tautological, a capacity to realize which is nevertheless essentially not yet realized. If freedom is identified with the capacity to decide before any decision is taken, then this is not, for Descartes, a category mistake but rather a gradual one. Such a gradual mistake occurs if it is assumed that the *actuality of the possibility* of freedom is worth more than or the same as the *actuality of the actuality* of freedom. The actuality of the possibility of freedom is the lowest degree of freedom because in relation to freedom it necessarily falls behind the actuality of the actualization of freedom. Freedom as really possible is—ontologically—less real than freedom as really realized.

One consequence of this criticism is that to identify the mere capacity of freedom before and beyond its realization with freedom is not only a gradual theoretical error but also has practical ramifications: Theoretical indifference can and must lead to practical indecision.[48] Descartes can infer this because he assumes that every (theoretical) understanding of freedom has practical im-plications.[49] Freedom in the sense of indifference (as capacity) is freedom in the state of its gradual lack, freedom in the state not of its complete absence, but in a deficient state, where the defect is a defect of cognition (*cognitione defectum*).[50] This means that indifference must also be a defective state with regard to the cognition of what real freedom is, since if I interpret the actual-ity of the possibility of freedom as the *one* form of freedom, I delude myself regarding the proper actuality of freedom. I am undecided, indecisive. *To act undecidedly* and irresolutely means to act and judge in an inconstant, volatile manner. *To be undecided* means not to act but to hesitate. The comprehen-sion of freedom as capacity of choice is therefore the lowest degree of the ac-tuality of freedom since it arises from a cognitive defect and, practically, leads to hesitation, volatility, and impermanence of judgment and acting. That this *can* happen does not mean that this *must* happen, but rather that it is all the time possible that some volatility in my judgment or hesitation occurs.

Indifference describes a defective understanding of freedom that practically leads to indecision that is volatility or hesitation. To understand freedom as capacity of choice leads to indecision. This is why indifference names a subjective-practical problem. *The practical truth of the gradually erroneous un-derstanding of freedom as capacity of choice, as liberum arbitrium indifferen-tiae, is embodied in indecision.* The subjective truth of identifying freedom with freedom of choice is in hesitation[51] not in doubt.[52] Arising from this gradually erroneous understanding of freedom are practically more (gradual) errors, whose first categorical name is "indecision." In this manner, the defective un-derstanding of freedom becomes a sort of problematic transcendental of all my future (gradual) errors. Things go gradually, necessarily, and progressively more astray. In an astonishing passage from the second reply where Descartes emphasizes that when concerning "the conduct of life" indecision and hesita-tion have to be absolutely avoided, we see quite how truly practically problem-atic this can be:

> I do not think that we should always wait even for probable truths;
> from time to time we will have to choose one of many alternatives
> about which we have no knowledge, and once we have made our
> choice, so long as no reasons against it can be produced, we must stick
> to it as firmly as if it had been chosen for transparently clear reasons.[53]

Even if, subjectively, I do not see clearly, the true problem in and for prac-tice consists in the resulting indecision. Waiting and hesitation are the result of my defective cognition or lack in cognition. Indifference names for the sub-ject a theoretically problematic understanding of freedom as the indeterminate capacity of choice that leads to practically problematic consequences, namely to the volatility of my practice or to my abstinence from practice overall. Indifference must be decisively avoided. If this is not theoretically possible,[54] this nonetheless holds in any case for any form of practice.[55]

Indifference II: Apathy and Decisions Outside the Boundaries of Mere Reason

This very analysis must be supplemented by an analysis of the objective side of the concept of indifference. Indifference in Descartes is an interweaving of subjective and objective indifference. The objective side of the concept of indifference ("when there is no reason pushing me in one direction rather than another . . ."[56]) establishes a kind of equal validity of the side of the very object of (free) choice. One can assume that Descartes thereby implicitly takes up on the objective side of indifference the Stoic determination of so-called "middle things," namely, things that are neither good nor bad, neither evil nor good. The subjective side of indifference, then, is the lowest degree of freedom when the "object" of freedom, freedom's "thing," so to speak, is also indifferent, that is, neutral.[57] In Stoic terminology the neutral, indifferent things are called *adiaphora*. They are things that are non-differently, that is, indifferently, good and evil: neither properly the one nor the other. *Adiaphora* are things that are *as well as* and therefore *neither* the one *nor* the other.[58]

In Descartes the *adiaphora*-determination as indifference of the object-side is related to the indifference of the subject. The things that leave us indifferent are the things from which also emerge freedom in the form of an indeterminate capacity of choice. Freedom surfaces in the form of indifference, in the pure form of a capacity to choose, when at the same time the object of choice or the possibilities of choice are indifferent and of an equal validity. But in the form of the capacity, freedom has only its most minimal reality because it remains indeterminate, merely possible. The same holds for the object of freedom, namely, that it is in a state of indeterminacy where it has its most minimal reality for us as long as we do not—literally—decidedly relate to it. If we do not decidedly relate to it, the object remains indeterminate as much as freedom remains indeterminate without decision. Indifferent objects are in this sense pure potential, "objects." They are potentially good and potentially bad, potentially good and potentially evil. The relation of a theoretically indifferent and practically undecided subject to a theoretically indifferent "object" thereby even becomes itself potential or indeterminate. And thus we see how in Descartes indifference names the concatenation of potentially good or bad objects and potentially yea- or nay-saying subjects. It names a concatenation of potentiality and potentiality, an indeterminate concatenation of indeterminacies. It marks a possible free relation to something that is possibly x or non-x, an object of freedom that could be anything. It is the categorical name of the relation of possibility to possibility, of potentiality to potentiality. And this form of relation is the lowest degree of freedom.

Two potentialities come together and form another—a potentiality of the potential relation to something potential—which all together lead to the lowering of the reality of freedom, and it is indifference that is Descartes's name for this third potentiality. A third potentiality which is composed of the theoretical understanding of freedom that leads to practical indecision and objective equal validity, the *libertas indifferentiae* and the *adiaphora*. Indifference is a possible relation of possibility to (anything) possible. It is therein what is furthest away from a realizing relation to reality. And it is precisely the multiplication and potentialization of possibilities that is the reason why we are dealing with the lowest degree of freedom here. *Indifference is the destitution of freedom by means of the multiplication of possibility qua possibility.*

Descartes's indifference is a state in which the subject does not know how it should deal with the object of its free choice because it does not know how this object can ultimately be determined, and therefore it only knows in a reduced manner what freedom is, since freedom without a determinate object of freedom is freedom before freedom. Thus, we are confronted with a form of freedom that on one side is reduced to the pure form of the capacity to choose and on the other to the pure form of the object of free choice. Through his critique of indifference Descartes criticizes the idea of freedom's identification with indeterminacy, with the mere form of the possible, with potentiality or with the capacity to do anything possible.[59] But it is precisely this elaboration, at least as announced in the fourth meditation, that is also supposed to give an elaboration of the origin of error; how can the thus far reconstructed argument contribute to understanding the concept of error? Descartes's answer reads as follows:

> So what then is the source of my mistakes? It must be simply this: the scope of the will is wider than that of the intellect; but instead of restricting it within the same limits, I extend its use to matters which I do not understand. Since the will is indifferent in such cases, it easily turns aside from what is true and good, and this is the source of my error and sin.[60]

Error has its source and origin in indifference, in an indifference which is linked to the scope of the freedom of the will; error is linked to freedom. But how precisely is this specified?

Initially, Descartes's claim that error originates in indifference means that error is a transgression of the limits of the intellect by the will: If the intellect is the capacity of judgment, then indifference designates a mode of willing in which the will wants something and is directed toward something which is located beyond the limits of the intellect and beyond the capacity to judge.[61] But how might this relate to the elaborations above? On the one side, indifference designates an indeterminate concatenation of two indeterminacies, and on the other, indifference is the source of error, because the will moves outside of the limits of the intellect and its judgments. Errors in judgment, practical errors, and falsities in general all originate in indifference; that is, they originate in the concatenation of a problematic comprehension of freedom which leads to indecisiveness, and which is linked to the equal validity of the object of freedom in an indeterminate way. Why? Because here there already exists a (gradual) error concerning the definition and identification of freedom. Error neither originates in the constitution of the will as such nor in the constitution of the intellect as such. Rather, error springs from a peculiarly averted collision, an avoided conflict between the will and intellect in which the indifferent will moves outside of the judgment of the intellect. One wills something of which one does not know what and how it is; one only knows that one wills it and that one does not know what and how it is, and because it is nevertheless willed, it is so willed in a way in which error is generated.

The will generates error in its transgression of the limits of the intellect, in being indifferent to them. It generates error when it wills without judgment or in indifference to judgment. The will then wills indeterminately and it is therefore a will that is separated from reason; it is a pure and in this sense an unjudging willing. Such willing is overtaken by error because the will wills but what it wills is indeterminate; willing without judgment becomes indeterminate willing. Why does such willing generate error? Descartes states:

> [T]his indifference does not merely apply to cases where the intellect
> is wholly ignorant, but extends in general to every case where the
> intellect does not have sufficiently clear knowledge at the time when
> the will deliberates. For although probable conjectures may pull me in
> one direction, the mere knowledge that they are simply conjectures,
> and not certain and indubitable reasons, is itself quite enough to push
> my assent the other way.[62]

Indifferently, the will decides in such a way that it ignores that conjectures are merely conjectures. The will disregards and ignores the intellect and becomes a will without knowledge and cognition, an unjudged willing. The deliberations, resolutions, and decisions of the will are decisions for indeterminate conjectures which cannot be recognized as such. They are decisions without judgments.

What does it mean to will outside of the limits of the intellect, outside of the boundaries of reason? The intellect, necessarily in a situation in which there is a cognitive defect, a judgment on and knowledge about indifference, must know that it does not know. For Descartes, the will ignores this knowledge when it wills without judgment, and indifference names a state in which I *know that I do not know how* I should decide, *because* I know *that* I do not know *what* the object of the decision is and this leads me into a state where I do not precisely know *what* freedom is and *how* to realize it, *but I decide nonetheless.* Or, at least I believe this is what I am doing. The will denies the knowledge (of the ignorance) that the intellect has.[63] Indifference, which stands at the ground of error, designates a state which might be described as follows: I *know that* I (subjectively) *do not know how* I shall decide—this is how the intellect judges—*because* I know—and this is how it continues—*that* I do not know what the (objective) purpose of my decision is. It is the *intellect* that *knows* all this. And it is precisely to this knowledge that *the will is indifferent.* If the will becomes indifferent to the intellect, ignores and denies this knowledge, it decides *as if* it knows nothing about it: The will decides in and out of indifference. The will decides in an indifferent way. Being indifferent, it decides outside and beyond the limits of the intellect.

Indifference is the origin of error because it describes a will that decides outside the boundaries of the intellect such that the form that defines decisions in general, namely that they are constitutively related to two opposing sides, is suspended. This is why the decisions of the indifferent will always already imply an error about the very nature of decision, and with this an error about the concept of freedom. So in this sense, indifference is the source (or origin) of error. But as soon as there is indifference, error has at the same time always already occurred. Indifference as ground and origin of error is not simply a misjudgment, it is rather the suspension of the constitutive two-side-form of judgment. It is therefore the suspension of the two-side-form of decision and thus also of freedom. And because of these suspensions, the indifferent will is an inconsequent will. The ground of error (indifference) is in this way also the disappearance of error as error. Error here disappears through the suspension of (i.e., the indifference to) the two sides of the (or any) distinction. And with this move, the will also suspends the distinction between true and false. To err, thus, is not only to will irrationally or a willing against better judgment; error is also not simply akrasia or weakness of the will. For Descartes, error rather lies fundamentally enclosed in the indifference toward error and truth. Put differently: Error is the assumption that one can suspend this distinction—the distinction between true and false—at all.[64] The origin of error consists in the assumption that it is possible to will beyond the distinction of true and false, beyond the distinction of good and evil[65] in a rational manner. Error arises when error disappears.[66]

Decision-Forming: Decisions in, because of, and against Indifference

Against such a background, how is it possible to make the difference that Descartes wants and needs to make in order to break with the other danger of indifference, namely the danger that arises from and is, indeed, indecision and hesitation? How is it possible to differentiate between a free decision taken even though I do not know how and nonetheless stubbornly stick to it, and a decision that my will takes in and because of an indifference to the distinction between truth and error?

If Descartes is consistent here, the answer must be that there are two fundamentally different types of decision. When I decide freely, I necessarily decide for one of the sides that are on offer. This holds even if I decide even though I do not know how to decide. But if I decide not only out of indifference, but in an indifferent manner, this is a decision that, ultimately, cannot *in stricto sensu* be a decision.[67] Here, my will exceeds the limits of the intellect— that of which I know that I do not know—and this happens when I decide but neither have good reasons for my decision nor am able to conceive of the absence of good reasons as a good reason for the decision, that is, as a reason that necessitates me to decide even though I do not know how. These are decisions that are neither decisions nor do they want to be. They suspend intellectual judgments. They are decisions in and out of indifference.

But here we must be more precise. The decision that is and wants to remain a decision, even if it goes wrong, generates a truth, even if such a truth may be the truth of the committed error. This is not, however, the case for the second kind of decision. Here, the will undermines the distinction of truth and falsity, transgressing the limits of the intellect. In this case, to suspend and ignore difference is to err. But to err here is not error in the sense of a mistaken judgment, but error with respect to the difference of truth and falsity, as suspension of the structure of judgment. *The origin of error is indifference to error and truth; it is indifference to the difference between the two.*[68] The indifference at the ground of error is ignorance in relation to or denial of the difference between truth and error and consequently ignorance of truth and error itself. If this distinction is ignored, as it is by the will that wills indifferently, the actuality of the distinction of the capacity to make judgments is suspended. It is taken to be a merely possible distinction. Yet it is this distinction that is for Descartes constitutive of freedom.

I am freer when I incline to one of the two sides of the choice; I still decide freely when I take the absence of my inclination and determination of my choice as ground for a—in this case a presumably contingent—choice, since in this way I can still generate truth, even in the case of error. But without the difference of true and false there is no decision (in a strong sense of the term), and without decision there is no freedom. For Descartes, the origin of error implies an error about what freedom is. This error is error about the essence of freedom, namely that freedom essentially consists in deciding. The error lies in the reduction of the essence of decision-making to its lowest grade, and as such to a mere form of decision which has no material consequence whatsoever. Thus are we mistaken with regard to the essence of decision. But if the essence of freedom and the essence of decision are misunderstood, so, too, is the concept of error,[69] as, in this chain, we are led to assume that there is *in stricto sensu* no error at all. It is precisely this assumption that is an error about what error is. Indifference is the lowest degree of freedom and the cause of all errors because, for Descartes, it designates an error about the essence of freedom and with it also about the essence of error. Indifference is the erroneous transcendental of all my errors.

It is important to note here that, in Descartes, one therefore deals with three different forms of decision:

There are in the first instance *not-indifferent decisions* that are, due to the existence of knowledge and insight or due to the necessity of decision, *decided in their pursuit, even against objections*, because they rely on the better reasons. This is the *highest grade*—the paradigm—of *the actuality of freedom*. The infinity of the free will is condensed and concentrated because of the judgments of the intellect on one side of the decision.

There are in the second instance *decisions in and against indifference* that are taken even though one does not know how to decide. But these decisions stick strictly to their own being-decided, because they consolidate the (practical) necessity to decide at their ground and are thus *decidedly opposing all objections*.[70] This is *the middle grade of the actuality of freedom*. There are thus decisions out of reasons that are indifferent to other reasons and decisions that take the absence of reasons as a reason to decide. Paradigmatically, Descartes elaborated the latter in his *Discourse on the Method* in the following manner:

> Likewise, lest I should remain indecisive in my actions while reason obliged me to be so in my judgements . . . I formed for myself a provisional moral code [*morale par provision*] consisting of just three

or four. . . . [One] maxim was to be as firm and decisive in my actions as I could, and to follow even the most doubtful opinions, once I had adopted them, with no less constancy than if they had been quite certain. In this respect I would be imitating a traveller who, upon finding himself lost in a forest, should not wander about turning this way and that, and still less stay in one place, but should keep walking as straight as he can in one direction, never changing it for slight reasons even if mere chance made him choose it in the first place; for in this way, even if he does not go exactly where he wishes, he will at least end up in a place where he is likely to be better off than in the middle of a forest. Similarly, since in everyday life we must often act without delay. . . . Even when no opinions appear more probable than any others, we must still adopt some; and having done so we must then regard them not as doubtful, from a practical point of view, but as most true and certain, on the grounds that the reason which made us adopt them is itself true and certain.[71]

Decisions out of and because of indifference have the absence of inclinations and good reasons as their ground. They can be decisions for the "most doubtful opinions" and out of contingency, because the strict insistence on and fidelity to them enables the generation of a truth (even if it is that of their falsity).[72]

We observe how *decisions* of the first type are decisions that are *free and oriented* by clear and distinct cognition, whereas *decisions* of the second type are not oriented by clear and distinct cognition but are nevertheless free decisions that therefore *create orientation*. They overcome the indecision and the hesitation[73] that manifests as instability of the decisions of the will, as they are in their *pursuit also persistent against objections* and they overcome the indifference at their origin. An elucidation of the decision of the third type will follow.

As-If Decisions: Decisions in and out of Indifference

There are decisions because of good reasons and decisions in and against indifference (viz., in the absence of good reason as good reasons). The actual problem of indifference, as should have become clear, is related to another, or third type, of decision. It is here that we encounter decisions that do not take their own status as decisions seriously, and thus *render indistinguishable decisions and non-decision*. The ensuing analysis will allow us to grasp more adequately, through the third type, the practical side of the problem of indifference: There are neither reasons for these decisions nor do they take the absence of reason as a reason. Rather, these are decisions that are neither related to reasons nor to self-justification; these are decisions that stand at the origin of the concept of error and suspend the distinction between true and false. They are *decisions in and out of indifference, that is, decisions in a perpetuated state of indifference.*[74] Being neither really executed nor realized decisions, they repeatedly reproduce the initial state of indifference, a persistence in indifference in an ostensible movement. They are decisions that ultimately do not really decide anything, leaving everything open. Anything is possible. Anything goes. Decision as no decision; no decision as if decision.

By means of the concept of indifference, Descartes criticizes two things: non-decisions that find their practical appearance in the forms of indecision and hesitation, and decisions that are undecided decisions, *as-if-decisions.* As-if-decisions are not negations of decisions, they are not non-decisions[75] (if I decide as if I decide, I do not simply not decide), rather, they are decisions without real practical and material consequences, decisions after whose pursuit things are not really any different from before. As-if-decisions are *decisions without decisions.* They are not negations but privations of decision. And thus Descartes can also address error as privation: "For error is not a pure negation, but rather a privation or lack of some knowledge which somehow should be mine."[76] Not only should the cognition and knowledge about what a decision is be mine, but I should also know that as soon as I only as-if-decide, I do not really decide. And yet because I am indifferent, this knowledge is inaccessible to me. And thus I do not know what I know. Such knowledge is inaccessible because I act outside of the boundaries of the understanding, and therefore I have suspended the knowledge about what I do. "I can make judgments only about things which are known to me."[77]

A remark by Martin Heidegger concerning the concept of privation, that he translates as deprivation (*Beraubung*), is instructive here for Descartes's use of the term "privation," since for Descartes, the privation that is error does not happen to human beings in a simple external manner. Heidegger remarks: "What has been deprived [*das Beraubte*] is not merely the 'object' of deprivation, but rather its ground." Exemplarily, Heidegger enlists the following things for "what happens to us as 'privation'": "death—life; forgetting—retaining; being silent—speaking; poverty—possession; unhistorical—historical."[78] Privation designates a loss that is not simply external or accidental for the deprived, but essential. A loss, if one may say so, of substance. But Heidegger's phrasing entails a further twist: Life is not only the object of the privation whose name is death—death does not simply deprive life externally—life is at the same time the ground on which and the reason as to why privation takes place. Life is the ground on which death takes place and is the reason why there can be death of life. Death kills life because it has been lived, so that life is neither

only the object of an accidental privation by death nor the substance of a substantial privation; rather, it is itself at the same time the subject of privation.
Life is the subject of death that is its privation. Life spends itself, and precisely
this is death. The privation is thus not only *immanent* to life but *from its very
ground* linked to its substance, one of its possibilities that it itself brings about.
Therefore, error is nothing that happens due to external reasons, and the
"battles" that are fought when "attempting to overcome all the difficulties and
errors"[79] are not battles fought against an external enemy. Rather, they are
battles against an internal enemy, battles against the indifference which results, as has been elaborated, from a specific understanding of freedom and
its practical consequences. But how does this relate specifically to the concept
of privation?

Descartes writes in the fourth meditation that "there is nothing in me to
enable me to go wrong or lead me astray; but in so far as I participate in nothingness or non-being . . . it is no wonder that I make mistakes."[80] This means
at least three things: First, lack and privation are not external to me but essential, because as a human being I am not perfect, which is to say I am not
God. My being always already participates in a nothingness, in what *is* not in
the highest sense.[81] Human being is (I am) a privation of God and therefore
has a lower grade of reality,[82] which is why, when human beings err and understand their error as error, they can become conscious of their own limitation, and can infer God as the one who lacks lack. Second, to make a mistake,
I do not need a separate capacity that I would actualize and realize in erring.
Error is a privation. Third, error neither originates in the intellect nor in the
will as such. This becomes clear to me "when I concentrate on the nature of
God," for then "it seems impossible that he should have placed in me a faculty which is not perfect of its kind."[83] Error is not inscribed in any of my faculties as such, rather it holds that "in this incorrect use of free will may be
found the privation which constitutes the essence of error. The privation, I say,
lies in the operation of the will."[84] Error originates in a way of *using* the intellect and the free will. It is practical, its practice is privative, and its conceptual
and categorical name is indifference.

This can furthermore be read in two ways: First, it can be read such that
the privation which is error originates in indifference because human beings
are not only will *and* intellect, but rather a compound of body and soul; the
ground of error and also of indifference would then lie in Descartes's infamous
dualism that would ultimately amount to a kind of defective human condition. But in this first case, the concept of privation would no longer hold what
Heidegger asserted, that the deprived is the ground of its own becoming-
deprived. Man would not be the ground of privation that is error, but rather

privation would result from being human as such, which in turn would make God—the creator—its ground. This would ultimately mean that God would be the ground of our privation: Error would be a structural feature of the dual human constitution in which man would never be subject of privation, rather always only its object. It would thus also no longer hold that error would be a privation that—in the sense of Heidegger's interpretation—is brought about as privation only and through the use of what is proper to man. Rather, the finite and limited constitution (of man) would as such be a defect. Consequentially, error would be unavoidable.

According to this interpretation, Descartes's project could not but have been doomed to fail from the beginning. It is here we may encounter the second reading, which we may extrapolate from another remark by Descartes, namely that sometimes there "is undoubtedly an imperfection in me," precisely in cases when "I misuse that [my, F.R.] freedom and make judgments about matters I do not fully understand."[85] Not only does privation originate in use, this use is, furthermore, an exercise of freedom. My use and my understanding of freedom is the reason and ground for the privation I suffer in error. The name for this use of freedom that leads to privation is indifference. But does this not ultimately testify to a certain limitation of freedom and refute the above elaborated analysis of free will outside of the limits of the intellect?

Descartes states over and again that freedom is not limited as such, but rather it is infinite. At the already quoted passage of the fourth meditation he claims:

> It is only the will, or freedom of choice, which I experience within me
> to be so great that the idea of any greater faculty is beyond my grasp;
> so much so that it is above all in virtue of the will that I understand
> myself to bear in some way the image and likeness of God.[86]

The freedom of the free will is so unlimited that—"when considered as will in the essential and strict," that is formal "sense"—it is in God not "any greater than mine."[87] That God's will cannot be coerced by and through nothing means that the same holds for us: "[W]e do not feel we are determined by any external force."[88] But if the freedom of my will is formally not inferior to God's, then it must be true that such freedom is so free that it is able to deprive itself of itself. This means that the ground of error, even and especially the error about freedom, is freedom itself. Whereas indifference designates the lowest degree of freedom, namely a freedom that understands and determines itself so that this leads to a privation of freedom, and error is the effect of a privation that grounds in indifference, namely, in a specific understanding and use of freedom, the freedom of the free will is so great that it cannot only will outside of the boundaries of the intellect in an indifferent manner. This way of willing can even lead to a privation of freedom, to its lowest grade. Indifference is self-privation of freedom by means of freedom. One can therefore supplement the series of Heideggerian privations of "death—life," and so on, with another couple: "indifference—freedom."

The freedom of the will is so great that it knows a mode (indifference) in which it does not realize itself but reduces itself to a minimum,[89] to a "non-being," to a "nothingness" in which "I participate."[90] Indifference designates the understanding and the practice of the free will through which it becomes the subject and ground of privation and experiences a privative reduction into its lowest grade, which originates in error. Indifference designates the most *privative mode of freedom*. It generates the *form* of error because it already relies on an error about what freedom is. I misuse free will (*liberi arbitrii*) when I assume that this form of freedom is already freedom in its fullest grade. I first judge erroneously about what freedom is, losing in this way the distinction of true and false. I even lose the insight into what I am doing: I do not know it, but I am doing it. Even though "now we know that all our errors depend on our will" (when it exceeds the intellect's limits), we "often wish to give [our, F.R.] assent to something which . . . contains some error."[91] I do know, but often I do not know what I know. The error I have committed and that makes me indifferent is therefore a structurally unconscious error, an error that is the most difficult to first recognize and then clear out. In indifference one is confronted with a free will that wills beyond the intellect all that's possible and therefore nothing really.

We can thus recapitulate: *There are (1) non-indifferent decisions from good reasons; (2) decisions grounded in but directed against indifference, and (3) decisions in and out of indifference.* The last type of decision relies on an understanding of freedom as the indeterminate capacity to do whatever is possible and on the assumption that this is already the highest degree of freedom. But this last type of decision is effectively a privation of freedom. Here, freedom as the purely indeterminate capacity of choice amounts to nothing effectively. A nothingness in which we in some sense always participate, a nothing in and of freedom, no(-thing of) freedom.[92]

The Practice of Indifference

Is there a specific way in which this nothing of freedom appears? What does a practice of freedom look like which in its pursuit realizes a privation of freedom? What is a practice in and out of indifference? These questions demand that the conceptual implications of the claims thus far elaborated are made explicit vis-à-vis the concept of a practice of indifference.

Let us begin with a simple as well as fundamental characteristic: Unlike non-decisions and also in difference to the above mentioned first two types of decision, within indifference one is confronted with decisions that are revisable, which resemble "a traveller who upon finding himself lost in a forest . . . wander[s] about turning this way or that."[93] But decisions that are fundamentally revisable are such that they can also be revoked, time and again. Decisions that can be revoked are indifferent to their own being(-decisions), and in a formal sense thus are and remain fundamentally indeterminate.[94] To revise the title of Robert Musil's novel, this, then, is a *practice without qualities*. The practice *seems* to gain determinations, but because they are and remain revisable, the determinations remain on the level of a lessened, diminished form of determinateness. They are determination on its lowest grade. This lowest grade is that in which determination is conceived of only as potential determination, as a revisable determination, and which in this sense cannot ever know determination as really determined. The practice of the indifferent will is a practice in which every determination is negotiable, everything is equally valid, anything is possible; nothing makes a difference, and nothing is ever ultimately determined. The practice of the indifferent will is a practice without real error or truth.

Such a practice of the indifferent will realizes, in its strict sense, a *freedom without freedom*, which is to say that it realizes the lowest degree of the reality of freedom, its mere and empty form. Such a practice of the indifferent will is about a seeming, a pseudo-realization of freedom which constantly shies away from real realization. It is in this sense a practice that tries to realize *freedom as indeterminate capacity*. It is a practice without real decisions, without real partiality, and, because it moves outside of the boundaries of the intellect, it is a practice without judgments. To conceive of and to determine decisions as revisable—a realization of freedom in the mode of mere possibility—is the consequence of an understanding of freedom as capacity that indifferently (viz., in a revisable manner) relates to potentially indifferent possibilities of the realization of this freedom. And this is the ground of all error.

Because it is revisable, within this form of practice anything is possible in principle; all commitments can be revised. However, even this happens in a perpetuated indifference because, beyond the capacity of judgment, there are no criteria for Descartes by means of which one could even still distinguish when, if, and why something ought to be revised. Through the kind of decisions that are none, the state of indifference is not only perpetually reproduced but is indeed never left. We seem to move, but do not make a single step. This is a practice without intellect and judgment, a practice in which freedom remains in a state of potentiality, even though it appears to be actualized. It is an essentially indeterminate practice because determination is not essential to it. Its determinations are therefore never real determination but only ever have a possible reality.

In such a practice of the practically indifferent will, because the judgments of the intellect and its distinctions are suspended, there are not only no longer any determinate commitments, but also because of this there is no normativity—neither divine nor self-grounded. Each determination is doubly indifferent (indifferent in both senses of the term). This is a practice that may appear, with Habermas, "normatively de-cored [*normativ entkernt*],"[95] but that ultimately, more precisely, is a privative form of practice. Such a practice is one in which the privation that freedom repeatedly brings upon itself is repeated. It is a practice that in its pursuit—that is, no pursuit of freedom and thus no pursuit at all—viz., in its static reproduction—is constantly manifesting the privation of real practice. But if this practice does not know normativity—and certainly no normativity of freedom, whatever this may be—what kind of practice is this? One can give two answers to this question, a structural one and one that derives from the actual text of Descartes's works.

The structural answer can be articulated as follows: If the practice of indifference (which is actually a situation of indifference because in it there is a perpetuation of the given state of affairs) is a practice whose agents understand themselves as if they were free, even though they are not—or only to the lowest, least real grade—then this is a practice in which there is a peculiar inadequacy between self-understanding and reality. It is thus a practice whose understanding of practice differs from the practice itself, and this difference is the reason for the specific constitution of this practice. The agents of this practice consider themselves to be free, but, due to this problematic understanding of freedom, they are engaged in a practice that is precisely not what it is assumed to be. To rephrase: The theory of the practice that its agent produced is constitutive of a practice that deviates from its very theory, and yet which is nevertheless produced by this theory. Here, a certain understanding of freedom generates a practice that is no longer really a practice of freedom or a practice of its realization. The name for that which introduces this deviation, this error, is indifference. To rephrase once more: Indifference describes the imaginary relation of the indifferent subject to the real conditions of indifference in which they live. This is, obviously, a well-known definition of ideology.[96]

Indifferent subjects indifferently relate to their freedom which is the real condition of their existence, and they understand it (imaginarily) in such a way that this understanding produces a reality that subsequently and erroneously appears to them as reality and as a practice of freedom. This is a representation of reality that as representation transforms this very reality. Descartes's critical analysis of indifference can thus be read as a critique of a specific ideology of freedom and of the (individual but also social) privative practice that follows from and is legitimized by it. The practice that one can describe (with Descartes) as the practice of indifference is an ideological practice of freedom in which one thinks and acts as if one were free, as if one were deciding, but in which one is at the same time not free, does not act, and does not decide.[97] Descartes's critique of indifference is a critique of ideology.

In looking at Descartes's actual text a quite different answer arises, which can be found precisely where Descartes describes the initial situation of his own enterprise. This situation is one in which, in philosophy, "there is still no point . . . which is not disputed and hence doubtful," in which "for the other sciences, in so far as they borrow their principles from philosophy . . . nothing solid could have been built," in which one may be surprised "considering how many diverse opinions learned men may maintain on a single question," a situation that is inhabited by "alchemist[s]," "astrologer[s]," "magician[s]," "frauds and boasts of those who profess to know more than they do."[98] It is a situation in which there are no reliable criteria as to what one can and should assume to be true. A situation in which, because the distinction of true and false is itself unclear, faint and normatively ineffective, unreal and inefficient, a diversity of different positions strive for interpretational sovereignty in answering to all possible questions. This is a situation in which progress is to "proceed" until one "at least recognize[s] for certain that there is no certainty."[99] In this situation one is "like a prisoner who is enjoying an imaginary freedom while asleep; as he begins to suspect that he is asleep, he dreads being woken up, and goes along with the pleasant illusion as long as he can."[100]

In short, the situation of the practice of indifference is the initial situation of Descartes's philosophical project—at least that of the *Meditations* and of the *Discourse*. It is a situation in which opinions oppose opinions, doctrines oppose doctrines, and each commitment is potentially possible and thus revisable, a situation in which all criteria for judgments and decisions of the will are lacking; it is thus a situation in which it is permanently unclear if one is mistaken or not, if one is free or not, if one is mistaken about freedom or not.[101] This means that the practice of indifference is, structurally, the situation in which the founding act of modern philosophy takes place. And it means that modern philosophy is philosophy emerging from a situation of indifference, from a misuse of freedom.

But if modern philosophy critically turns against what appears unchangeable and most natural in such a situation to establish stable, clear, and distinct criteria of how to judge and decide freely, this also means that the practice of indifference describes a constitutively premodern situation.[102] It is a situation that, for Descartes, is therefore akin to our own childhood, in which we "had to be governed for some time by our appetites and our teachers, which were often opposed to each other and neither of which, perhaps, always gave us the best advice."[103] This situation is determined by a specific imbalance in power, in which

> [t]he world is largely composed of two types of minds for whom it is quite unsuitable. First, there are those who, believing themselves cleverer than they are [and] if they once took the liberty of doubting the principles they accepted and of straying from the common path, they could never stick to the track that must be taken as short-cut, and they would remain lost all their lives. Secondly, there are those who have enough reason or modesty to recognize that they are less capable of distinguishing the true from the false than certain others by whom they can be taught; such people should be content to follow opinions of these others rather than seek better opinions themselves.[104]

This, then, is a practice of perpetuated and permanently reproduced error in which one party (the dominant one) presets erroneous opinions and the other takes them on. In this sense the practice of indifference describes a situation in which there are only vacillating and erroneous understandings, determinations, and heteronomous determinacy, because there are neither self-grounded nor absolutely grounded commitments and decisions. The choice to belong to a side (or which side to belong to) thus becomes a choice between two evils. It is a choice between two evils because it is a choice where there are only opinions, no truth, at stake. It is an indifferent choice.

If one party is constantly deflected from the path by external impulses and the other is fully determined by externality, we can see here that such a form of heteronomous determination can be thought in and for Descartes in analogy[105] with the heteronomous determination by and of our own body, a body that will never bring us any certainty. The practice of indifference is a practice of heteronomous determination in which ultimately—because the indifferent will suspends the judgments of the intellect—even the distinction of body and will (or mind) must collapse; here, too, the distinction between self-determination and autonomy is lost. In such a practice one acts not only as if one were free (freedom is reduced to its lowest grade) even though one is not truly free, but the collapse between the distinction of free will and body also leads to the fact that one ultimately acts as if one were (without free will) a mere body vacillating from one external impulse to the next.

Human beings, when or if they are indifferent, do not act as human beings, as truly free beings. They act in their own self-understanding as if they were free and at the same time they act in reality—paradoxically—as if they are not free. They act as if they were free, but the way in which they understand freedom leads them to act as if they are not free, as if they are not free beings. Humans acting indifferently act as if they were animals. Indifference is the name of the peculiar privation of free beings, their being in a state in which they act as if they were not free.[106] An exit strategy from this is necessary.[107]

There is a third option, which Descartes famously believed might be opened up through *methodical* doubt. With Descartes, modern philosophy begins with the will to free itself from premodernity, from the situation of indifference. Its motto might be "Nevertheless I will work my way up."[108] Descartes demonstrates that error results from indifference, and indifference designates a problematic comprehension of freedom that on the one side is admittedly not a *necessary* and unavoidable human destiny, but on the other, because of the constitution of human spirit (as will and intellect), can never be completely eliminated and can therefore always contingently resurge. One can derive from Descartes's analysis the following series of points:

1. Descartes's critique of indifference articulates the diagnosis that there can be and that there is a privative and reductive understanding of the concept of freedom, an understanding that comes with practical consequences of its own.
2. His project locates the task of modern philosophy in its negative form in the critique and overcoming of this understanding. To be able to do so it needs a precise analysis of it.
3. This implies that one can also delineate the, or more moderately, a, task of modern philosophy in a positive manner. This task is to think freedom in a non-indifferent way.
4. The negative-critical and positive-affirmative sides are connected with the founding act of modern philosophy.
5. This begins (negatively) with a critique of the premodern understanding of freedom. The latter is condensed in the assumption that freedom has its full reality already as and in the form of a given capacity. The consequence of Descartes's critique can then be reformulated as follows: Modern philosophy begins with Descartes with a critique of the premodern myth of the givenness of freedom as capacity.
6. If modern philosophy (of freedom) begins with Descartes by confronting the myth of the given, this philosophy is not premodern and mythic, but modern and rationalist.

7. The rationalism in Descartes which is thus constitutive of modern philosophy designates the project of exorcising the premodern myth of the givenness of freedom as capacity. It is in and through this act that modern philosophy commences. For Descartes, the further development and differentiation of philosophy still stands under the condition of this exorcism.

8. Any philosophical position that falls for this myth in whatever form is premodern and not rationalist.

The method of doubt, then, is certainly the most famous methodical operation of how to get from the exorcism and critique of the myth to a positive articulation of a concept of freedom.[109] However this is understood, it is critical to remark here that Descartes does not simply begin with an elaboration of the positive side of the concept of freedom, but that this is preceded—in search for certainty on which then also freedom is grounded—by a critical traversal of deception and error and its ground: indifference.[110] Or, in Descartes there is no positive concept of freedom without the negative-critical traversal of the premodern-mythical understandings. Descartes himself describes this operation of traversing (of/in doubt) in the following manner: "I think it will be a good plan to turn my will in completely the opposite direction and deceive myself by pretending for a time that these former opinions are utterly false and imaginary."[111] This strategy makes error conscious so that in a certain sense fire is fought with fire, namely, (unconscious) deception with (conscious) deception, indifference with (another kind of) indifference.[112] This is supposed to sublate and overcome the identification of freedom with an indifferently given capacity, and the whole question will now be how one conceives of the move from (ontic) indifference to (ontological) indifference.

Irrespective of how we may judge the failure or success of the Cartesian enterprise according to Descartes's own criteria, we can generalize for post-Cartesian philosophy what Descartes himself remarked in his first meditation:

> But it is not enough merely to have noticed this; I must make an effort to remember it. My habitual opinions keep coming back, and, despite my wishes, they capture my belief, which is as it were bound over to them as a result of long occupation and the law of custom.[113]

There is a permanent threat of regress even for the Cartesian and post-Cartesian philosophy of rationalism, a relapse into the premodern understanding of freedom. The myth of the givenness of freedom as capacity threatens to return as if it had a right to do so after the long practice and intimate relation we have had with it. This may be because this myth has a peculiar, perhaps-too-evident, effectivity, because it seems so difficult to exterminate that even the insight into its mythical kernel does not make it disappear. Like ideology, the myth returns even after it has crumbled, and in this way the "possibility of relapsing . . . is always given."[114] One must always be attentive, in order that this permanently threatening danger might be opposed. Remembering the critique of indifference, one must repeatedly (once more . . .) traverse the dominant, customary opinion. In (the history of) modern philosophy, the destiny of modern philosophy, the destiny of rationalism, is permanently at stake. And this is why it might not be surprising that another great thinker of radical change, Immanuel Kant, will make—*encore*—another attempt of criticizing this very myth, after its return.

2

Kant and the Fall into Natural Necessity

[L]and was unstable, the sea unfit for swimming, and air lacked light, shapes shifted constantly.

— OVID, *METAMORPHOSES*

Just as trees continue to grow in an impenetrable wilderness when human hands don't cut them; so the human being also grows wildly, for he has by nature a tendency to sink back to animality.

— IMMANUEL KANT, *MENSCHENKUNDE ODER PHILOSOPHISCHE ANTHROPOLOGIE: NACH HANDSCHRIFTLICHEN VORLESUNGEN*

What if I never break?

— INTERPOL, "LIGHTS"

From Despotism to Anarchy to Indifference

In 1781, almost 150 years after Descartes's far-reaching critique of the (premodern) identification of freedom with a given capacity of choice under the name of indifference, Immanuel Kant published his *Critique of Pure Reason*. On the first pages of the preface of the first edition, a resurgence of the Cartesian critique of indifference is immediately recognizable, even if the systematic context as well as the problem initially take on quite different shapes; Kant speaks of indifference in the first preface of this epochal work, which was supposed to introduce the critical project, the project of the critique of reason in general.

As is well known, Kant begins his preface with the statement that human reason is confronted with, is literally molested [belästigt] by, questions that due to its own nature it can neither avoid nor silence. What is the character and ground of this unavoidable molestation of reason? Kant, in the very first lines of the preface, delineates: "Human reason has the peculiar fate that it is burdened with questions which it cannot dismiss, since they are given to it as problems by the nature of reason itself."[1] The ground on account of which reason cannot dismiss the questions it is confronted with is the very constitution of reason. Reason cannot not pose (or give itself up to) these questions. And at the same time, these questions are of such a nature that reason "also cannot answer [them], since they transcend the capacity of human reason."[2] Reason is a capacity that appears to be brought, through its constitution, to the point where it is confronted with its own limits and incapacities. Reason is by nature like a small child,[3] constantly asking question upon question from whose answers only further questions follow. It constantly asks "why" and is never satisfied with an answer, however simple, and "Because the questions never cease,"[4] reason is led into areas that escape its grasp. Initially, reason is, by way of this structure, led out of the realm of experience and out of the realm of that which can be verified by means of experience. Because it questions the ground and cause of the objects of experience which as such lie beyond experience as such,[5] reason enters the kingdom of principles.

Although reason now "takes refuge in" these "principles,"[6] it simultaneously continues to question further, even more thoroughly, incessantly, questioning the ground and cause of these principles, their "why." This constant compulsion to repeat the question that knits together rational questions (viz., questions of and in reason) with rational questions is now the ground for changing the capacity of reason into a peculiar incapacity. The compulsion of reason to repeat its questions drives it into metaphysics that is, at first sight, the opposite of any rational undertaking. For in metaphysics "[reason] thereby falls into obscurity and contradictions";[7] its obscurity arises from leaving behind the clarity of the experiential.

As soon as one begins to establish claims regarding what is to be found beyond the clarity of experience, contradictions emerge, since beyond the experiential, as a matter of principle, anything can be maintained so long as there isn't any rational criterion of evaluation. However, reason does not have such a criterion at its disposal. The problem of reason consists in its being driven, due to its own questions, to assume principles that it can no longer possibly validate or evaluate. This is a real problem because it is thus no longer clear; namely, it remains obscure, according to which method, and even whether, these principles can at all be verified. For Kant this dilemma is the reason why metaphysics became "[t]he battlefield of these endless controversies,"[8] which could not have been settled previously for the very same reason. It is in the nature of reason to run riot, and it is precisely this rioting that brought about a bellicose battle regarding the interpretational sovereignty over the answers to the questions of reason,[9] which is the starting point of the *Critique of Pure Reason*: the absence of rational normativity and of the normativity of reason make a battlefield out of the field in which reason necessarily seeks final answers.[10] On the battlefield, various conflicting party factions are struggling with one another, parties that Kant himself describes in political terms.

First and foremost there exist numerous "dogmatists," who attempt to rule the metaphysical arena in a despotic manner,[11] for as soon as the normative space is missing, dogmatically represented assertions appear that are ultimately uncritical and unexamined "prejudice[s],"[12] providing the only form of the final grounds and answers to the questions of reason. The dogmatists rule despotically over the dominion to which they lay claim because their regiment only knows "law and force without freedom,"[13] as Kant will later define despotism. The dogmatic prejudice (dogmatic because uncritically assumed) as to how the questions of reason have to be answered rules as a law that is defended with all (rhetorical) force without accounting for or counting with freedom (not even with the freedom of insight). Since there is not only one dogmatic position but several, these are driven into conflict, and thereby "traces of ancient barbarism"[14] over the seeming justifications and foundations of metaphysics return to the competition. On the battlefield of metaphysics "no combatant has ever gained the least bit of ground, nor has any been able to base any lasting possession on his victory"[15] when and because the barbarism is structurally determined as "force without freedom and law."[16] For the struggle of different despotic dogmatists, who from the beginning have relinquished all freedom of cognition and insight, internally turns out to be a conflict that no longer answers to any superordinate law. In this way, in metaphysics, first freedom and then even the universal law or superordinate normativity are lost, and even the idea of a law that is binding for all dogmatists or a law that binds all dogmatic positions together is undermined by the conflict itself. What remains is a sort of an intellectual tussle over metaphysical dictatorship.

In this way the metaphysical territory "degenerated through internal wars into complete *anarchy*."[17] Kant defines anarchy such that in it "law and freedom without force"[18] prevails. At this point such a definition comes as something of a surprise since it initially seems to contradict the previous determinations. But the anarchy that arises through the constant struggle for dictatorship establishes, in the seeming lawlessness of this permanent conflict, the law of this very struggle, the law of a conflict in which freely chosen dogmatism fights against dogmatism. Since all (dogmatic) sides, however, keep to the rules of the conflict because they nevertheless seek to convince the other (dogmatic) positions, there is ultimately no true authority. One seems to take the affair dogmatically seriously, but ends up in an endlessly willed "mock combat."[19] And for Kant it is precisely this structure, namely that the serious demeanor of the dogmatists turns into a redundant and unserious game which is unserious because it will never know any victor, that brings the skeptics onto the scene.[20]

The skeptics are "nomads who abhor all permanent cultivation of the soil" and "shattered civil unity from time to time."[21] The skeptics infer from the discursive constitution of metaphysics that all dogmatism not only remains empty but also arbitrary, and they ultimately abdicate the competition between positions entirely. Because the skeptics have withdrawn from the struggle, they ultimately have no effect for and on metaphysics or on the questions of reason, which in turn makes possible the easy return of the struggle of the competing dogmatisms. But with empiricism, notably with Locke's, things seem to change. Locke, according to Kant, attempted to draw up an apparently similar *"genealogy"* of metaphysics that sought to understand it as a necessary consequence of a *"physiology* of the human understanding." However, this genealogy was shown to be "false,"[22] for metaphysics is not to be derived from "the rabble of common experience."[23] Such a derivation also joins the dogmatic assertions with respect to the constitution of understanding and reason, of which, by Locke, the latter are not even adequately distinguished. For already the assumption of a nature of the understanding, or of reason that is not justified in any way and is uncritically assumed from what our experience has to offer, is, due to its structure, a repetition of "the same old worm-eaten dogmatism."[24] Thus Locke becomes nothing more than another dogmatic belligerent in the now already overpopulated battlefield, which he, like all the others, willed to seize. What appears therefore to be a new solution to the problem is shown to be just the same problem in a new guise. Things seem to have moved; nothing changes. The history of philosophy is stuck at its beginning; but it repeats, we might say, first as tragedy and then as farce.

The Mother of Chaos and Night

Out of the consequences of this situation, which is at the same time the initial situation of the project of the *Critique of Pure Reason*, Kant resumes:

> Now after all paths (as we persuade ourselves) have been tried in vain, what rules is tedium and complete *indifferentism*, the mother of chaos and night in the sciences, but at the same time also the origin, or at

least the prelude, of their incipient transformation and enlightenment, when through ill-applied effort they have become obscure, confused, and useless.[25]

The result of the peculiar, repeated and repetitive, indulgences of reason is indifferentism, which is characterized as the mother of chaos and night, and *at the same time*, as the origin of or the prelude to an approaching transformation. How are we to understand Kant's characterization? It can initially be said that metaphysics as the realm and discourse in which answers are supposed to be given to the questions of reason shows and yields a structural indifference as its internal constitution. In this, and in an equally valued and bad infinite way, one avowed dogmatism is strung together with and maintained against the next and the only way out appears to be skepticism. Then, there ultimately remains only the ungrounded and arbitrary choice between, on the one hand, one of these avowed dogmatisms and, on the other hand, the fundamental skepticism. One stands before the choice between two evils that can only evoke tedium since one cannot not choose falsely.

One can only choose falsely in this choice because there is a choice between, on the one hand, the constant repetition of the eternally same dogmatic structure, which leads to no result and no real answers, and, on the other hand, the general abstract doubt about the truth content of any metaphysical position, which does not represent anything essentially less dogmatic. If one opts for one of the sides, one involuntarily appears to end up on the other. The choice between dogmatism and skepticism becomes, therefore, a structurally indifferent decision, and it is precisely this equal-valence (*Gleich-Gültigkeit*) of the false that brings indifference, more precisely the indifferentists, on to the scene. For "the inescapable experience of *many* dogmas, all of which claim to possess *the* truth, is skepticism."[26]

This remark from Hannah Arendt enables us to grasp more precisely the situation Kant describes in which, confronted with the problematic choice between two evils, indifferentism decides to not decide on either. The indifferentist acts just like the proverbial Buridan's ass, who, despite being hungry, cannot decide between two equidistant and equisized stacks of hay and therefore starves in front of them. The indifferentist decides to not decide.[27] It thereby takes the equal validity of both wrong options at their word and makes itself indifferent to them. Indifferentism delineates a position that reacts to a choice that can scarcely be characterized as such. Indifferentism is Kant's name for the decision to decide neither for siding with the dogmatic quarrels that are endlessly following one another and that can lead only to skepticism nor with the skepticism that in its turn against dogmatism turns out to be dogmatic.

Indifferentism is described by Kant as the mother of chaos and night. Why? Initially, we can assume this is the case because indifferentism makes clear that one can choose between only the dogmatic chaos or the obscurity of skepticism vis-à-vis the questions of reason, and that these are the only two possibilities to choose, and so it is thus better not to choose at all. As Kant conceptualizes it in another context: "[I]f common reason ventures to depart from laws of experience and perceptions of the senses it falls into sheer incomprehensibilities and self-contradictions, at least into a chaos of uncertainty, obscurity, and instability."[28] The indifferentist seems to agree with Kant and repeat his judgment. When one enters the territory of metaphysics, there is ultimately only a chaos of uncertainty and obscurity. Indifferentism is the mother of chaos and night in the sciences because its decision against taking a decision for either dogmatism or skepticism structurally implies such repetition that characterizes the discourse of metaphysics, and which in itself repeats the endlessly inquisitive structure of reason in a modified manner. This is not just the preservation of the metaphysical chaos as it is found, but even worse than that, indifferentism produces chaos and obscurity with respect to what is or could be maintained and thought in the science of metaphysics in general. By way of this (repetitive) production of chaos and obscurity, it becomes all the while increasingly obscure as to why there is metaphysics at all. It becomes obscure why reason compels human beings, through its questions, into this situation and why metaphysics is thus a matter of reason in the first place. Decided indifference, in the double sense of the term, renders it unclear and indistinct whether it might ever be possible to pursue metaphysics as science, to pursue metaphysics in a scientific and rational manner, and it renders opaque why this is even a relevant issue at all. Indifferentism thus characterizes a position that asserts, because of the failures of the dogmatists and the skeptics, that it is indifferent to the questions of reason. But from this perspective, indifferentism would be not the mother but the registrar of chaos and obscurity. How can one therefore properly understand Kant's claim?

The decisive punchline of Kant's claim becomes comprehensible when one turns to what he states after the above cited passage: "[T]hese so-called indifferentists . . . always unavoidably fall back into metaphysical assertions, which they yet professed so much to despise."[29] Why does indifferentism entail a fallback into metaphysical assertions? This relapse occurs because in the indifferentist's decision to not decide, the decision to decide in favor of none of the available options is nevertheless still a decision. Indifferentism maintains that one can decide against the options offered and, through taking distance from them, see appear an alternative to what is presented as the only possible option. Here, it becomes thinkable that there can be more than what there is: If one can decide that one does not have to maintain either of the two sides of the choice offered, then not everything is lost with the forced choice between the two, and a new possibility emerges. The emergence of indifferentism is therefore good news.[30] Indifferentism still affirms the capacity of reason, even in the act of negating the choice and thus the difference between dogmatism and skepticism, although it seems to decide against this capacity, for it shows thereby how reason is not condemned to remain in a state of dogmatic or skeptical incapacity. But indifferentism is the mother of chaos and night because it neither sees nor knows what it does. It obstructs the alternative in the act of its disclosing. For indifferentism assumes that it is not deciding and does not notice that it nevertheless decides against the offered options of decision. It doesn't know it, but it does it. It does not know what it does.

Indifferentism thus feigns indifference where it does not, maybe cannot, exist. This is why only a further *dogmatic* position arises from indifferentism, which assumes that reason can be indifferent toward this decision; yet this is in itself a dogmatic and unexamined assumption. It leaves reason in dogmatic disorder and in a deep slumber, even after it has made arrangements to awaken it. Indifferentism leads thereby—and this is why it is the mother of chaos and night—to a sort of "dogmatic slumber,"[31] to a dogmatism that knows nothing of its own dogmatic character and from which Kant himself was awoken by encountering and being irritated by David Hume's philosophy. Therefore, indifference is for Kant more than the apparent expression of an incapacity of reason that results from its previously dogmatic or skeptical *use* (and understanding).[32] And this is why, despite his problematizing description of the state of metaphysical discourse, Kant can still maintain that indifferentism—about which more will be said—is the "prelude [*Vorspiel*]," that is, it is the sign of a coming transformation. Indifferentism is an ambivalent phenomenon because, on the one hand, it shows something other than the given alternatives, but on the other hand, it distorts these alternatives again, because it misunderstands itself and assumes that one can simply not decide and be indifferent toward the answerless questions of reason. Against this Kant insists: "[I]t is pointless to affect *indifference* with respect to such inquiries, to whose object human nature *cannot* be *indifferent*."[33] Reason cannot by any means be indifferent.

Kant's thesis means to say that even when there is indifference there is never any true indifference. No human being can be indifferent toward the questions raised by reason. As far as the theoretical interests of reason are concerned, Kant seems to maintain against Descartes that the problem which Descartes identified with the concept of indifference cannot even exist as a problem. Kant therefore interprets even indifferentism as a symptom of the interested dealings of reason with the problems resulting from its own questions, and within

a historical background wherein a general state of impossible indifference resulted from previous metaphysics. This is the case, as

> the effect . . . of its ripened *power of judgment*, which will no longer
> be put off with illusory knowledge, and which demands that reason
> should take on anew the most difficult of all its tasks, namely, that of
> self-knowledge, and to institute a court of justice.[34]

There is an apparent indifference because reason, no longer satisfied simply with metaphysical assertions, has attained a degree of reflexivity which
compels it to examine all the answers to its questions by means of rational judgments and thus in a universally comprehensible manner. Because neither
dogmatism nor skepticism can be rationally tested, one chooses to not choose.
Thus begins the "age of critique,"[35] and here and in it, an unperceived and
unthought possibility presents itself. Kant insists that there cannot be an indifference of reason toward the questions of reason if indifferentism misunderstands itself, for even the indifferentist chooses and decides. Because there
have not previously been any answers to the questions of reason (this is what
the indifferentist claims), reason should put to rest the questions that it seems
driven by. This is an indication of novelty and enlightenment because it makes
palpable that the use of reason opposes what we take to be evident and thereby
shows that we can not only reject the options that are presented to us, but even
(critically) examine them. Indifferentism is therefore the symptomatic expression of a burgeoning critical age; it systematically marks the limit and limitations of the unguaranteed undertakings of metaphysics, since it demonstrates
that reason is in the position to maintain a critical relationship, at least in the
sense of taking distance, toward these very undertakings.

Indifferentism indicates a new path, and "this indifference, occurring amid
the flourishing of all sciences . . . [is] a phenomenon deserving our attention
and reflection."[36] Understood in such a way, the project of the *Critique of Pure
Reason* emerges out of indifferentism, albeit from the last of all dogmatic-
metaphysical holdouts, but at the same time the critical project begins from
arguing for the impossibility of indifference for reason and human beings with
regard to all theoretical concerns.[37] Chaos and night are therefore the last, inherently erroneous, preconditions for a true and critical examination of the
theoretical use of reason which will aim to institute clarity and order, structure
and enlightenment. The *Critique of Pure Reason* is meant to deploy and im-
plement precisely this post-indifferentist project, which therefore makes it "a
treatise on the method, not a system of the science itself."[38] For the first time it
pursues metaphysics in a rational way, a way adequate to reason. This means,
for the first time ever, that it pursues true metaphysics.

Indifference is the surmountable prelude that proceeds to ground true (as in, critical) metaphysics, which at the same time also leaves behind a condition of possibility that can only be left behind.[39] Critical metaphysics thus begins by understanding indifferentism better than indifferentism understands itself. It adopts the critical distance to the previous metaphysics which indifferentism establishes and at the same time avoids any unwilled and unconscious regression back into it. The critical metaphysics of Kant's first critique begins with the insight that there is and cannot be an indifference of (or in) reason, and it is precisely this insight that becomes the condition of the affirmation of the true beginning of metaphysics.

As Far as Possible

With this volte-face Kant picks up a moment that already appeared in the Cartesian critique of indifference: that the situation of indifference is the starting point for the grounding of the critical project, namely that it is the foundation of true modern philosophy. But here we should and have to be more specific. For Kant, indifference and indifferentism are not merely premodern forms of thought; rather, by taking a critical distance from the apparently exclusive set of options, the indifferentists precisely mark the point from which modern philosophy's necessary overcoming of all previous undertakings, and thereby the beginning of a true (rationalist) metaphysics, can be conceived at all. Indifference and indifferentism are therefore—and here Kant is pointedly emphasizing in a manner different from Descartes—an index not only of its own overcoming but also an indication of the overcoming of the premodern form of philosophizing. This overcoming is accompanied by what appears to be a fundamentally non-Cartesian orientation, namely that there can be no indifference as far as reason and human beings are concerned. However, Kant, in contrast to Descartes, thinks that human beings and reason cannot be indifferent toward freedom, nor God, nor their own immortality. Does this ultimately mean that the problem that was posed by Descartes no longer exists for Kant? Did Kant systematically fence in and cast aside the problem of indifference?

Many things point to this conclusion, since Kant maintains the impossibility of indifference not only in theoretical matters but even with regard to practical concerns of reason.[40] On the subject of a necessary faith in God as constitutive of the moral disposition in his *Critique of Pure Reason*, he already writes that "no human being is free of all interest in these questions."[41] Which is to say, we cannot be indifferent vis-à-vis our belief in the existence of God. In his *Religion Essay* he makes this point in even more elaborate ways: "Yet an end proceeds from morality just the same; for it cannot possibly be a matter of indifference to reason how to answer the question, *What is then the result of this right conduct of ours?*"[42] This means that for Kant there is and can be no equivalence and indifference in moral matters. The same holds for real, historical matters: "Nevertheless, in regard to the most distant epochs that our species is to encounter, it belongs to human nature not to be indifferent about them, if only they can be expected with certainty."[43] And not only theoretical cognition, practical orientation, and historical understanding, but even natural matters seem to be constitutively unaffected by indifference. In his early *Universal Natural History* Kant already writes:

> From the most sublime class among thinking beings to the most despised insect, not one link is indifferent to it; and not one can be absent without the beauty of the whole, which exists in their interrelationship, being interrupted by it.[44]

There *is* no indifference. Or, to take Kant's formulation more precisely: At least nature, history, freedom, and reason seem like they must be free of indifference to be what they are. Any form of indifference would be an interruption.

In the same way in his *Critique of Practical Reason* Kant maintains:

> The human being is a being with needs. . . . But he is nevertheless not so completely an animal as to be indifferent to all that reason says on its own and to use reason merely as a tool for the satisfaction of his needs as a sensible being.[45]

For Kant, human beings are animals, albeit animals that are *not completely animals*, because they can never be indifferent to what they are told by reason. Whereas animals are indifferent toward the rules and questions of reason, human beings are not. Kant thus situates something like the beginning of the history of humankind, with recourse to the Christian narrative, as the expulsion from paradise, which, among other things, is the transition from "the crudity of a merely animal creature" to its own and autonomous positing of ends. First and foremost, this positing of ends leads to and makes possible the distinctions of good and evil, law and prohibition, because it breaks the indifference of the always already equally valued goods that God bestowed on nature, and it inaugurates "the history of *freedom* from evil" as, henceforth, a "*work of the human being*."[46] Human history thus begins with the introduction of the distinction of good and evil and with the breaking away from the equivalence and indifference of animal life. If human beings were indifferent (toward reason and freedom, to good or evil actions) then ultimately, to follow Kant, they would not be different from, indeed they would entirely be, animals. Equivalence and indifference in rational matters (inclusive of both the-oretical and practical matters) would mean that one is no longer concerned with human beings but with animals.

Equivalence and indifference therefore mark the threshold of the transi-tion between human beings and animals and vice versa. Breaking away from indifference is not only constitutive of modern philosophy in terms of its es-tablishing a critical metaphysics, but also, from a historical perspective, it is constitutive for history as history, for nature (at least from the human stand-point), and ultimately even for human beings as human beings. The matter could of course be laid to rest here: Human beings would always be human beings and never indifferent; animals would be animals and always indiffer-ent. However, in Kant's *Religion within the Boundaries of Mere Reason* (pub-lished in 1793), we find a remarkable comment that immediately complicates things massively. After the preface that introduces this essay, in which Kant proves the necessity not so much of religion as the idea of God "[s]o far as . . . [it] is based on the conception of the human being as one who is free but who also, just because of that, binds himself through his reason to unconditional laws,"[47] "Part I" is titled "Concerning the indwelling of the evil principle along-side the good, or, Of radical evil in human nature."[48] On the very first pages of this essay, Kant initially distinguishes different (theoretical) perspectives on history. On the one hand, one might assume that historical development pro-ceeds from "the Golden Age" to "the decline into evil . . . in an accelerating fall" and already discerns the lurking "destruction of the world . . . knocking at the door," or, on the other hand, one assumes "that the world steadfastly (though hardly noticeably) forges ahead in the very opposite direction, namely from bad to better."[49] Kant then mentions that the latter perspective cannot be validated on the basis of the facts of experience since the majority of expe-rience doubtlessly speaks against any progress toward the good. Therefore, the real motivation for such a view of history lies in recognizing either its moral lessons, or its faith in an ultimately good human nature. But at the same time, Kant goes on to claim, however problematic the optimistic view of history ap-pears, it is similar to the pessimistic view (that of history as decline) insofar as by means of experience alone neither can the latter ultimately be verified or validated; rather, the doubt always remains as to whether everything will not still turn out to be good.

Kant maintains that both these interpretations are based on a more fun-damental assumption that concerns the nature of human beings. One either understands human beings as evil by nature so that history necessarily devel-ops toward the worst, or one shares the perspective of the moralists and opti-mists and maintains that human beings are naturally kind and good beings.

However, Kant adds, there is a further possibility. This is that both assumptions of human nature are false. Thereby one may legitimately ask "whether a middle ground may not at least be possible, namely that . . . the human being can neither be good nor evil, or . . . that he can be both the one and the other."[50] One's view of history depends on an implicit interpretation of the human nature whose history is history. These interpretations seem to cancel one another out so that human nature can either be good, evil, or neither (i.e., neutral and indifferent), or it can be partly evil and partly good. At this point Kant raises the question whether an indifferent human nature ultimately must be thinkable. Does indifference become not only the surmountable (dogmatically pre-) metaphysical condition of true metaphysics, but also the natural-human foundation of all free human actions and thus of freedom in general?

As one might expect, Kant consistently denies the validity of any of these questions, since he shows how what ultimately remains unclear in all these assumptions is precisely what is meant by human nature in general. He develops this argument by explaining why and to what extent one calls and can call a human (being) evil. This is so "not because he performs actions that are evil (contrary to law), but because these are so constituted that they allow the inference of evil maxims in him." A human being—not only its actions and conduct—is evil or good *if* its maxims are. To be sure, actions are observable, but maxims aren't. Thus the judgment "cannot reliably be based on experience"[51] that someone is a good or evil human being. So, to what does one refer in speaking of a good, evil, mixed, or indifferent human nature? Kant answers as follows:

> [B]y "the nature of a human being" we [can only] understand here the subjective ground—wherever it may lie—of the exercise of the human being's freedom in general (under objective moral laws) antecedent to every deed that falls within the scope of the senses [and this must] in turn, itself always be a deed of freedom (for otherwise the use or abuse of the human being's power of choice . . . could not be imputed to him)[52]

The nature of human beings is decided on its subjective ground. This ground is the foundation of the maxim which determines the actions of human beings as good or evil. It characterizes the "site" where an act of freedom takes place. And to answer the question that Kant posed, fundamentally, he thereby rejects any objective or objectivizing understanding of the nature of human beings. This means that the nature of human beings, the nature of which one speaks when one says that human beings are by nature good, evil, or indifferent, cannot be understood as one would speak of a "determination through *natural causes*,"[53] precisely because one speaks of free beings. The nature of human beings is never simply, in an equivalent and indifferent manner, the given nature of all human beings. Rather, the nature of human beings is such that there is "a first ground (to us inscrutable)"[54] in it, which is inscrutable because for human beings there are no external determining causes and there is no "natural incentive" which could establish why a human being assumed this or that maxim as its own. For Kant, there is a nature of human beings because every human being chooses freely their own good or bad nature through their maxims (i.e., in the form of a "universal rule. . . . , according to which he wills to conduct himself").[55] And even human nature, as the humanly *"innate"* "character of its species,"[56] is not free from this dimension of choice. The human being is still responsible for its innate character because it must be regarded as a free being.[57] Thus, its innate character is attributable to the human being even if it did not consciously choose it to be so,[58] for it always remains "alone its author."[59] Later in the same essay, Kant calls this free choice, which determines the innate nature of human beings, an *"intelligible* deed before all experience."[60]

There is, then, an act of freedom prior to all (experiential) actions from freedom. This constitutes the nature of human beings because it is essential to the human being to choose, even to choose its own nature. At this point Kant concludes the introductory reflections of the first part of his *Religion Essay*. But, before the first subsection of the first part begins, he adds a remark. This remark stands out from the entirety of the rest of the *Religion Essay* because where each introduction of the four main parts is followed by unnamed or no more specifically defined than enumerated "sub-parts" (as in the first part), by "sections" (as in the second), by "divisions" (as in the third), or by "parts and sections" (as in the fourth), and each of these "parts" concludes with a "general remark," the remark following Kant's introductory reflections is the only one that follows an introduction (which is, we should remember, the introduction of the entire essay).

At first this remark seems to fulfill the task of summarizing what Kant believes he has already shown. It begins by establishing that "a disjunctive proposition"[61] resides in both hypotheses investigated in the opening examination of human nature (the human is good *or* evil). As Kant had already remarked, it is unclear and unconclusive to show whether human nature really concerns an irreducible disjunction[62] in which there are two and only two mutually exclusionary possibilities of determination ("the excluding *or*"[63] between good or evil), *or* whether there can still be indifference or a mixture of good and evil in human nature. Is it thus not possible that the disjunctive distinction between good or evil is only one side of the distinction, on the other side of which there could be a more fundamental indifference? Or both good and evil? "Experience even seems to confirm this middle position."[64] It not only seems that one is justified in doubting the disjunctive logic of good and evil regarding human nature, but what is more, experience seems to indicate precisely another possible interpretation. Kant then writes something that is noteworthy in all the details of its formulation:

> It is of great consequence to ethics in general, however, to preclude, so far as possible, anything morally intermediate, either in actions (*adiaphora*) or in human characters; for with any such ambiguity all maxims run the risk of losing their determination and stability.[65]

A lot depends on, so far as [it is] possible, precluding indifference in morals. This means that, above all, Kant distinctly speaks here of indifference in a subjective sense, that is, of indifference with respect to the subjective practice of reason. But this passage is equally noteworthy because it remains unclear as to the standard by which it can be established how it is and will be possible to avoid *adiaphora*, namely, the moral, intermediate things, in actions and characters.

From the Human to the Animal

Kant maintains that all maxims run the risk of relinquishing their determinacy and stability if there is or can be indifference in human actions and characters. That he speaks of actions *and* characters shows that the intermediate things in morals can concern *adiaphora* and indifference. This not only means indecision and irresolution as well as decisions in and from indifference, but also concerns the problem that either a both-and mixture of good and evil, or a neither-nor in actions and characters, can arise. As described by Kant, the effect of this is unambiguous: intermediate things in morals—namely, moral indifference of actions and characters—jeopardize all maxims. For there is an ambiguity that Kant attributes to maxims of moral indifference which results in their being either neither good nor bad, or partly both at the same time, and this ambiguity alters something in the very functioning of maxims in general. More precisely: These indifferent maxims destabilize the function and constitution of maxims as such, since, for Kant, maxims are those universal rules in accordance to which actions are formally determined, and they are constitutively related to the moral law (and this means to the categorical imperative). Maxims can only conform to the moral law if they conform to its form since they prescribe "not the what and wherefore of something that happens but rather solely of which sort and manner, with what form they ought to be concerned."[66] If, however, maxims become ambiguous and ambivalent with respect to their form, then the following two things become problematic: the status of maxims as maxims and their relationship to the moral law (and also thereby the status of maxims as maxims of either good or evil actions).

Maxims become indeterminate and imprecise and ultimately unstable, and thus their status as maxims is at stake. This occurs when or if there are (or can be) intermediate things, indifference, and *adiaphora* in human nature, as its subjective determining ground. The same holds for as long as and if there are actions that one can call neither good nor bad, but rather both at the same time or neither. For if there are indifferent actions, there must be indifferent maxims (and vice versa). In his own words, Kant presents this danger of a destabilization of maxims as the destabilization of the subjective ground which was introduced to avoid the assumption of an indifferent nature of human beings and thereby to avoid indifference. We might even specify this intellectual interrelationship as follows: If indifference and equivalence arise at the exact point that should make indifference categorically impossible, then the impossible arises. Indifferent actions and an indifferent nature of human beings arise such that this nature can no longer be what it must be to be human nature. Consequently, there is indifference or a mixture of good and evil in the act constitutive of freedom for every human being (the act constituting the choice of his nature); there is a destabilization of the determinacy and stability of its maxims, which emerge from the choice of its own maxims. Maxims thereby run the risk of losing their status as maxims and the human being seems to run the risk of losing its status as human. In other words: Human beings lose that which makes them human, namely their freedom. Why should this be the case? In a remark that Kant not only adds to this remark but a remark added to this second remark—that is, a footnote to the footnote—there is an initial answer to the question:

> A morally indifferent action (*adiaphoron morale*) would be one that merely follows upon the laws of nature, and hence stands in no relation at all to the moral law as law of freedom—for such an action is not a *factum*, and with respect to it neither *command*, nor *prohibition*, nor yet *permission* (*authorization* according to law), intervenes or is necessary.[67]

This is a far-reaching and no less astonishing remark, which is yet conspicuously uncommented upon. In an initially simplified reformulation, one could say: As long as human beings act in such a way that their actions are morally equi-valent, that is, indifferent, then these actions are no longer actions that derive from freedom. Indifference not only changes the status of the maxims but also the status of the very actions that follow from these maxims. It is a mode of changing the ontological status of actions. It is not that they are merely unfree actions, but rather that they break away from the relationship to freedom and its law, since this law—the moral law—claims, among other things, that an act of freedom cannot contain indifference with respect to moral matters. Were there or could there be indifference, then the bond between action and freedom is or could be severed; so, in other words, there is no relationship between freedom and indifferent actions. Recalling the initial difference between human beings (as free and non-indifferent) and animals (as unfree and indifferent beings), one can thence conclude that there is "no relationship" between the human being and the animal. For, according to the law of freedom, animals are indifferent, that is, they merely act in conformity with nature.

That there is no relationship between freedom and morally indifferent actions is an astonishing thought because it implies that, as long as (or if ever) morally indifferent actions arise, these actions are based on maxims that no longer appear to be maxims proper. These actions not only no longer have any relationship to the law of freedom and thereby have no relation to freedom itself, but they can also no longer be recognized or classified as being truly human performances. Indifferent actions are not performances accomplished on the basis of freely chosen maxims of one's own will, which are in conformity with the moral law. In this sense, morally indifferent actions cannot ultimately be classified as actions in the proper sense, since what evades them is precisely what makes (human) action into the action (of human beings), namely its constitutive relationship to and with freedom. If there is "*indifferentia actionis*," as it is called in the lecture notes for Kant's lectures on moral philosophy, then there are "actions whose value amounts to nothing (zero)."[68] Indifferent actions are the *zero point of, the nullification of action as action.*[69] From this, then, Kant can acknowledge the following: If indifferent actions arise, they occur in conformity with mere nature, that is, ultimately with mechanical laws. If there is indifference in practical relations, there is thus a fall into natural necessity; if there are morally indifferent actions, human beings no longer act as they must or ought to act as human beings. If morally indifferent actions could or indeed do arise, then they no longer concern actions from freedom (viz., they no longer concern actions); they (would) ultimately fall outside the field of morality. In this case, such actions are rather mere effects of natural laws, results of the natural causality that for Kant also determines all animal behavior,[70] and human beings would no longer act as (and like) human beings, but rather they would behave like animals.

Looking also at Kant's *Anthropology*, published five years after the *Religion Essay*, it becomes clear that these reflections are neither narrowly concerned with an abstract, conceptual reconnaissance of possibilities for thinking, nor are they an abstract thought experiment standing beyond all practical reality. In the context of his discussion regarding "the deficiencies of the mind in the capacity of cognition"[71] and the "complete mental deficiency"[72] which leads to the transition to "mental illnesses," Kant, at one point, notes the following:

> Complete mental deficiency, which either does not suffice even for animal use of the vital force (as among the *Cretins* of Valais), or which is just sufficient for a mechanical imitation of external actions that are possible through animals . . . is called *idiocy*. It cannot really be called sickness of soul; it is rather absence of soul.[73]

If indifferent actions in morals lead to a fall into natural necessity and human actions regress to a sort of animal behavior, then the above passage reveals yet another interpretive dimension: that, therefore, in a peculiar way, indifference would constitute idiocy in precisely the sense Kant gives to this concept.[74] This would also mean the following: Indifference does not only lead to the loss of maxims, not only to the loss of the relationship to the law of freedom, not only to the loss of the peculiar nature of action, not only to the loss of the human being, but it also leads to the loss of the soul—the trait specific to the human being. For Kant, then, indifference is not sickness of the soul, but rather like imbecility, it is the lack and loss of it. Indifferent action is soulless behavior, and soulless behavior is precisely reducible to and derivable from a form of causality in conformity to natural law, since this determines the sphere that seems to be mere externality. If the soul, freedom, and its law, and thus ultimately reason are missing, then nothing more than mere external relations remains. As a result, the series of losses that Kant characterizes with the concept of indifference in morals (in actions and characters) show that for him, as for Descartes, when it arises, indifference brings about a peculiar and far-reaching privation. For Kant, indifferent actions are so constituted as if they were only a moment within a causal chain. They are actions not truly distinguishable from causal mechanisms.

If it is imaginable—and Kant's remarks imply exactly this possibility—that human beings *can* act in a morally indifferent manner,[75] then it is also thinkable that human beings can act as if they were not free, thereby behaving and performing as if they were soulless animals.[76] From this point of view human beings for Kant can be and become idiotic. Human beings can be and become so idiotic that it is no longer possible to recognize anything human in their behavior but only see in them the irrational and soulless performances of an animal. Human beings can behave—if there is indifference in action and character, i.e., what must be expelled and avoided so long as possible because "indifference point[s] to . . . stupidity"[77]—in such a way that their practice is not worked out through freedom but rather determined in a natural manner. This practice characterizes their peculiar idiocy.

Kant proceeds to claim that human beings can behave so that they are determined in a merely external manner. For him, such behavior characterizes a fundamentally privative mode of human practice that deprives human beings of all human determinations.: Human beings can act indifferently (idiotically) and thus behave as if they were merely animals. Kant's reflections make it possible to think that there is the possibility of such a privation, and that the name of this privation is, as with Descartes, indifference. This is the profound consequence of these Kantian reflections: Human beings can regress to animal behavior if there are morally indifferent actions.[78]

It is crucial here to bear in mind the further qualification of indifferent actions made by Kant. How exactly are we to understand his claim that morally indifferent action "is not a *factum*, and with respect to it neither *command*, nor *prohibition*, nor yet *permission* (*authorization* according to law), intervenes or is necessary"?[79] What can it mean that morally indifferent action is not a fact? This seemingly obscure observation becomes intelligible if one recalls that at one point in the *Critique of Practical Reason* Kant speaks of an "undeniable" and "sole fact of pure reason,"[80] by which he refers to the fact of freedom of the will. That morally indifferent action is not a fact in the sense of a fact of the freedom of free will means that such action does not concern a f-*act* of freedom. It does not concern a (f)act, namely, an objective act or a factually becoming objective of freedom, because it does not concern an act but merely a thing. Morally indifferent actions are not facts (of reason), not facts (of freedom) in the conceptual sense, but are rather matters of nature, natural matters. So what always holds for true actions (embodying freedom) precisely does not hold for morally indifferent actions, namely that they stand in a constitutive relationship to the moral law. If this is the case, then it must mean, as Kant convincingly concludes, that neither commands nor prohibitions can hold for indifferent actions.

It is noteworthy that Kant also excludes indifferent actions from the sphere of what is merely permitted. Indifferent actions cannot be classified as merely permitted actions, since they lack the categories applicable to what the law holds as permitted when there is a relationship to the law in general: what is not prohibited by the existing juridical laws and is neither prohibited nor sanctioned by the moral law. However, it is precisely this relationship to the law that precludes indifference, and thus indifferent actions are situated beyond command, prohibition, and permission.

Indifference, Equanimity, Apathy

When indifference arises, it thus seems to present a problem for Kant. However, it has remained unclear up to now whether Kant's remarks only concern a sort of negative thought experiment, or are rather a positive determination of the indifference problem. In order to delimit the problem of the intermediate things—indifference and *adiaphora*—in actions and characters more precisely, namely, to delimit their possibility, it is helpful to distinguish indifference from phenomena which, at first sight, are similar to indifference (at least in Kant's account). Such differentiation is not an external way of proceeding, since Kant himself separates indifference from two other "conditions," namely equanimity and apathy. Indifference in the sense of equivalence leads to neither equanimity nor apathy as Kant consistently ranks these latter states as higher.

To begin with apathy. As characterized by Kant, "The principle of apathy, is an entirely correct and sublime moral principle of the Stoic school,"[81] since what is maintained by it is that "the wise man must never be in a state of affect."[82] Here, and this is an important insight of the Stoics, apathy characterizes freedom from affects and passions. Since any "affect, considered by itself alone, is always imprudent,"[83] since "[p]assions are cancerous sores for practical reason"[84] and are "without exception *evil*,"[85] the absence of affects and passions becomes a fundamental condition for the authority of reason as well as for morality. Apathy gets rid of the evil that is brought to human beings by passions—namely the danger of merely subjective, non-universalizing maxims for action—and is therefore only apparently an absence of inclination (for the good). Since every passion is formally evil, it must be maintained that the absence of passions is the condition for the possibility of true morally good and rational action. Apathy is, as the absence of passions, the disposition toward and precondition for good.

Thus, although "[t]he word 'apathy' has fallen into disrepute, as if it meant lack of feeling and subjective indifference with respect to objects of choice," for Kant "*moral apathy*"[86] does not characterize a condition in which there is not an inclination toward good or evil, nor in which there is no good or evil. Apathy is not indifference and must therefore "be distinguished from indifference"[87] as it characterizes a necessary precondition of virtue, for "[t]he true strength of virtue is a *tranquil mind* with a considered and firm resolution"[88] to follow the moral law.[89] Apathy is not the fundamental indifference toward feelings and decisions but rather characterizes the calm mind that is the precondition for virtuous and moral action. Apathy is one of the conditions for a true moral decision, whereas indifference undermines and suspends such a decision. While indifference is the phenomenon of the privation of action, morality, etc., apathy is a constitutive component of what Kant calls "*health in the moral life*."[90] And so, if passions characterize the sickness of moral life, its cancer, and if apathy is the expression of respect for the law and thus the health of moral life, then indifference and equivalence characterize its death. Indifference mortifies moral life; apathy keeps it healthy.[91]

Indifference is not apathy, nor equanimity. As far as equanimity is concerned, Kant writes the following: "Indifference means stupidity; equanimity means strength of mind and understanding."[92] Indifference is thus distinguished not only from apathy and the formally evil passions but also from equanimity. How, then, does Kant define equanimity? He defines the equanimous as those "who do not lose composure, who are not agitated by affect," and equanimity as a disposition "that does not become happy or sad; yet all the time has a joyful and valiant heart, not soft-hearted, not nostalgic."[93] Equanimity characterizes a state of mind which could at first appear to be, or be like, indifference. It is a state of mind that is neither sad nor happy, but at the same time it is not simply the absence of both. Rather, an equanimous subject is a composed subject, a subject who cannot be brought from composure to movement, to affective e-motion, but is rather a subject who attains joy through the pursuit of rational and moral principles. The equanimous subject is constantly joyful and valiant and neither weak nor apologetic in its judgments, for the equanimous subject knows that its judgments are based on rational maxims, and thereby joy is for it the result of rational and free deliberation. In this way equanimity describes a state that, on the basis of its attachment to principles, is resistant toward movement through affects, albeit without being entirely indifferent or insensitive, for this disposition even contains certain sensations. Therefore, Kant opposes equanimity, on the one hand, to the sensuousness that describes a condition in which one is overcome by influences through external things or passions in a non-self-determined manner. Yet he also opposes indifference, on the other hand, to sensibility (*Empfindsamkeit*),[94] so that indifference characterizes a complete deficiency of the capacity of sensation. Indifference is based "on the deficiency of feeling (the absence of feelings) or [is] the [kind of] indifference opposed to stimulations"[95] that leads to stagnation and indecision. Equanimity, however, can be sensitive, but really can only be sensitive when it is "judging" and is therefore never "passionately sensitive." Indifference ultimately regresses to "the weakness" of sensuousness, whereas in equanimity is characterized what Kant calls an "ideal disposition."[96] It is an ideal disposition because it is an idealization of disposition, a feeling of judgment, a *judgment with feeling and reason* in which the composure (of the moral law) remains preserved and arises in it through the capacity of judgment.

Whereas indifference abandons judgment either because it does not lead to any feeling at all, or because it leads to a mixture of feelings without direction and determinacy, equanimity exhibits a form of "contempt toward the stimulus [sic] of life," which is "its means of sustaining it." Equanimity concerns a form of apathy but, as Kant specifically states, not "the apathy of indifference"; this latter is the apathy that, according to Kant's earlier reconstructed definition, does not deserve the name of apathy, but rather concerns the apathy "of equanimity which is attached to duty with all seriousness, yet attached to enjoyment with coldness."[97] Equanimity has an ideal, idealized, and idealizing relationship to feeling and sensation. This is because the feeling and sensation with which equanimity is accompanied are always already the result of a rational and free judgment from principles and are only worth considering in relation to these in general, which does not exclude these in an abstract and merely negating manner, but rather it is related to them in judging and is thereby always already at a distance from them. In this way, equanimity characterizes not a particular quality of character, or a merely subjective constitution of a disposition but, on the contrary (as referred to by Kant) is "the (self-) feeling of a healthy soul"[98] in general. So moral health implies moral apathy and equanimity. Kant proceeds to explain the latter in a more far-reaching sense in the light of its fidelity to principles and idealization, as the "philosophical sort of disposition"[99] in general. Critical philosophers are equanimous, and, in the moral sense, healthy. Their task, precisely therefore, is to speak up and to speak for and to judge human reason. Or more precisely, they have the task of letting human reason speak and judge for itself.

With hardly any variation in its formulation, the distinction of indifference and equivalence from apathy and equanimity seems to repeat and express what already became clear in the beginning—not only of this chapter, but also at the beginning of Kant's critical undertaking. Namely, that critical philosophy does not contain indifference because it emerges from its overcoming. Critical metaphysics (i.e., the only true metaphysics) begins where the impossibility of indifference is cognized, understood, posited, and thus recognized precisely as an impossibility. Critical philosophy begins with the impossibility of indifference, for what it consistently undertakes to emphasize and present is that the constitution of reason and freedom cannot be indifferent and equivalent. There cannot be any idiocy, stupidity, deficiency of feeling in reason and freedom, since they must contain soul, reason, and an apathy of equanimity. The matter would once more seem exhausted if there were not another surprising passage in Kant's *Reflections on Anthropology*, which, yet again, fundamentally alters the picture that has been drawn up to this point.

It is in this passage that we learn why indifference is still, continually, a real problem for Kant. In brevity, and yet, as one can readily predict, in the most equivocal manner, Kant asserts the following: "The indifferent seem to be equanimous, that is, philosophers."[100] The equivalent and indifferent person can appear to give and sustain the impression that he is a philosopher, that he *seems to be* a philosopher. This means, then, that what Kant established as the symptom of the forthcoming departure from dogmatic (non-) metaphysics, and as the harbinger of the entrance of true metaphysics, namely indifference, is also not exhausted after and with the beginning of the critical project. Rather, there is a return to what is already exhausted, what the critical and true metaphysician already believed she had left behind, which returns directly within the midst of metaphysics: There is "a relapse into one of the already sublated determinations"[101] which the critical project constantly warded off. This means that the indifferent, in maintaining the pretension or giving the impression, that they are already critical philosophers, therefore present themselves next to and among the first true philosophers,[102] or, as if they belonged to the same species. And this makes for potential chaos and disorder. Why? Because the indifferent thereby introduce into critical philosophy precisely that which, according to reason, has no place in it. A peculiar indistinguishability arises between the philosophers and the indifferentists, an apparent (viz., in appearance) and presumed equivalence and indifference. A fundamental problem, which was part of the dilemma of the previous metaphysics, is thereby repeated in philosophy with the pseudo-philosophers of indifference. This problem means that not only philosophy and the use of reason are endangered but so too is (the existence of) morality. In the place of an idealization of feeling, this problem becomes potentially indistinguishable from a defect in feeling and conviction within philosophy. Can philosophy then remain a battlefield between the equanimous and the indifferent?

Indifference in Philosophy: Latitudinarians, Indifferentists and Syncretists

Against the background of this question, it is helpful to turn to a passage in Kant's *Religion Essay* which follows the negatively formulated explanations on the morally intermediate things—indifference and *adiaphora*. It is precisely in this passage where Kant added the remark (in the general remarks) in which he defines the existence of the morally intermediate things such that they are bound up with a regression to actions merely in accordance with the laws of nature. After Kant remarked that all maxims risk losing their determinacy and stability so that there is indifference in moral matters, he goes on (in the body of the main text of the first remark) to say:

> Those who adhere to this strict way of thinking are commonly called *rigorists* (a name intended to carry reproach, but in fact a praise); so we can call *latitudinarians* those at the opposite extreme. These latter, again, are either latitudinarians of neutrality and may be called *indifferentists*, or latitudinarians of coalition and can then be called *syncretists*.[103]

The defenders of the critical project and of true metaphysics are rigorists. After the failure of all dogmatic metaphysics and the emergence of indifference, the first true philosophers are rigoristic in their activity. They are rigoristic because they pursue dogmatic metaphysics in a new and different manner, namely in being dogmatists grounded in principles rather than being dogmatists in the uncritical sense.[104] They critically examine principles at every step in a reflexive manner, especially with respect to the fundamental disjunction between good and evil,[105] their mode of activity and constitution, and the capacity as well as the demands of reason: "Rigorism . . . involves an uncompromisingly bivalent view of moral life, according to which every imputable act and morally responsible agent must be characterized as either good or evil."[106]

In contrast to this, the position of the indifferent in philosophy splits into two. The critical metaphysicians wage a war on multiple fronts. There is not only the classical dogmatic metaphysics, but there are also (at least) two antirigorist parties, two antipodes to the rigorous modes of thought.[107] With respect to the introductory passage, it is worth noting that Kant subsumes the representatives of indifference, on the one side, and the so-called syncretists, on the other, under the common category of the latitudinarian. As a term, this was used originally for a group of English theologians in the seventeenth and eighteenth centuries who defined themselves as undogmatic free thinkers, seeking to take an intermediate position in the conflict between the Church of England and the puritanical Presbyterians, representing an indifferent attitude toward church dogmas.[108] Etymologically, the term derives from the Latin "*latitudo*," which means wide and space to move. Taking up again the already introduced distinction between the neither-nor-indifference and the both-and-indifference, Kant distinguishes the latitudinarians of neutrality from the latitudinarians of the coalition. Whereas the rigorists separate characters and actions into good and evil in philosophy, the indifferentists (as Kuno Fischer summarizes) maintain that "the human being is neither good nor evil by nature, . . . the syncretists: the human being is both good and evil by nature."[109] If both "so-called *indifferentists* . . . unavoidably fall back into metaphysical assertions,"[110] then the foundation of even these assertions lies precisely in the (problematic metaphysical) assumption of the existence between good and evil of a discretionary power. Both kinds of latitudinarians doubt the strict disjunction between both, which in turn maintains and must maintain rigorism. This doubt, which is valid for Kant in every doubt, implies an "opposing ground or a mere obstacle for holding something to be true" and is either the expression of the subjective "condition of an irresolute disposition," or "the [objective—F.R.] inadequacy of the grounds."[111] Why is this a problem?

A further definition that Kant provides of the latitudinarians provides an answer; he maintains the following: "He is a latitudinarian who considers the moral law in such a way that he could proceed with his frail actions, who feigns permissive laws."[112] The latitudinarian, the indifferent of philosophy, not only pretends to be a philosopher, but she also fabricates and formulates laws which subsequently enable him to pretend that she thinks and acts according to laws. Precisely on the basis of this redoubled fabrication, she can pretend to be a philosopher and appear as such. If this maneuver succeeds and both the latitudinarian and the indifferent are held to be philosophers, it follows that their concept of (the moral) law is not and cannot be such. The latitudinarian feigns having a concept of the moral law as well as thinking and acting in conformity with it, but this concerns, rather, a pretended concept (here is the fabrication), because the most unstable action can still not correspond to it. Therefore, the feigned law cannot correspond to the true concept of law. Through this semblance of philosophy, the latitudinarian brings into the law not only semblance but also a peculiarly dangerous vacillation, for she introduces concepts that seem philosophical but are not, because they are ultimately not concepts but fabrications.

As a result, the fundamental concepts of philosophical discourse and thought risk becoming unstable themselves, because instead of reason what rules is a peculiar conceptual permissiveness, which suggests that thinking and action would stand under a strict and unwavering law. However, as Kant writes in a famous passage, the freedom of this law would ultimately exist in "making an *exception* to it [the moral law] for ourselves . . . to the advantage of our inclination."[113] This means that the concepts of the fake philosophers are feigned concepts to which they pretend. A feigned concept of the moral law is evidently not a true concept of the moral law, as the constitutive and strict logical disjunction (between good and evil) on which the moral law is based for the rigorists is suspended in it. Through such fabrication, appearance becomes something else. Through this fabrication, both the concept and the law (as well as everything else) fall into indeterminacy and vacillation. Through philosophy, what is introduced into practice is the constant possibility of the exception by law; there is constantly the possibility of actions by which the moral law cannot find any practical application, so that these actions do not ultimately stand in any real relationship to this law. Since for Kant "*lex* is" valid and must be "that for which there are no exceptions,"[114] indifference and *adiaphora* are thus produced.

With the vacillation of its fundamental concepts, philosophy itself falls into vacillation, and, seeking to explain only the constitution of reason and rational practice, so too does the everyday practice of human beings. This means that Kant can assert: "Moral *latitudinarii* are dangerous human beings."[115] They are dangerous because they introduce semblance, fabrications, and agreeable formulations of the concept and law into philosophy and human practice. And an essential ground of all error, for and in Kant, is precisely this semblance. Consequently, the following: Indifference introduces error into philosophy, and this is not an error concerning an external object but is rather error concerning morality, freedom, reason, and philosophy.[116] Such thoughts can be more precisely formulated with respect to the distinction between the latitudinarians of neutrality and the coalition, between indifferentists and syncretists,[117] as follows: The first maintain that there is neutrality in moral characters and actions, and thus one would have to decide either against good and evil, the second claim one does not have to (be able to) decide in general. Indifferentists suspend the process of decision because they suspend the disjunction on which any *free* decision is based, and, as a result, they abandon morality in general. Their position leads to that which must be avoided as far as possible: to a neutrality of actions and characters in moral matters. For neither reason nor philosophy, properly understood, is able to abstain from decisions in the interests of morality. Indifferentists proceed to the abolition not only of morality, but also of reason, freedom, and philosophy.

Kant also characterizes the syncretists as "false peacemakers . . . who want to satisfy everyone by melting down the different creeds . . . [who] are even worse than sectarians, because they are basically indifferent to religion in general."[118] The syncretists are just as indifferent as the indifferentists (with respect, at least, to religion and the ends established in it), only they establish their "philosophical position" in a different manner. They establish a merely feigned, false peace between the formerly conflicting dogmatic and metaphysical positions, on the one hand, and—as explained—in the conflict between the individual inclinations and preferences and the moral law, on the other hand. This state of peace is false and feigned because it is brokered by proceeding from the problematic assumption that one can peaceably bring everyone into agreement.[119] The syncretists suspend any disjunction, replacing it with a potentially endlessly extendable conjunction, the price of which establishment is not that no real position (neither for X nor against X) is attained, but rather the contrary, namely that everything is treated as indifferently as good or evil. Thus obedience to the moral law can be unproblematically accompanied by the selfish pursuit of their own pathological inclinations. It is precisely such an assumption, on syncretism lines, that is the expression of indifference toward morality, toward faith in something held to be most essential, as well as in a rationally arranged world in general.

Indifferent syncretists are worse: even worse than those who turn away from creeds in an abstractly negative and sectarian manner, since they deny God, reason in the world, and the freedom of humans. They are worse not only because they turn away, in a sense, from the rational religion and the religion of reason without making this recognizable, since they claim to not relate to a fixed position for or against it, but also because the truth of their position is summed up precisely in their turning away from the religion of reason, whereby they cannot do anything other than relate to a will that does not take a position. For Kant, they are worse because they turn away from reason and religion, and at the same time they veil this turning away, making it unrecognizable. They are worse because they—just like the indifferentists—make it to all appearances possible and thinkable to suspend the distinction between truth and error, between good and evil.

However, the real problem, the real error, consists precisely in the fact that even as they can present themselves as peacemakers they bring a still more fundamental disorder, confusing the difference between war and peace, confusing the categories of human reason and the constitutive concepts of philosophy. And because it is not initially discernible as such and not perceived as such, the problem of such a disorder is all the more great. For Kant, both latitudinarians are ultimately inconsistent, even if this inconsistency is presented as a logically consistent possibility. However, "[c]onsistency is the greatest obligation of a philosopher,"[120] and therefore the following is valid:

> In cognitions of reason everything must be determined exactly
> (*stricte*). . . . Broad determination leaves a certain play for error, which
> still can have its determinate limits [*sic*], however. Error occurs
> particularly where a broad determination is taken for a strict one, e.g.,
> in matters of morality, where everything must be determined *stricte*.
> Those who do not do this are called by the English *latitudinarians*.[121]

Latitudinarianism produces error since it cancels the strict rigorism of determinations and definitions both of morality and reason, and thus ultimately of philosophy. Latitudinarianism is the tendency in philosophy of what appears to be philosophy to abolish philosophy.

For philosophy, there can be neither neutrality nor a peace treaty between good and evil. The fundamental error already consists in assuming that it is possible in general to take up, in moral questions, a neutral or peacemaking position, and to thus go on to represent indifferentist or syncretist attitudes as seemingly consistent attitudes. This error is once again error about error, which is an error that is worse than (any partial) error. It is *total* error. The persistence and intractability of indifference within philosophy, of which the paradigm is the figure of the latitudinarian, produces (and not only within philosophy but in practice generally) an omnipresence of the artificially produced "habitual disposition" of the phlegmatic temperament.[122] This is a temperament which no longer takes anything seriously, which stands for nothing, decides nothing, holds everything to be dispensable and negotiable, and so, without noticing or knowing it, it renounces its own freedom. This is pretended and feigned because indifferent philosophy produces the phlegmatic temperament, and thereby also produces the decline of morality, rational action, and a rational arrangement of the world in general.

At this point we might well assume that for Kant reason and philosophy will maintain the upper hand as before. However, as he mentions in the *Critique of Practical Reason*, we live in a

> *syncretistic* age, in which a certain *coalition system* of contradictory principles, replete with dishonesty and shallowness, is contrived, because it commends itself better to a public that is satisfied with knowing something of everything and nothing as a whole, so that it can turn its hand to anything.[123]

Indifference recommends itself and is (becoming) more popular. It is more easily satisfied. It disturbs and irritates nobody in its opinions and comforts, inducing no difficult decisions, letting the difficult questions of reason be forgotten. It does not necessitate any consequences in, of, or for either action or character. In this way, even as the forms of latitudinarianism sustain a problematic form of the democratization of reason and morality, this works agreeably for the public, as anyone can join in, indifferently, with what they think, what they assume, or how they act, since it no longer pertains to the consequences and consistency in matters of morality. In this way latitudinarianism produces what Adorno, more than a century later, will call "half-education."[124] It produces, through its ever-expanding series of pretensions, the pretension of knowing, which is not knowing but which is still presumed to be knowing. From such a knowing, even without its being noticed as such, any resulting statement, any relating to or defense of a position, is thus made impossible. In an apparent and peculiar manner, what is also made impossible is a defense of reason, of freedom, and of philosophy. This is because here, pretended philosophy—the pretense of philosophy—is maintained as philosophy, indifference is as maintained as if freedom, inconsistency as (if) the use of reason, in a series of apparently worsening substitutions. For Kant, however, it is evident that the future not only of philosophy but also of freedom, reason, and morality depend on dealing with this problem, and also so far as possible, on keeping in check those who bring this problem upon humanity. What, then, is required is a *Critique of Indifferent Reason*. A critique of a conceptual impossibility and an impossibility of thinking.

Schmid's Critique of Indifferent Reason

In Leipzig in 1809 a Kantian by the name of Carl Christian Erhard Schmid published an essay that was this very critique of indifferent reason. This work appeared under the inconspicuous title, "Adiaphora, Scientifically and Historically Investigated by Carl Christian Erhard Schmid." Without being able to reconstruct this over-700-page work in its entirety and detail here, it is instructive to consider some of Schmid's reflections systematically and in the context of our previous discussion. Already on the first pages of the introduction, Schmid begins to establish that what he refers to as ethical indifference deserves a systematic and historical investigation and critique. Why? Since such an indifference was "often the object of serious and persistent conflicts since the earliest times,"[125] which historical fact indicates that morality "is completely other, distinct, depending on whether it either denies or maintains *adiaphora*."[126] Philosophy and thereby ethical life and morality is a battlefield, and any peace treaty as well as any attempt at final arbitration has previously failed. Hence there is an immediate "practical importance of this investigation"[127] for human beings, because the results will have a direct effect on real (and possibilities of) ways of life. Thus, Schmid's aim is clear from the beginning. And this aim is Kantian. Schmid proceeds to show the following: "Whoever honestly and courageously believes in the truth, they are sublimely above all doubts in its connection to all truth, as well as its necessary and essential relation to all good."[128] His investigative aim concerns the "deviance" both "of moral pedanticism" and "protecting" indifference.[129] It concerns a truly rational "philosophy of life."[130] And thus a critique of indifferent reason cannot be anything other than a philosophy of life, cannot be anything other than the philosophy of the life of rational beings.

In the first part of his essay, Schmid analytically treats the conceptual determinations of *adiaphora*. In the second and—in Kant's sense—synthetic part, he turns to the resolution of the analytically established problem. He first differentiates, in accordance with this division, the various fields in which there can or could be purely conceptual-analytic indifference in general: in the theoretical field, both in the aesthetic disposition in which one finds neither approval nor disapproval in an object, and in intellectual cognition that is analyzed into indifference[131] as a condition of the soul or of things or of thoughts, which are or act metaphysically or logically indifferent in this condition. The logical indifference of thoughts characterizes those thoughts that are neither true nor false, but are, rather, of a third kind.[132] Metaphysical indifference characterizes an indistinguishability (indiscernibile) of an object of cognition that can be understood as either quantitatively externally similar, or qualitatively the same in composition, such that this concerns in turn the inner determinations and relations of objects (i.e., the essence of objects, or the accidents of objects). Schmid presupposes Leibniz's assumption that what one cannot distinguish is ultimately not distinguishable, namely, is identical,[133] against the existence of metaphysically indistinguishable things. And against the background of these initial divisions, Schmid turns to indifference and equivalence. These concern him solely in the practical sense.

By practical, Schmid means the Kantian formulation that "everything depends on freedom," where there is an absolutely practical object that is determined as an "act of the power of choice in general" and a relatively practical object that is determined as "an object in which my free power of choice is actively expressed."[134] Practical indifference is a predicate that can be either (relatively) attributed to the (more precisely: this) object, or (generally) attributed to the act of the power of choice. As a result, Schmid differentiates the permitted as practically indifferent action, and subdivides it into technical content (neither individually agreeable nor disagreeable), pragmatic content (neither detrimental nor useful), and absolute content (neither purposeful nor unpurposeful). He goes on to distinguish it from merely legal and juridical indifference, and thereby turns to ethical indifference proper. From this, ethical indifference is to be understood in terms of either objective or subjective indifference, whereby the former characterizes something neither prohibited nor commanded, and the latter an action whose incentive is neither good nor evil.[135]

After detailed analytic subdivisions, Schmid concludes that everything which stands outside of the practical law objectively, "and (subjectively) [outside of] the maxims that execute this law, even if breaking away from adherence to all of my inclinations,"[136] is to be named as ethically indifferent.[137] Everything that falls outside of the sphere of morality is indifferent and equivalent for the freedom of the will and for the practical law. Non-moral objects and actions are morally irrelevant, and hence morally indifferent. Although this initially sounds undramatic, it means, as Schmid demonstrates in a profoundly renewed Kantian manner, that "both one's own as well as others' happiness and unhappiness belong to ethical *adiaphora*,"[138] since the rationally thought moral law *must* be indifferent toward my own or others' happiness or unhappiness—otherwise it concerns happiness (or blessedness) and not morality. Thus the duty called upon by any law concerns only the "*completion*"[139] of its compliance, that is, the moral perfection of the subject of the law. Subjectively, the completion of ethical education is required so that "*gradually everything and anything can become an ascetic adiaphoron.*" And "*it must because it ought to.*"[140]

For Schmid, the introduction of these distinctions or divisions, and the apparent exile of all morally irrelevant things from the field of reality, is only a precursor or precondition, in order that he can go on to establish that which conceptually falls outside of the moral sphere, which is nevertheless yet conceived as a part of this sphere. Only through the division in the first instance does it become possible in a second instance to realize a power of the free will subordinate to the moral law "throughout the entirety of nature."[141] This concerns a shift of perspective: Only from the perspective of morality can it be decided as to how something is associated with morally indifferent things and relations, and in order to have a precise concept of the moral perspective, it is necessary to separate this from what is morally indifferent *in-itself*. Only in this way can the question be answered of how what is morally indifferent in-itself, distinguished from the perspective of morality (i.e., *for us*, i.e., as a morally relevant field of objects), can be presented.

The second part of Schmid's essay begins by leveling "an investigative gaze . . . at the ground of all moral *diaphorie* and *adiaphorie* of actions in general."[142] *Diaphorie*—the disjunctive judgment of which Kant had spoken—is present as soon as and "*when something ought to happen.*"[143] The *ought*, here, means something distinct from no obligation, or necessary occurrences from natural laws or drives.[144] This *ought* is necessarily related to the freedom "that a character is, which is entitled to the human power of choice,"[145] which determination is not, however, an invention of philosophy or something feigned by philosophy, but rather "is *found* in consciousness,"[146] and philosophy merely indicates the task of clarifying this consciousness.[147] Freedom is so found because it is given to rational beings. That philosophy can only explain what is given means it can never prove the origin of this ought,[148] but rather the ought can only be released from itself, that is, proven through its practical adherence and actualization. Moral practice is a result of the freedom that is subordinate to the moral law. This means that practice as such is never guaranteed and settled and simply given: "[w]hoever does not will to think and act morally"—and the emphasis here should be placed on the willing—"must be and is certainly given over" to a "dissolution of all moral concepts in the empty, deceptive representation . . . of his *sincere* approval."[149] Which means the following: Whoever is sincerely evil, that is, an evil character, will subscribe to the doctrine that speaks and propagates talk of the dissolution of morals. Evil characters have a selfish interest in discrediting the thought of morality as such.

Schmid's position here is remarkable if one reads it in the context of Kant's critical analysis of the latitudinarians, as it implies that there are not only latitudinarians within philosophy because latitudinarianism characterizes a further logical possibility of thought, that is, a position that is purely taken up deductively, but also that latitudinarianism, the indifference in moral (and philosophical) matters, is the universal and theoretically disposed representation of an individual decision of the will against morality and thereby for evil. There is a latitudinarianism that is the symptom of a will which does not want to think and act morally, and therefore not only gives its sincere approval to the dissolution of morals but also enthusiastically participates in this dissolution. Latitudinarianism is not simply a further philosophical opinion of doctrine, it is, instead, a form of ideology. Why ideology? Because everyone finds in themselves "an irresistible, inner voice"[150] that tells them that only the obedience to the moral law allows for the realization of their own freedom. But one can also arbitrarily, that is, freely, decide against obedience to the moral law, and thereby be able to decide against the appropriate actualization necessary of one's own freedom. To be free, here, implies paradoxically freely deciding against freedom.

If this is the case, then one can also know that one has decided against that which one knows is the right and good thing to do. Because one has freely decided against freedom, one encounters a contradiction: one maintains that there is freedom beyond the decision (between good and evil), and precisely this a decision against freedom. And inevitably this contradiction is not represented as what it is. Rather, the latitudinarians produce a representation of human nature that is supposed to remove the contradiction without either truly sublating or overcoming it. Such a contradictory representation consists of an assumption that human beings are not always good or evil and are sometimes even both at the same time. This leads to the claim that human beings are either essentially separated from morality (i.e., human beings are beings that do many things and *only some* of these things are morally relevant), or that freedom (as the essence of human beings) is separated from morality (i.e., human beings are beings that are freely able to determine what morality is), or finally, that morality is separated from the distinction between good and evil.

If this danger, already foreseen by Kant, is thinkable, then the freedom of human beings is actualized in such a way that its actualization implies neither a decision for nor against morality or freedom. And since it is not represented, but rather it is maintained that there are decisions and that these decisions are not good or evil or both at the same time, the decision for evil at the basis of this representation is concealed. This decision is concealed because it is not related to such a human nature whose constitution is not always forced to one-sided decisions. We thus discern in Schmid a logical genealogy of latitudinarianism, arising from the free decision against morality and reason as well as the decision for the merely individual and pathological inclinations which simultaneously do not want to be such a decision. The culpability inherent in this decision knows that it represents the inexistence or artificiality of morals. But in order to avoid culpability, and to not be held responsible for any decision, a (pseudo-philosophical)[151] universal representation of human character and human action is created that allows for the suspension of morality (anthropo- as well as onto-logically). Through a universal representation of human nature the guilt of a merely individual and particular decision is removed.[152] Latitudinarianism, or indifference in morality, is the ideological justification of evil through the sublation of moral foundations in general, and, as Kant remarked, it is dangerous in precisely this sense. For the inexistence of the moral law necessarily leads to the "universal ethical indifference of all human action."[153] Against the ideologues of morals who are evil in the conceptual sense, Schmid insists the following: *"There is a real distinction (diaphorie) between ethical good and ethical evil."*[154] Thus the critique of indifferent reason necessarily leads to a moral realism.

Here Schmid investigates whether this moral realism can also be applicable to the involuntary actions of human beings. If this were not so, then there would potentially be "some indifferent actions of human beings."[155] Schmid strictly rejects this thought because the actions that appear to human beings as involuntary—for example, habits or digestive mechanisms—either imply voluntary changes of human nature (a habit is a habit because I made it so), or merely expire according to the laws of nature. If they expire naturally, then they do not seem to concern human beings as human, but rather human beings as "animal-human [*Thiermensch*],"[156] and thus seem to fall outside the field of ethical life. However, it also holds that since *"nature* is at work everywhere, so freedom is at work in everything," and therefore the merely natural functions of human beings are (at least potentially) subordinate to the free influence of the will. Where exactly the boundary between nature and freedom lies for human beings is therefore subjectively determined by the free decision of the human being—it always remains responsible for it in every case—and is objectively and conceptually undetermined.[157]

The boundary between nature and freedom is only subjectively determin-able.[158] Or, as Schmid indicates in a dialectical manner: "The human being must only be subjected to natural mechanisms because it wills it,"[159] that is, the functions by which the human being is mechanically determined are mechani-cally determined because the human *wills* that they are mechanically deter-mined. The conceptual point for Schmid lies (and herein may be found the answer as to how to clarify Kant's formulation "so far as possible") in establish-ing the following: "*We ought to observe no free action as physically-indifferent*, as indifferent for the entire world in all its consequences."[160] There *ought* to be no indifference in morality. This ought is what the law of freedom claims. The human ought not to understood itself as a human-animal. "It must give none [indifference]. . . . It could, nevertheless, give some. . . . But it ought to give none."[161] Schmid's conclusion is that, against indifference in morality, one can only refer to an ought and never to a must. Nothing prevents the human being from understanding itself as an animal, but it ought not to do this.[162]

Nothing prevents latitudinarianism: It must not be, can always be, yet it ought never to be. This ought posits morality in turn as "all-encompassing"[163] and yet also as something that is to be understood only gradually.[164] The ought also asserts that what arises in the universality of the ethical law is not knowl-edge but rather faith.[165] It *ought* to hold therefore that: "*No deed is morally in-different, or: there is no moral adiaphora of the deed*,"[166] for every action is the expression of a self-chosen and posited maxim of free will, which either is or is not subordinate to the moral law. It is maintained therefore that the true movement of universalization which Schmid adopts is the disjunction in-scribed in the ethical law. This means that decision ought to be everywhere and always—and (of course) to assume this is even a decision. This, then, is a decision which one cannot create from the world or the subject and is a deci-sion for or against indifference. This also means that morality was, is, and will always remain a battlefield.

Indifference and the Ideology of the Counter-Enlightenment

Against the background of this discussion of Schmid's essay, we can argue that for Kant equivalence, indifference, and *adiaphora* in morality all also desig-nate a problematic understanding of freedom, since the expression of indif-ference in morality and of latitudinarianism in philosophy and in practice is grounded on an understanding of freedom which strives to rid itself of differ-ent forms of decision. Freedom is understood either as a neither-nor or a both-and, and thus as a capacity for both in either a neutral or a composite form. One hundred fifty years after Descartes, Kant and Schmid repeat and realize with their critique of indifferent reason the Cartesian critique of the interpretation of freedom as an indeterminate capacity, adding a further dimension to the indeterminacy of this capacity, since it is not only an abstract negation of determinacy as the determination of freedom that is problematic in general, but also problematic is the abstract attitude that all possible determinations can be attributed to the capacity of freedom. This attitude is a moral attitude, for it is evil and veils its evilness. But what is decisive for Kant and Schmid is that freedom is a *factum*, fact, and is as such given to reason and the rational being, even as the givenness of freedom is nothing beyond its actualization. In other words, the true proof of the givenness of freedom is its actualization and therefore the givenness of freedom is a retroactive givenness, a givenness that is no longer distinguishable from a practical production of freedom.

To think freedom as neutral, or as everything mediated with anything, means to not think freedom, and also means to abolish it altogether. In Kant and Schmid, therefore, we find a far-reaching and complex analysis of an ideology of freedom as capacity. Under these auspices Kant remarks at one point in his *Reflections on Anthropology* that indifference is a *"voluptas non rationalis,"*[167] an irrational pleasure, a pleasure in and of irrationality and unreason. Indifference means understanding freedom as a capacity beyond the spontaneity of freedom, namely, understanding freedom beyond the act that realizes such freedom.

In philosophy there is no indeterminate freedom so long as it is true philosophy (i.e., rational philosophy and the philosophy of reason). Freedom always already implies an act (that determines what freedom is). A decision is already expressed if one negates this act of freedom in the manner of the syncretists and indifferentists, which is the expression of a decision whose character can be called ethically evil, and which is thereby symptomatic of the regression of the human being to the animal and to animal behavior. This is an effect of a peculiar ideology of freedom that is ideology because it arises from a free decision for the abolition of freedom whose motivation is its own self-obscuring. For Kant and Schmid such an ideology is ideological because it introduces a further self-incurred immaturity into the emergence from the self-incurred immaturity that is characteristic of enlightenment. To decide that freedom is to be understood as an undetermined or overdetermined capacity is regressive. This is the case not only because human beings become animals, but also because this interpretation is anti-enlightenment. This attitude does not display the courage to make use of one's own understanding. Counter-enlightenment and indifference seem to arise from fear or anxiety of freedom, which therefore seems to generate an interpretation of freedom for which courage is not a requirement. From Kant's and Schmid's diagnosis, then, the following conclusion is possible: that as long as human beings understand and act toward freedom from anxiety in such a way that they understand their freedom as so fundamentally undetermined that it can mean anything is possible—the equivalent of saying "anything goes"—then they act as if they were animals because they do not have the courage to take responsibility for their decisions, decisions in which, even in this indeterminacy, they are already implicated. This abolishes the sphere of morality, reason, freedom, and the enlightenment of their constitution, that is, philosophy. But so long as human beings become human-animals, they are no longer self-determined but rather determined by something other and thus heteronomous. This relationship of determination amounts to determinations that are given by nature.

The abolition of freedom through this counter-enlightened reinterpretation of freedom does not mean a regression to the premodern but to natural relations. It is a dogmatic metaphysics that denies it is such, since it pretends not to partake in metaphysics, as well as indifference toward it. In this way a perverse return to nature arises. For, as Schmid points out, any return to nature that is not an appropriation of nature is a relapse to nature as well as the abolition of freedom and humanity.[168] Indifference is and remains a problem in the history of rationalism—a problem whose problematicity is constantly expanding and cannot simply resolved by enlightenment. What the Enlightenment ultimately reproaches it with is that it is morally reprehensible—*It ought not to be!* But is this really the last word that philosophical rationalism has to say on the subject?

3
Hegel, the Dead Disposition, and the Mortification of Freedom

How we finally are over here I do not know to say. It is an indifferent status which, God willing, will not last long.

—CAROLINE PAULUS, LETTER TO HEGEL, DECEMBER 18, 1810

For there is also a peace that is indifferent to the depths of the spirit . . . but that which is only overlooked or despised is for that very reason not overcome. On the contrary . . . the harm . . . will be all the more dangerous.

—G. W. F. HEGEL, "FOREWORD TO HINRICH'S *RELIGION IN ITS INNER RELATION TO SCIENCE*"

Down in the dirt, nothing has changed.

—REFUSED, "ELEKTRA"

Indifference is always the worst.

—G. W. F. HEGEL, "ÜBER DIE BEKEHRTEN (VON ERNST RAUPACH)"

Encore: Relapse; or, The Last Latitudinarian

The disputation of Hegel's habilitation theses took place in 1801 at the University of Jena. The official subject of these theses was announced as "Philosophical Dissertation on the Orbits of the Planets" (*Dissertatio philosophica de orbitis planetarum*).[1] Here, even as the thirty-one-year-old Hegel does not at all explicitly take up the problem that Descartes brought about and Kant took up and

82

modified, namely the problem of indifference,[2] we nevertheless ought not to be deceived by the title of the subject that Hegel is dealing with. In these habilitation theses he explicitly addresses and positions himself vis-à-vis the philosophy of Kant, and does so in an unequivocally critical manner. It is precisely this self-positioning that permits us, here, a productive connection to the Kantian rendition of the indifference problem. For Hegel's early critique of Kant demonstrates why the indifference problem is a problem which persists at the heart of, thoroughly afflicting, Kantian philosophy. The following will be concerned with grasping the early Hegelian encounter with Kant in order to comprehend the extent to which Hegel presents a further, a novel, and a radicalized response to the indifference problem, which decisively takes place *after* Kant (and in a manner very different from that of Schmid).[3] We are, therefore, taking a further step in the history of philosophical rationalism.

Already in the first and probably best known of the twelve theses submitted, Hegel begins with a fundamental and far-reaching claim: "Contradictio est regula veri, non contradictio falsi" (Contradiction is the rule of the true; non-contradiction is the rule of the false). No truth without contradiction. This, a beginning which is a breathtaking rejection of one of the foundational principles and pillars of the whole of Aristotle's philosophy in only seven words. The implications of this rejection are manifold. The contradiction of which the early Hegel speaks is already not contradiction in a merely formal logical sense; rather, it designates, to formulate here cautiously, a "discrepancy of a particular kind."[4] Hegel's first thesis, about contradiction, means at least three things: First, truth is never truth beyond contradiction. Truth is the truth of the *or* of a contradiction. Contradiction is the medium of truth, so that there is no truth if there is no contradiction. Truth is brought forth by contradiction. Truth is thus a production and not a given. Second, this must mean that contradiction, or a singular contradiction, can be read as an index or as a symptom of truth, and this truth is a truth that exceeds the positions that are in contradiction. Third, this must also mean that if contradiction is truly the rule of truth that truth cannot eliminate contradiction.

This can mean that contradiction does not simply disappear but is (as Hegel will say later) sublated (*aufgehoben*). It can also mean that if a truth is contradicted, this truth is no less true. It is a characteristic of truth, rather, not only to arise out of contradiction but furthermore to be a one-sided truth, a truth which seems to be a contradiction. This, however, does not mean that it loses any of its truth-potency, so to speak, even as it potentially evokes contradiction and can be articulated in a one-sided manner or from a particular position. Truth arises from contradiction as truth of the contradiction and, because it does not dissolve contradiction, because it would otherwise also dissolve itself, it has the characteristic of one-sidedness, which, at least seemingly, contradicts the concept of truth. These are some of the fundamental features of the concept of truth that the early Hegel brings up in his first habilitation thesis.

From these determinations one of the punch lines of the thesis is perhaps predictable: that truth no longer stands in an exclusive and precluding relation to falsehood. But does Hegel, here, fall precisely under the Kantian definition of indifferentism or latitudinarianism? Does (this early) Hegel stand on the side of indifference and thus orient himself against Kant and Kantian philosophy? To begin with, we should note here whereas the implications of this thesis certainly undermine any stiff distinction between truth and falsehood, they in no way undermine the distinction of truth and falsehood as such. Hegel does not therefore fall into the category of the indifferentists. The distinction of true and false explicitly depends on the distinction of contradictoriness and non-contradictoriness—a distinction abandoned by the indifferentists (or at least the indifferentists in Kant's account). Hegel's point, on the contrary, consists in claiming that there is no pure truth and no pure falsehood, that is, the two-sided-form of the distinction is never a simple two-sided-form but rather it multiplies itself internally if one follows the truth (of contradiction). Truth is always truth of the not-true. Consequently, falsehood consists in assuming the purity of the distinction of true and false, which is an error to which, from Hegel's perspective, even Kant fell prey.

In the following theses, Hegel proceeds from this point by initially stating that the syllogism is the principle of idealism, the square (viz., the quadrangle) is the law of nature, and that the triangle (viz., trinity) is the law of spirit. To this he adds two theses on arithmetic and gravitation. It is in his seventh thesis that he finally returns to and attacks Kant's philosophy: "Philosophia critica caret ideis et imperfecta scepticismi forma" (Critical philosophy lacks the idea, and it is an incomplete form of skepticism).[5] This thesis can be better understood in relation to the definition of the idea that Hegel gives in his sixth thesis: "Idea est synthesis infiniti et finiti et philosophia omnis est in ideis" (The idea is the synthesis of the infinite and the finite, and all philosophy is philosophy in and of ideas). All philosophy is philosophy of the idea and thereby it is a philosophy, which grasps, conceives of, and articulates the relation between the finite and the infinite. It is thus philosophy not only of the idea, but philosophy *in* (the form of) the idea, that is to say its (presentational) form itself is the form of the idea, because it is a finite articulation of the infinite. In this way, philosophy is the synthetic articulation of both, and it thereby grasps the infinite in a finite way and form of articulation. And it is this which is a contradiction, namely, an index of truth. Philosophy is *idea-ology*;[6] philosophers are "militants of the idea."[7]

How then to read, against this background, Hegel's seventh thesis that is critical of Kant? First, for the early Hegel Kant has a problematic comprehension and a problematic idea of the idea, because in his (Kant's) conception there is no mediation of the finite and the infinite, but only a peculiar mark of infinity in a being that is conscious of its own finitude and limitedness. Although Kant famously introduced the postulates of reason being the idea of freedom, of God, and of the immortality of the soul, this does not establish any mediation, only making explicit the difference between the idea and mere finite consciousness. There is something infinite in us finite beings (the idea of freedom, for example), but we can never cognize it adequately, thus we have to postulate it, because otherwise a deficient form of practice would result from its absence. Kant has, therefore, according to his own belief, demonstrated the necessity of the postulates for rational and moral beings, namely, beings that realize their rationality practically. Yet he did not realize any mediation of finitude and infinity, rather, expressed only the apparent insight that such a mediation is needed but ultimately impossible. Kant's postulates of reason therefore remain tainted with and within the sphere of finitude.

It is this claim that Hegel articulates in his eighth thesis: "Materia postulati rationis, quod philosophia critica exhibet, eam ipsam philosophiam destruit" (The matter of the postulates of reason, which are exhibited by critical philosophy, destroys this very philosophy). Hegel derives this from the fact that Kantian philosophy lacks the actual concept of the idea: Kant's philosophy remains stuck in finitude, postulates the infinite, but thereby destroys the philosophical character of its own project, because a philosophy can only be philosophy of and in the idea, that is, as a realized—and not only postulated—mediation of finitude and infinitude. For Hegel, then, Kant's project fails because he (Kant) believes it is possible to sublate or at least evade the contradictions that derive from the finite constitution of human beings by means of the postulates of reason and thus his project does not do what philosophy must do, namely, conceive of a synthesis of finitude and infinitude. Kant "remain[s] within the abstract dichotomy of infinite and finite,"[8] and in this way the actual philosophical claim is not fulfilled, but rather ignored. Kant's attempt to avoid contradictions and antinomies leads to the result, if we follow Hegel's above-cited definition, that his philosophy becomes problematic or false. And since no philosophy as philosophy of and in ideas can be false (as philosophy articulates the truth of contradiction), Kant's project is deprived of the status of philosophy.[9] This is a scathing verdict. The commencement of the first real philosophy as metaphysical science is, contrary to what Kant believed, no commencement of philosophy but just another turn of the dogmatic-metaphysical and pre-philosophical screw.[10] The beginning failed.

But how does this diagnosis relate to the characterization of Kant's philosophy as an incomplete skepticism? Does this not explicitly go against Kant's self-understanding and explicit repudiation of skepticism? By answering this question, we move toward a first indicator of the discussion of the indifference problem. This is also, at first, a remarkable claim, particularly in the light of the recollection that Kant had systematically introduced skepticism as the position and attitude, which, proceeding from the failure of the previous dogmatic attempts in metaphysics, sought to turn away from metaphysics altogether. However, Kant also claimed to have pursued the first true metaphysics in a non-dogmatic and critical manner. So, why should his project still be a form of skepticism and an imperfect form at that? Hegel's response can be parsed as follows: Kant sought to position his own philosophical-metaphysical endeavor against the badly infinite succession of dogmatic, pre-metaphysical and pseudo-philosophical positions but also against the refusing stance of the skeptics; Kant took a position also against positions that took a distance against previous dogmatic pseudo-philosophies. Already for Kant, the skeptics assumed that the only thing that is certain is that nothing is certain, but with this assumption (because they took this as a peculiar certainty of its own) they regressed to just another dogmatic-metaphysical position. Kant thus took a skeptical distance from the pseudo-philosophical commitments as well as from the skeptics of these dogmatic commitments.

In Hegel's reading, Kant attempts to be methodically more consequent and consistent than the skeptics (who rejected dogmatic metaphysics because they dogmatically believed in the certainty that nothing is certain) and so, in this reading, Kant then takes on himself a skeptic position with regard to the distinction between the badly infinite repetition of pseudo-metaphysical positions and the skepticism in view of the former. But it is here that the problem of indifferentism emerged. This problem took the following contours: a set choice between the different pseudo-philosophical positions and just another, namely skeptic, pseudo-philosophical position, whereby the indifferentist enters the scene, rejecting altogether the choice between the two equally unsatisfying options. The indifferentist thereby assumes that human beings can be indifferent even to the very questions Kant believed were inherent to the structure of rationality as such and unavoidable.

To avoid the position of the indifferentist, Kant not only repeated the skeptic gesture toward the problematic choice between skepticism and dogmatic metaphysics, but he also introduced undeniable facts of reason from which in turn he derived the postulates of reason. Or, Kant took the first step in the right direction, but shied away from going any further. To use Lenin's famous formula, he took one step forward and two steps back.[11] And so for Hegel, Kant is a skeptic (of dogmatic metaphysics and skepticism), but in an incomplete form, because he wanted to escape indifferentism (which avoidance restrained and limited his skeptic gesture) by means of the postulates, ultimately becoming precisely that kind of skeptic that practices unacknowledged dogmatic metaphysics. The expression of this systematic weakness of Kant is thus that indifferentism shall not be but cannot be avoided. And this shatters his philosophy. This is why Hegel's eighth habilitation-thesis in its entirety reads: "Materia postulati rationis, quod philosophia critica exhibet, eam ipsam philosophiam destruit, et principium est Spinozismi" (The matter of the postulates of reason, which are exhibited by critical philosophy, destroys this very philosophy, and this is the principle of Spinozism). Kant is a Spinozist against his own will. Why? Because he unwittingly introduces substantial claims into reason and thought, which lead to a substantial determination of the very nature of reason as well as of the nature of nature (and the course of the world) and which find their expression on the postulates of reason that ultimately regress to being dogmatic contentions of existence. In this sense, Kant's thought, and what was supposed to be the beginning of philosophy, is a regression.

Kant's thought regresses because of the skeptical rejection of the problematic choice between previous pseudo-philosophical metaphysics and skepticism. It regresses because he tries to be the first to do actual (philosophical) metaphysics (in scientific form). But because he tries to escape indifferentism by being a skeptic in view of the distinction between dogmatic metaphysics and skepticism, he ultimately does not side with skepticism, as he appears to, but rather, in an unacknowledged manner, with dogmatic metaphysics (as his own critique of skepticism had indicated). This turns his position into just another dogmatic metaphysical position, speaking of assumptions of which he has to contend that rational beings cannot not make. His skepticism concerning the problematic choice is incomplete, and as such it is dogmatically metaphysical. What, then, might we name Kant's unwilling dogmatic metaphysical position? For Hegel, it is Spinozism. Why Spinozism? Hegel will later remark: "[I]n Spinozism . . . this world or this 'all' simply *is not* [*ist gar nicht*]. Certainly the 'all' appears, one speaks of its determinate being [*Dasein*], and our life is a being within this existence [*Existenz*]. In the philosophical sense, however, the world has in this view no actuality at all: it simply *is not*."[12] The contradictions that Kant revealed in his antinomies ultimately have no actuality except in and for the merely limited perspective of a finite being. The antinomies neither concern actuality nor do they have a relation to it.[13] Hegel's thesis thus implies that the beginning of (post-Cartesian) modern philosophy, as described and pursued by Kant himself with his critical project, namely, the Copernican turn in philosophy, is a failed turn, a beginning of philosophy that fizzled out.

Kant's newly begun modern philosophy is thus a repetition (of Spinoza and dogmatic metaphysics) and therefore neither really a new nor a first commencement of philosophy. Kant's postulates in the last instance represent for Hegel a repetition, as Dieter Heinrich remarks, "of Spinoza's theory of an immanent necessity of reason immanent to the world."[14] Kant postulates the rationality of the world (God must have necessarily arranged the world rationally so that we can act in it), but he can only postulate this because he simultaneously denies its recognizability. But with this peculiar repetition, and against its will, the business of philosophy, namely the production of a synthesis of finitude and infinite, (formally) fails from and at its beginning. Kant noticed, rightly, that the previous attempts within the field of metaphysics were just bad infinite repetitions of unfounded and unjustifiable contentions about infinity, but he does not succeed in escaping this logic because he ultimately not only hypostatizes the finitude of human cognition and reason, but in the same move he also substantializes it. Infinity exists only because of and through faith (in— the form of—the postulates) and not because of and through knowledge or thought. Knowledge and thought are separated from infinity, and herein lies, if one likes to put it this way, the peculiar subjectivist bias of Kant, which bias led him to substantialize the supposedly objective and unchangeable form of subjectivity, namely, finitude. The form of subjectivity becomes thereby the only and unique actual substance, which is why Kant is a Spinozist who substantializes form.[15]

With respect to the problematic choice between dogmatic metaphysics and its skeptical rejection, Kant, precisely because of his initial taking distance from skepticism, was not skeptical enough, siding too much with dogmatic, Spinozist metaphysics in order to avoid the danger of indifferentism. Since for him there is both finitude (for finite beings) and infinity (for the postulates) even though only the latter ought to be actual, Kant becomes the last latitudinarian. His position is an imperfect skepticism that is mixed with dogmatic metaphysics and is thus fundamentally indistinguishable from the former metaphysics *à la* Spinoza.[16]

In reading Hegel's abovementioned habilitation theses in the context of this discussion, it seems that Kant ultimately formulated a problematic resolution to the indifference problem, in which the only option was to assert—so far as possible—that indifference ought not to be, but such an "ought" has no real conceptual force but merely a moral force. From the perspective of the early Hegel, Kant describes the first dogmatic-metaphysical position that expresses a consciousness of the problem of the difficulties with dogmatic metaphysics, but at the same time the form of this expression remains incomplete. This incompletion derives from the fact that Kant was not logically consistent enough as a skeptic with respect to dogmatic metaphysics and its assumptions, and thus also inconsistent regarding the prevailing skepticism. Kant was—with respect to the skeptical influence on his formulations—not systematically and consistently forward enough, because he tried to dispel and avoid all contradictoriness.[17] In this way the truth of Kant lies in his falsehood, and this criticism will have far-reaching consequences for the determination of the indifference problem.

First, however, it is important to clarify what the execution and realization of skepticism in a complete form might mean for Hegel. Structurally, this must mean (against Kant) to reject the distinction between dogmatic metaphysics and skepticism, and to do so even more radically than Kant. It must mean an increase of rejection. This, however, can only be done if one accepts from the outset the peculiar contradiction of having a choice only between two false options. And this means to choose—and to understand the choice—differently from Kant. One has to be more Kantian than Kant, and thus has to decide in a way that is different from his, which, again, can only be done if one does not (as Kant did) opt for metaphysics (metaphysics as science) but instead for skepticism.[18] From this, then, may arise a truth of the contradiction of metaphysics and skepticism, and the bad infinity of the one side of this distinction that ultimately regresses to finitude is transformed, as it is brought into a new and differently synthetic relation with the infinity of skeptical doubt.[19] One must opt for skepticism because it is only skepticism that offers the option of vanquishing the wrong options, namely, the falsity of both options which are at hand. Although it does not (and cannot) mean that the skepticism is the right option, it is however that option that allows us to see that there are only wrong options. And that from this point we can get the truth of the contradiction; the truth that lies in our having only wrong options to choose between.

Inverted and Complete Skepticism

In 1802 the *Journal for Philosophy*, co-edited by Hegel and Schelling, published a text by Hegel on the relation between skepticism and philosophy. The occasion of this was the publication of a multivolume project written by Gottlob Ernst Schulze (a professor of philosophy from Helmstedt), which took the publication title *Critique of Theoretical Philosophy*. Hegel's text in response was a review, and he reviews in a strict and annihilating manner. A reading of this text allows us to draw some conclusions about how the early Hegel images a complete skepticism, how he imagines, through this, the real beginning of philosophy. In this text he not only investigates Schulze's oeuvre but also "the relationship of skepticism in general . . . to philosophy."[20] He posits that such an investigation is necessary because "the concepts ordinarily current about it [the relationship of skepticism to philosophy] are extremely formal ones, and the noble essence of it, when it is genuine, is habitually inverted into a universal bolthole and talking-point of unphilosophy in these latest days."[21] What it means to be and think skeptically has been forgotten (this is Hegel's diagnosis), and not only Schulze's neo-skepticism but also Kant's incomplete skepticism are symptoms of this forgetting, symptoms of the forgetful inversion that has befallen skeptical thought.

Such skepticism, symptomatic and inverted into an unphilosophical evasion maneuver, no longer follows even the proper conduct of skeptical thinking. One way in which such an inversion took place consists of the transformation of skepticism into a quite trivial subjectivism; in its most problematic versions that Kant referred to as indifferentist, it only knows one criterion of truth, namely the "assent" of and the "success"[22] with the audience. But this is "the death of Speculative Reason."[23] The today forgotten Schulze is a paradigmatic name of this sort of inversion, against which Hegel puts forward the following thesis:

> Without the determination of the true relationship of scepticism to philosophy, and without the insight that scepticism itself is in its inmost heart at one with every true philosophy, and hence that there is a philosophy which is neither scepticism nor dogmatism, and is thus both at once, without this, all the histories, and reports, and new editions of scepticism lead to a dead end.[24]

Hegel's claim is rather remarkable. Initially pointing out that without the precise determination of the relationship between skepticism and philosophy, Hegel notes skepticism itself is not and cannot be properly and adequately understood. But, and here one encounters a surprising emphasis, philosophy is at the same time neither skeptical nor dogmatic and is therefore both at the same time. Hegel modifies the perspective on the choice Kant deemed so problematic: If one has to choose between skepticism and dogmatic metaphysics, one has to reject both, but not to replace them with a yet to be determined third, but rather to relate dogmatic metaphysics and skepticism in a novel manner. One does not choose one of the two but rather rejects them both individually. Why? Because one seeks to form a new universal out of them.

Yet with this answer might Hegel not ultimately be speaking in the same register as the indifferentists and latitudinarians? He at first rejects the choice between skepticism and dogmatism (like the indifferentists) in order to choose both at the same time in the next step (like the syncretic latitudinarians). Such a reading fails to recognize that Hegel, in his answer, aspires to another solution. A solution that emerges through a different mediation of dogmatism and skepticism which leaves neither unchanged. Neither indifferentists nor syncretists change anything in the givenness of the choice. So the philosophical rejection of which Hegel speaks and which leads to the point that both options are chosen changes the givenness of the options of the choice;[25] it does not only take the contradiction between the options of the choice seriously, but it also takes seriously that the only choice is to choose wrongly and that therefore there does not seem to be a choice, and this is a contradiction. This is what allows for the possibility of choosing differently.

To rephrase: First, one must be more skeptical than the skeptics, which represent the obverse of dogmatic metaphysics in the given choice. Although this might seem to be like indifferentism, it is ultimately solely a skeptical trait, since, as Hegel seeks to show, with it the constitution of the choice at question is modified. By being more skeptical than the proffered skepticism, one is able to establish a new and different relation to both of the two options of the choice. Why? Because when we are more skeptical than the skeptics, we are more dogmatically skeptical, and this changes the meaning of dogmatism. What Hegel aims at is thus a new provenance of a kind of dogmatic metaphysics-skepticism.[26] He does not need to position himself against the indifferentists and the latitudinarians because he attempts to remain indifferent, against the conventional shapes of skepticism and dogmatic metaphysics, such that he can unify skepticism and dogmatic metaphysics in such a way that a genuinely novel philosophical position is created—one that is different from any latitudinarian or indifferentist medley. A novel philosophical position that mediates the finite and the infinite. This is why Hegel writes that "a true philosophy necessarily involves a negative side of its own, too, which is directed against everything limited," which makes "a true philosophy . . . infinitely more sceptical than this scepticism"[27] (i.e., the skepticism that Hegel is attacking). And of course, this move also holds for the limited choice between skepticism and dogmatic metaphysics.

The philosophical work that Hegel takes to be a proof of both this idea and of the existence of true philosophy is none other than Plato's *Parmenides*. In this dialogue—even though or perhaps precisely because it famously leads him to no simple resolution to the question he treats[28]—Plato is not concerned with "*doubting* these truths of the understanding . . . , but rather he is intent on the complete negation of all truth of such a [and here lies the emphasis, F.R.] cognition."[29] Thus it can be learned from Plato that not merely the content but even the form of cognition must be questioned in order to actually be able to think skeptically, for only then does it become clear that there is not only one given form of cognition but potentially no predetermined and stable form of cognition at all.

For Hegel this skeptical punch line exceeds even the form of doubt and doubting that modern thinkers like Descartes and (albeit in a different manner) Kant invoked and performed. True doubting doubts even the seemingly unchangeable form of doubt (*Zweifel*) and thereby becomes despair (*Verzweiflung*).[30] So what is at stake is not a vanquishing of doubt, but a real sublation of all false certainties, and precisely this genuinely negative part of skepticism, which enables and shall enable true philosophy, "is the free side of every philosophy,"[31] the side of its freedom. This is because, as a result, there is a freedom even from the previous forms of philosophical thought and doubt (and freedom); the radicalization of skepticism, its effectivity, is so dogmatic it ultimately avoids all dogmatism and even the dogmatism of skepticism itself. This, then, produces a peculiar contradiction. For philosophy to be philosophy, it must challenge the form of philosophy without being able to relate to any given form of doubt or of philosophy beforehand.[32] In this way, this movement transforms the options of dogmatism at choice. But how can one still know what one does in such a practice of perpetual negation?

The answer is that one cannot know in advance. But according to Hegel, "since every genuine philosophy has this negative side," it "eternally sublates the principle of contradiction"[33]—it is philosophy because it does not rebuff skepticism. So (reading Hegel here) philosophy is philosophy if Aristotle's' principle of contradiction does not pertain to it. Philosophy is truly philosophy when it becomes philosophy of contradiction, when it becomes radicalized skepticism.[34] For the early Hegel, philosophy exists when one takes seriously that the contradiction between skepticism and dogmatism cannot be avoided but instead must be traversed. One thus traverses the fantasy that it can be avoided. The contradiction between dogmatism and skepticism must be traversed; traversed in such a way that the skeptical part of every philosophy leads to the point that philosophy is freed from all stable assumptions and presuppositions (about what it is, how it operates, etc.). Only in this way can a true beginning of philosophy be made. This is the beginning that Kant did not actually achieve and that the *Phenomenology of Spirit* will, then, be supposed to prepare us for.

True philosophical skepticism then means that any form of givenness must be dismissed, even that of the certainty of being able and knowing how to doubt as well as all certainty concerning its form. But "this skepticism" (the true and originally conceived skepticism) has its "positive side wholly and only in character, and in its complete indifference towards the necessity of nature."[35] Negative—radical—skepticism allows—positively—the demonstration that the skeptic liberates herself even from that which appears to be an unavoidable natural given, the given nature of a thing, of a practice, discourse, thought, or

of reason. Radicalized skepticism, and this is Hegel's point, is more dogmatically skeptic than traditional skepticism, and it thereby allows an entrance into
a metaphysics that therefore will no longer remain dogmatic. In this way, Hegel
shows a positive and productive effect of "the indifference of spirit,"[36] which
amounts to a radicalization even of Cartesian doubt. Such indifference is not
based on an identification of freedom with the capacity to choose, neither does
it end up in equivalence. Rather, such indifference frees itself from everything
which seems to be substantially attributed to the concept of freedom. The traversal of skepticism in this way makes a productive use of indifference by
freeing freedom from all substantial determinations; skepticism in this sense
is the liberation of freedom from dogmatism. But at the same time this indifference is not yet (cannot yet be) philosophy; it is only its preparation. This
indifference of spirit, this radicalized skepticism, is only "the first stage of
philosophy,"[37] that is, it is the preparation for the actual, constructive, commencement of philosophy. What has happened here to the substance (of
freedom) must also happen to the subject (of freedom).

It is crucial to keep in mind at this point that indifference has to be traversed so that it becomes possible to be conscious of "the freedom of Reason"
elevated "above this necessity of nature, in that it cognizes this necessity as
nothing, but at the same time it honors necessity supremely."[38] Hegel's punchline is twofold: radicalized skepticism doubts even the form of doubt and thus
all givenness, even all those seeming givens which arise in the process of doubting, and in this way it must ultimately abolish itself, at the point that it does
not want to introduce a supreme form of givenness (of doubting) (for example
that what is given is that there is no givenness). It is precisely in this "extreme"[39],
in this self-sublation, in this "pure negativity, which is, *per se*, a pure subjectivity",[40] that, in order to be able to begin, philosophy must "keep itself (*sich zu
halten)*"[41] and persist. What Hegel thereby aims for is a form of dogmatic skepticism that dogmatically eliminates all presuppositions, all givens. Or in his
words, what is at stake is a "subjectivity of knowledge, which direct[s] itself
against knowledge."[42]

A reversal of knowledge in knowledge against knowledge that subjectifies.
In the act of thinking the liberation of freedom not only skepticism and dogmatism but also indifference seem to be peculiarly reconciled. The problem
that plagued the modern history of rationalist philosophy, at least in the guise
of Descartes and Kant, seems to disappear again. It seems, even, to have been
sublated. But is the indifference problem really resolved in this manner? Despite
this systematic point that seems to solve the Kantian problem, Hegel continues
to speak of equivalence and indifference. Is this the return of the sublated, or,
encore, a relapse?

Empty Promises, Unphilosophy, and Superstition

In a formulation in which he defines the achievement of philosophy, Hegel articulates the following thesis: "[P]hilosophy is in fact the very discipline that aims at liberating man from an infinite crowd of finite purposes and intentions and at making him indifferent with regard to them whether such matters are the case or not."[43] As radicalized and consequently as skepticism, philosophy makes us indifferent, in a positive and good way. It brings about an independence from the things on which we otherwise (potentially) depend. Philosophy liberates us from dependencies by rendering us indifferent. But, nevertheless, "Hegel does certainly not overlook that the majority of people are rather indifferent, if not hostile to philosophy,"[44] and a peculiar problem arises. There is, similar as there was in Kant's diagnosis, an indifference articulated toward philosophy. An indifference toward the philosophical indifference which liberates from objective dependencies. This means that there is an indifference toward the liberation that philosophy is able to generate.

In a letter of 1810, one of Hegel's friends, Pierre Gabriel van Ghert, even goes so far as to diagnose that, not only in the Netherlands, but in all regions, people present a "complete indifference which does not have any clue of philosophy."[45] The indifference toward philosophy is also an indifference to (philosophical) liberation. If, for Hegel, philosophy is the discipline that thinks (and liberates) the concept of freedom and thus the reality of freedom, then the drying up of the "need of philosophy"[46] that was around the same time conjured by Hegel produces an indifference not as form of freedom, but rather as against freedom itself. Human beings can become indifferent not only towards philosophy but even towards their own freedom and liberation,[47] which latter indifference is expressed in the indifference to the former (i.e., philosophy and its claim to liberation). This indifference is thus not only peculiar but also contradictory, as it is directed against one's own freedom and therefore desires a relation of dependence. With an allusion to de La Boétie one can reformulate this as follows: Human beings desire their dependence as if it were their freedom.

So, despite the response to indifference that resulted in the dilemma between dogmatism and skepticism in Kant, a problematic form of indifference with respect to philosophy arises here, and it is a form of indifference that is no longer intra-philosophical but is extra-philosophical. It is a worldly and profane indifference toward philosophy.

Kant had assumed that the indifferentism and latitudinarianism in philosophy was representative of the philosophical expression of a free decision for evil, which, as such, even needed an intra-philosophical expression. Philosophy, which could only plead for the good, was thus internally threatened by a pseudo-philosophical enemy that ultimately proved to be an ethical enemy. Hegel, now, indicates that there can be an indifference and deadness in the general life of the people, which is, initially, in a purely external manner directed against philosophy and does not even have need—or care—any more for a philosophical expression. People become indifferent to the questions that philosophy raises and to the answers it has to offer. What Kant deemed unthinkable ("reason cannot be indifferent to the questions it raises"), occurs. Things turns out worse than previously thought. And this is an expression of one's indifference to one's own freedom.

The indifferentism that Kant described therefore returns here in a transformed, that is, unphilosophical manner.[48] Further to this, Hegel diagnoses that the reason for this indifference to philosophy (and consequentially also to freedom) derives from a (social) fatigue, because it can happen that a "deeper philosophical need" is "worn down" such that there is "indifference, and even . . . an outright contempt for philosophy as a science."[49] The need of and for philosophy disappears through exhaustion, fatigue, saturation, which opens up the ground for the indifference toward and the contempt for philosophy. But where does this fatigue come from? At one point in the *Phenomenology of Spirit* Hegel gives an answer to this question in passing, writing about "the boredom and indifference which tend to result from the continual awakening of expectations through unfulfilled promises."[50] The disappearance of the need of and for philosophy that is (silently) expressed in the general indifference toward philosophy is the result of a particular symptom of fatigue grounded in the fact that philosophy constantly and repeatedly raises expectations and makes promises but disappoints. The exhaustion of the need of philosophy is thus the result of falsely aroused expectations.

This, then, is a fatigue of philosophy, because without philosophy these disappointed expectations and promises would not have existed at all. Philosophy thus brings into the world not only expectations but also disappointment, disappointment that exists only because of it. Philosophy is disappointing and disappointments tire (us) out. The answer to the question as to why there is indifference to philosophy is, therefore, that if there is philosophy and it produces a need to fulfill the promises it itself made, then this philosophy must be blamed for the indifference with which it is confronted. Philosophy is guilty of the fact that there is indifference toward philosophy because the permanent disappointment that arises from it is tiring. At the ground of the indifference toward philosophy there is therefore a disappointment that has the structure of a peculiar kind of fraud.[51] As soon as philosophy begins to appear to people as if fraudulent, as if it were charlatanry or as mere sophistry, philosophy erases the need for it, which is the punishment that is inflicted for this crime which is otherwise unavenged. With this move, philosophy does not only incapacitate the need for it, but also, subsequently and additionally, incapacitates the need and desire for freedom and liberation. Fatiguing, philosophy wears out the desire for freedom and enforces the desire of dependency as true freedom.[52] If this is the determination of the form of the disappointment that philosophy generates, what is its content? What is at stake in the promises of philosophy whose disappointment can have such far-reaching consequences?

At another point in his development Hegel himself gives an answer to these questions, addressing not a philosophically educated but a general audience, namely, precisely that kind of audience that proves or will have proved indifferent toward philosophy. In an address on the occasion of the annual graduation at the Nuremberg Egidien-Gymnasium, Hegel talks about that "which the newer upheavals of the time [Zeitumwälzungen] have so often precipitated," namely "indifference, hopelessness and the loss of the otherwise so powerful faith that the citizen can do something for the universal Good, even of his own town."[53] In view of the dedication that the Nuremberg population had shown when earlier that year protesting against the closure of the Gymnasium, Hegel adopts a rather optimistic tone. What is remarkable here is that Hegel indicates another reason for the indifference, hopelessness, and loss of faith in one's own autonomy and freedom, and that reason is the transformation and upheavals that were determining the time. In this way, philosophy alone is not at fault; rather, philosophy *and* historical developments stand at the ground of the indifference toward both. But what is more important, if it is not only philosophy but also historical developments that produce indifference, is that it must also be true that not all philosophy, not philosophy in general, produces indifference. Rather only a specific philosophy produces indifference, and this is the specific philosophy of this specific time. Or, we might say, indifference happens first as historical development and then as philosophy. And this philosophy is the philosophy of a time that itself produces indifference and hopelessness.

Adding another twist to this argument, in 1810 Hegel wrote to Friedrich Niethammer: "Fate does presently follow the method with us to stall our expectations so long that it is indifferent if they are satisfied or not."[54] For Hegel, the times—the first years of the new century—also have the disappointing and deceptive character, in a structurally comparable sense, of the then present philosophy: The historical transformations produce expectations and promises (for example of freedom and equality) that are either fully disappointed or that remain for so long in the status of mere expectations and promises that it becomes indifferent if what had been expected and promised happens or not. One just has to recall the long-term outcomes of the French Revolution or, even worse, that no such revolution ever happened in Prussia. The time for which Hegel evidences an indifference toward philosophy and a universal hopeless deadness is that same time in which he undertakes his own philosophical project. Like Descartes and Kant before him, but somewhat differently, Hegel's philosophical thinking begins against the equivalence and indifference of his own time.

This time is a time of indifference, characterized (due to the empty promises) by the prevalence of what Hegel once called "the universal deception of [oneself, F.R.] and others."[55] But how do the universal indifference and hopelessness and the indifference to philosophy relate to one another if both are the product of a universalized appearance of fatigue with regard to the disappointed expectations and promises that both historical development and philosophy produce? Recall, perhaps, in answer to this question Hegel's infamous definition of philosophy, namely that it is *its own time apprehended in thoughts*."[56] Philosophy apprehends its own time in thought. But does this also hold for the philosophy that produces disappointment? Hegel's early criticism of Kant is instructive in this respect: It is not only that Kant, too, ultimately regressed to dogmatic metaphysics, but that, thereby, his philosophical project is an expression of aroused and subsequently disappointed expectations. With Kant what appeared was the promised way out of the badly infinite succession of dogmatic metaphysical positions—finally, philosophy could become an actual science!—but this, only at the price of being again immediately disappointed, and of falling back into the very same bad infinity.[57] One can give Kant the credit that he recognized the regressive tendency as a problem of previous attempts in metaphysics, but his own project failed against the standards he himself had set. Whereas in contrast with previous metaphysics, Kant at least failed and was able to fail, failing in a new way. But, nevertheless, the failure of Kant's project, resultant from his self-set task, became an expression of further disappointed expectations and more empty promises.

There is here a repetition or peculiar apprehension within philosophy of that which is also the determining feature of its time. As the philosophy of this time is a sort of adequate expression of its time it is precisely therefore an inadequate form of philosophy. Here, one can observe a kind of quaint reflection insofar as the *philosophy* contemporary to the beginning of the new century does not *apprehend its own time* in thought but apprehends *in empty promises and disappointing expectations*. It is precisely this misapprehension that provides an adequate expression of the indifference of the time itself, and which nonetheless can only reinforce and amplify it. Thus the expression of philosophy that produces indifference within an already indifferent age produces a peculiar redoubling of indifference—a base and a superstructure indifference, to use Marxian parlance—which makes the latter ever more problematic and fundamental. A relapse out of indifference into greater indifference—if indifference can know degrees—pervades the different spheres of spirit.

We are now able to give an answer to the question regarding the contents of the expectations and promises that philosophy arouses and disappoints: They are expectations and promises that philosophy is truly and actually philosophy and that it is, its own time, apprehended in thought in such a way that it has something to say about the transformations of its time. The badly infinite structure of the battlefield that is philosophy constantly disappoints this very promise, and, worse, now it becomes irrelevant whoever wins. The battle has become boring. Philosophy has then either nothing to say about its time (and is not then apprehension proper of its time in thought), or it has only always the same thing to say about its time (which means it has ultimately nothing to say about its (specific) time). It then never stops speaking about it; it speaks about it in such a way that it has nothing to say about it; the time does not at all affect—nor thereby condition—its form of thought.[58] Philosophy never stops talking, but its speech is empty and becomes (empty) chatter,[59] and, as the early Hegel already notes, "the frightful [entsetzliche] chatter" to which philosophy has regressed is "endlessly prolonged in this key and inwardly vacuous, has become so wearisome [langweilig] that it is now utterly devoid of interest."[60] To do philosophy in such a way that it is empty promises apprehended in thought cannot but generate indifference. This is why

> the degradation into which philosophy has thus sunk appears doubtless at a first glance to be only an affair of supreme indifference, an occurrence confined to the trivial field of academic futilities; but such a view necessarily makes itself at home in ethics, an essential part of philosophy; and it is then that the true meaning of these views makes its first appearance in and is apprehended by the world of actuality.[61]

Against this background, since it happens when the view of the indifference of philosophy has already become an essential part of actuality and reality, we can understand how Hegel is able to offer a post-factum analysis of how the conversion of philosophy to chatter has taken place. This conversion happens in "[a]n age which has so many philosophical systems lying behind it in its past" that it "must apparently arrive at the same indifference which life acquires after it has tried all its forms."[62] The lifeline of philosophy, after all its previous attempts, after all the badly infinite played through articulations of all possible dogmatic forms, comes to be exhausted and saturated.[63] Hegel therefore determines the time of deadness and indifference to philosophy in such a way that there is not only fatigue because of the repeatedly disappointed expectations brought about by historical transformations and in face of the empty promises of philosophy, but also that philosophy itself is essentially saturated, exhausted, a clear symptom of which is that even philosophers are or have become indifferent to philosophy. Philosophy becomes the very boring academic chatter it always seemed to be.

This extra- and intra-philosophical indifference originates from the fact (as we have seen for Kant, and then for Hegel in such a way that Kant is culpable of precisely that which he sets out to dispel) that the many badly infinite variations of philosophical thought have saturated all its forms, whereby philosophy itself becomes exactly as saturated as it previously appeared to be. Faced with the dogmatics, skeptics, indifferentists, syncretists, and the many other academic "philosophers" that all give different answers to the particular questions of the age and to the general questions of reason without ever giving real answers, not even the "philosopher" believes in (the existence, relevance, and actuality of) philosophy any longer.[64] In this way an arbitrariness concerning that in relation to which human beings for Hegel cannot reasonably react arbitrarily is put into practice, one which is not concerned with a preexisting canon of questions of reason, but more fundamentally is concerned with one's own freedom. Here appears what seems to be a will to be unfree. And as Hegel once put it in a letter to Altenstein, this tendency yields the following result: "The caprice of the understanding and the arbitrariness takes priority, this immediately leads either to simply indifference to philosophy or to a fall into subtleties [Vernünftelei]."[65] The exhaustion and saturation of philosophy generates indifference to it and thus generates precisely the arbitrary attitude to believe in and claim whatever seems most opportune.

Everyone within such a generalized state of indifference looks for the individual "philosophy"—a *contradiction in adjecto*—that suits him or her the best simply because no one cares any longer for philosophy as (universalist) philosophy. Arbitrariness, expressed in and because of the bad infinite constitution of all previous philosophy, is thereby redoubled. Arbitrarily and indifferently one chooses an arbitrary and indifferent "philosophy" because one gives priority not just to the caprice of the understanding but even more to the diverse interpretation of what may, opportunistically, be meant by understanding. If philosophy appears in this way to the public, as just another arbitrary opinion in the realm of opinions, as an empty promise made and never kept, and if this generates indifference to philosophy, then there is the recursive effect that ultimately makes philosophy into what it seemed to be, namely that it is just an arbitrary opinion. Philosophy is thereby replaced by what Hegel calls *unphilosophy*.[66] Unphilosophy takes the form of philosophy but subtracts from it its content, its—dangerous—substance. It is a philosophy without philosophy, mere chatter.

Thereby for Hegel unphilosophy is never entirely or really distinguishable from arbitrary belief[67] and thus has a direct link to superstition. For superstition gets rid of the form of philosophy but seeks to arbitrarily retain its substance. Superstition is the dogmatism of everyday life. Superstition is also the flip side of unphilosophy. This is why times of indifference, which are times of indifference to philosophy, are also times of superstition:

> For this is precisely where superstition has its ground: in the fact that human beings are not indifferent to external things—and they are not indifferent when they have no inward freedom, when they do not have true independence of spirit. All that is indifferent is fixed, while all that is not indifferent, all that belongs to right and morality, is jettisoned and given over to caprice.[68]

If there is indifference to philosophy, there is dependence on external indifferent things that thereby become essential for me. But because I cannot be indifferent to those things anymore—for not only would such an indifference be the proper merit of philosophy, but within an immediate relation to the world these things are immediately the only thing that matter—I cannot avoid offering interested interpretations of these things and of their connectedness. However, because these interpretations are born from relations of dependence, the external things become the ultimate determining factor of their own interpretation. They become the actors. Human beings that are indifferent to philosophy do not believe anymore in philosophical interpretations of things, *but they believe nonetheless*[69]—for example, they believe that things are ultimately and forever like this or that; they believe that they do not believe anymore in the questions and answers of philosophy, but in this way they believe not to believe, and thus they repeat precisely what they wanted to withdraw from. It is pertinent at this point to recall Hegel's words: "[T]he indifference of things to one another . . . is not their true relation but a semblance."[70] Which means that the indifference to philosophy (and even the indifference of philosophers to philosophy) is also not a true relation, and rather is ultimately only a semblance: a semblance of indifference and disbelief. Why? because there is an inversion of indifference on one side and on the other there is a misunderstood and unconscious belief, superstition, which in German is *Aber-glaube*—literally a *but*-[or nevertheless]-*belief*. Superstition solidifies and petrifies not only itself but also the dependence from those things which result from the inversion of indifference. It is as if thinking: "I do only care about things I should be indifferent about and am indifferent about the things that do allow me to care or be indifferent in the first place, namely freedom."

By the production of the semblance of indifference and the unknowingly yet arbitrarily chosen superstitious dependence, the indifference produced by unphilosophy goes precisely in this sense hand in hand with an increase of the dependence on the indifferent external things, which is why these things do not appear (or seem to be) indifferent any longer. In this way, an attitude is produced that is indifferent to that to which one cannot be indifferent to: to freedom, thought, philosophy. And in this way, and against one's very own will and belief, one slides into unphilosophy, which is then no longer simply a negation of philosophy but which constitutes itself positively in the absence of philosophy. When there is no philosophy, there is either unphilosophy (the form of philosophy without content, empty chatter) or superstition (empty content without rational form), and unphilosophy and superstition are what (does not) fill(s) the gap left open by the lack of philosophy that is symptomatically indicated by indifference (that is produced by philosophy and its time). In indifference to philosophy, superstition and its flip side, the empty unphilosophical chatter, are established to offer a kind of *Ersatzbefriedigung*, a surrogate satisfaction. They represent a reduced, wasted, version of philosophy from and for the unfree everyday life. This is the inversion specific to times of indifference. That which is essential becomes indifferent and that which is indifferent becomes essential.

What this means is that something appears to be essential, even though it is essentially indifferent. For example, "what and how much I possess" is no longer "a matter of indifference"[71] but becomes of the highest significance to me. It should not matter to me as the true end is a life to be led within a collective organization of free and equals and aimed at a collective good, but through the state of indifference my focus shifts. In and through indifference the indifferent life becomes essential for me, even more essential than the fundamental questions pertaining to a rational and ethical collective life. It is easy to see here how Hegel not only assumes that this leads to a degradation of philosophy into unphilosophy and its flip side, superstition, but also to a peculiar decay of universal (and individual) life. This is because one's religious and rational convictions are equally dependent on external things in a twofold sense due to their being determined through arbitrariness: Dependent on and clinging to external things, one thereby has an external relation to one's freedom, which one then, therefore, sees determined by external things, by how much and what I possess. Freedom thus depends entirely on the constitution, consistency, and concatenation of external things. Imagine now that in times of indifference, of unphilosophy, and superstition a philosopher comes along, who desires and proclaims to do actual, to do real, philosophy! For Hegel it is clear who this philosopher is. He is Hegel: "Common sense cannot understand speculation; and what is more, it must come to hate speculation when it has experience of it; and, unless it is in a state of perfect indifference that security confers, it is bound to detest and persecute it."[72] There is either perfect indifference to philosophy and speculative thought brought about by unphilosophy and that offers the security of unfreedom, as in superstition, or there is disgust and abhorrence for actual philosophy that cannot be reconciled with one's indifference and that thereby cannot be pacifistically unified with common sense and its superstitious constitution.[73]

If it indeed has the ability to disturb the security of indifference—a formula wherein one should hear resonate the old Platonic definition of philosophy as corruption of the youth—true philosophy will be despised and persecuted because actual philosophy reminds, remembers, recalls, and marks the contradiction as truth of indifference and whoever is indifferent as desirous of their domination as if it were their salvation. For Hegel, philosophy that is actual philosophy not only has the structure of a battlefield, but it is also at the same time despised and persecuted from outside. Philosophy cannot but produce contradiction (as the early Hegel demonstrated with regard to the very concept of truth) because this is where truth lies, and is what any true philosophy has as its object. This is even more the case because as actual philosophy, it is philosophy against indifference, even against the indifference toward philosophy, and therefore it is a philosophy of multiple truths of multiple contradictions. Philosophy that recalls and insists upon the contradiction inherent in the indifferent attitude to philosophy can therefore produce only contradiction. This is—encore—the beginning of philosophy.

The battlefield of philosophy is therefore not only philosophy itself, but also the actuality, Wirklichkeit, that seeks to remain indifferent toward it as it is. The consequences of Hegel's analysis of indifference toward philosophy are directed against the structure of the universal and universalized deception of oneself and of the other, but—and this is conceptually unavoidable—this enlightenment is not simply one-way. At one point in the Phenomenology Hegel even asserts that the contradiction of the disgust and security of unfreedom can lead only to a problematic reaction toward the intervention of philosophy, thus leading in a direction other than the beginning of true philosophy. Philosophy's intervention against the indifference toward philosophy can also make things worse: Not only can there be a retrieval of what has been inscribed into the chain of unphilosophical and superstitious substitutions; there can also be a problematic reaction to the intervention of philosophy. Such an intervention can produce an even greater relapse, "a flight back"[74] "into the wilderness of the nearly animal consciousness, which is also called Nature or innocence."[75] There is a reaction of flight toward the philosophical disturbance of indifference. This flight is a flight back to nature, which is just as (indifferent as) it is. The price for undertaking this flight is to return to the wilderness and proximity of animality, for the animal is precisely that which cannot change or conceptually grasp its own nature. Indifference, which produces the age and unphilosophy, leads to a regression toward the animal consciousness. Thus, in Hegel, there is also a peculiar regression of the human being to the animal which is brought about through indifference and equivalence. This regression needs to be understood.

The Indifferent State of Nature: On the Objective Regression of Time into Space and of World to Environment

The indifference to philosophy that arises out of both philosophy and historical transformations, and which was generated in large part, as demonstrated, by the history of philosophy itself, can produce a peculiar relapse of human practice into (proto-)animal(istic) behavior. But this is a regression, a relapse, that is *produced*. Or, for Hegel, ages of indifference see a relapse into an artificially (or historically) produced state of nature, which is a regression to a state of illusory innocence as if "before" the historical and philosophical Fall of man that brought about all the disappointment. The concern with fall from within history out of history is what instructs any critique of the premodern within the history of rationalism. This means that indifference thus leads to and cannot but imply an imminent de-historicization. It leads to an omission of history and of historical consciousness.[76] But in this way it becomes clear that this indifferent state of nature is ultimately not a state of nature, but it is a state that is generated by history and the predominance of unphilosophy, in short: There is a state of nature if there is no actual practice of thought (like philosophy, or art, or religion for that matter) and if the material historical conditions present us with a strange stuckness themselves. Everything moves; nothing ever changes. The indifferent state of nature and its assumed innocence is a product of history that itself now comes with the promise to be able to cast aside the contradiction whose premonition philosophy gives.

The desire of indifference that seeks to avoid its own contradiction drives the indifferent into an artificial state of nature in which the end of history has always already taken place, in which everything hinges on purely external relation to externalities,[77] and all essential difference has disappeared. Yet, since a purely external relation to externalities is also one way of defining what ultimately is an object,[78] so the relapse and regression is thus not only a regression from culture or spirit into nature but also one from subject to object. And this *artificial* natural space in which these objects are located, because it is an artificial *natural* space, is without history and thus without time proper. Indifferentiation is thus artificial naturalization, produced regression. "The externality in which the concept is pre-eminently to be found in nature brings with it the total indifference of difference,"[79] so that the only differences that can exist are ultimately not of qualitative but of quantitative nature: There might be stronger, heavier, denser, etc. objects, but no objects that are essentially and qualitatively different.

This state of nature implies an indifferent and objective leveling down, whose ultimate determining ground is quantity, which is precisely why the question of how much and what I possess becomes more important than most things or perhaps even than anything else. For distinctions as distinctions, namely, as qualitative, can no longer exist if it is held that that which exists is the sole thing which is and can be. Just as in nature, for Hegel, what is lost in and for such a state is actual time, and therefore also history and the consciousness of time and history. There is a dumb squandering of the objectively indifferent, of the always the same. One can see here why the element of nature is space (and not time).[80] Yet this is a particular kind of space, a space in which there is "a coexistence of indifferent points without relation,"[81] a space in which time and history have collapsed into the flatness of spatial de- or in-differentiation. For space has "the form of *indifferent juxtaposition* [*Nebeneinander*] and *quiescent subsistence*, the temporal, by contrast presents itself as the form of *unrest* [*Unruhe*], of the *internally negative*, of the *successiveness*, of *arising* and *vanishing*."[82] There is rest and subsistence, rather than succession and unrest, an indifferent juxtaposition that potentially extends infinitely and which generates a peculiar security. Notably, this security is the security that there cannot and will not be a qualitative difference and therefore that there will never be any succession, no change.[83] This is the security of indifference and hence of unfreedom. One lives in an a-temporal space where historicity is elided. Security here implies the lack of temporality.

For there is no emergence in indifference and deadness, no becoming and disappearing, there is only a generalized disappearance of time that leads to an indifferent parallelism, which one may read as being comparable to the status of atoms in Democritus before the swerve. An atomism before the clinamen.[84] There is an absorption of time that results from indifference as well as a reduction to the one and only dimension of space, of spatiality (hence—social—atomism). Indifference in and toward philosophy thus generates further indifference, to time, history, becoming and vanishing. Indifference seems infective, an infective regress, a regressive infection, creating a world interior of a peculiar kind of naturality. It might not be surprising that this is the interior which some have identified as the very form in which capital organizes space.[85] The seemingly—"seemingly" because indifference is a semblance—unchanged and unchangeable nature of historical transformations and of philosophy that find their expression in indifference produce at the same time a universal spatialization and de-temporalization. Indifference produces a spatial turn that is a productive relapse into artificial nature, since "nature . . . is morally indifferent,"[86] and the space of indifference and of those who are indifferent is thus no longer a space of freedom and can only be a space of (external) dependency. Indeed, Hegel noted in his ninth habilitation thesis: "Status naturae non est iniustus et eam ob causam ex illo exeundum" (The state of nature is not unjust and therefore one has to exit it). One cannot know the distinction between just and unjust in the state of nature, and it is precisely therefore, due to the concept of freedom (and of free beings), that is necessary to leave it. A distinction must be made, a cut introduced, for freedom, quite precisely, does not consist in the indifference toward these concepts or their abandonment, but in establishing a relation to them, in generating their determination.

Hobbes had already emphasized that the state of nature is a state before the existence of right, and hence concepts of right and normative principles cannot be valid in it. Hegel, however, in contrast to Hobbes, does not think that our natural constitution and selfish will to defend our life (effectively functioning as the sole norm orienting us) forces us to accept the rational insight that we must leave the state of nature. This would mean that there is a path that leads from nature to right because it is innately (logically) suitable.[87] On the contrary, Hegel's argument is that the state of nature as such is indifferent: There is nothing unjust about, no injustice, and thereby no freedom, in nature. When there is at least injustice out of which one can conceive of what just(ice) is, there can be freedom. There is no freedom without the freedom to be evil and unjust. However, the representation of the state of nature is not a representation *of* any actual state of nature but rather a representation always already conceived from the perspective of culture (for example, as Hobbes is often read, as justification of the present state of things). In this way the state of nature is a cultural representation of a peculiar paradisical (or hellish) state before the fall into culture (and before the introduction of the distinction between good and evil); it is the representation of a phantasmatic, pre-free, pre-conceptual primordial state of innocence. Yet this thought is not particularly innocent. According to Hegel's argument, one must leave the state of nature because one has always already left it in a certain way. Freud will later show that such a phantasmatic primordial state constantly repeats and reinforces the assumption of the (sexual) innocence of children from which it is necessary to free ourselves.

The age of indifference that Hegel describes establishes a similarly phantasmatic state of nature and suspends freedom. It thus also suspends the distinction between justice and injustice and is in this sense no longer an age-in-time (*Zeit-Alter*). It constitutes a world in which there is not and cannot be freedom, a world that has abandoned the normative criteria for distinguishing between justice and injustice. And such a world is, strictly speaking, no longer a world. It is, rather, a world that has regressed to an environment. Since only human beings live in a world, those who live in this non-world-environment, a context which is poor of world, bear a strange resemblance to animals (for only animals live in an environment).[88] And, as Hegel will polemically argue in the preface to the *Phenomenology of Spirit*, there are clearly ways in which human beings can act that lead to a "trampl[ing] underfoot of the roots of humanity," when someone refers to what she feels as norm as what is supposed to be true. This is so because if he refers to the "oracle within his breast," man "is finished and done with anyone who does not agree," and implies that "the anti-human, the merely animal, consists in staying within the sphere of feeling, and being able to communicate only at that level."[89] Thus, the suspension of the domain of the concept and a productive regression to an animal that speaks in the language of feelings, which might be the paradigm of a truly private language, the peculiar language spoken in the artificial state of indifferent nature.

In this peculiar state of nature, what prevails is precisely that which prevails in the nature of the environment reduced to mere spatiality, the environment without history: a mere conformity to mechanical laws. For "with the term mechanism Hegel conceptualizes the togetherness of individuals who behave indifferently to one another,"[90] which means that regression is not only from free to unfree being; Hegel posits not only a regression of subjects dependent on things but also a regression that transforms subjects into specific kinds of objects. The shift from history into wilderness and nature, from the world to environment, indicates a peculiar relapse of subjects not only into dependence on objects and objective conditions but also into the state of bodily objects. Free beings become bodies, become indifferent bodies in an indifferent juxtaposition of bodies. Such subjects lose precisely what makes them subjects—their singularity through freedom. When they turn away from freedom and become indifferent toward it, they become the objects that in turn become the purely external things on which they in turn become dependent. Indifference in this specific sense objectifies. Indeed, one might venture to say that it alienates (in a very particular way). And with this objectification there comes a dependency on and from external things, simply because the objectified subject becomes one such thing.

"Thus," writes Hegel, "there arises the contradiction of a perfect *indifference* of objects to one another and of an *identity of determinateness* of such objects."[91] They are all indifferent, each one to another, but they became all the same, and without any individualizing criterion any longer they therefore (conceptually, that is) start "repelling each other in the unity. This is the *mechanical process*."[92] With the relapse into indifference, subjects become indifferent objects, yet a contradiction arises because they are as individuals only determined by the concatenation with others in which they do not however count as individuals but only as indifferently the same. The mechanical process that governs this artificial state of nature places the particular objects into a general concatenation, but at the same time it implies only a formal and general concept of particularity—namely, a formal equality and thus substantial indifference. For Hegel, objectively, within the state of indifference, there is not only a step from temporality to spatiality, from the world to the environment, from the disappointment originating in history to the omnipresence of nature, from freedom to external arbitrariness, but there is also the insight that what is at stake is a peculiar process of objectification, reification, and mechanization. Human subjects are turned—and turn themselves through their resistance to any disturbance of their indifference—into paradoxical (because at the same time artificial and natural) objects that are located in a timelessly stable and indifferent space of a mechanically governed environment. We end up in an object-oriented ontology, the ultimate indifferent style, in which everything is just an object among objects.[93] This is a formal and objective determination of this regressive status which results from indifference. It remains, therefore, to ask: What does this amount to from the perspective of the indifferent subject?

Subjective State of Nature: Tarrying and Indecision

In a passage of the *Phenomenology of Spirit*, which was precisely the philosophical work that was supposed to introduce Hegel's system and thus move away from indifference into actual philosophy, Hegel writes the following:

> The frivolity and boredom which unsettle the established order, the vague foreboding of something unknown, these are the heralds of approaching change. The gradual crumbling that left unaltered the face of the whole is cut short by a sunburst which, in one flash, illuminates the features of the new world.[94]

If frivolity (*Leichtsinn*) and boredom occur, this is a sign of change. Even the boredom which is brought about by philosophy is thus greeted by Hegel with a surprising optimism. A flash, a flash-like transformation must and will occur, which will illuminate something hitherto unseen. In another text, Hegel states: "Philosophy enters the scene at a time where the spirit of a people has worked itself out of the indifferent apathy."[95] There is indifference to philosophy, but it is precisely this indifference that is a potential sign or symptom for a true beginning of philosophy; Hegel can be seen to repeat Kant's claim about indifferentism as mother of chaos and the night, albeit in a modified manner. And in a similarly optimistic manner he explains "reason cannot stand still at such indifference,"[96] and we are forced by the rationality of reason to sublate the contradiction in which it subsists. In the face of Hegel's apparent optimism in these passages it is nevertheless important at this point to sketch out the fundamental effects and defects of the constitution of subjectivity in times of indifference, since in this state "[t]he individual appears completely vegetative because any particular relation is a matter of complete indifference."[97] This state is the state in which subjects are like objects. But what kind of will is decisive and determinative in the time of indifference if there simply cannot be a freely determined or freely determining will? It is in fact possible to read Hegel's definition of the will at an early (conceptual) stage in such a way that it offers an answer to this question. In serving as an answer to this question his overall formulation will become clearer. In his *Philosophy of Right*, Hegel writes the following of this will:

> A will which resolves on nothing is no actual will; a characterless human being never reaches a decision. The reason for indecision may also lie in a tenderness of feeling which knows that, in willing something determinate, it is engaging with finitude, imposing a restriction on itself and sacrificing the infinite; yet it will not renounce the totality after which it hankers. However "beautiful" such a disposition may be, it is nevertheless dead. As Goethe says: "Whoever wills something great must be able to restrict himself." Only by resolving can a human being step into actuality . . . possibility is not yet actuality.[98]

The environmental space without history is inhabited by wills that do not decide anything and are thus not actual wills. There is a permanent hesitation and tarrying, and in this way the inertia of matter, filling the space, encroaches upon what is there otherwise, which is the nature and constitution of the will. The will becomes inert; it tarries and becomes indecisive. The artificial state of nature of indifference produces a "subjectivity that cloisters itself away,"[99] a subjectivity which is the counterpart to the pure externality of the circumstances, since in it exists merely an empty, beautifully meant (and therefore beautiful-soul-like) interiority, which at one and the same time amounts to nothing. It is a mode of the mortification of freedom. The indifference and equivalence of all possible options for action hinder the realization and reality of freedom. This leads also to an internal reification of freedom, a freedom which then consists only in the "indeterminacy of inner indecision."[100]

Against this attitude, Hegel states with regard to the great *historical* individuals that they do not choose but "*are* through and through inherently what they will and accomplish." They are what they will, and they are their deed, from which their life is indistinguishable. But the dead disposition and indecision consists in "the weakness in acting . . . , in the separation of the subject as such and its content."[101] The subject of (the state of) indifference, because it already became an object, no longer acts in any proper or full sense of the term, rather, it is separated from its content because it assumes it already possesses this indifference in and of itself, without (externally) realizing its content in any way. There is here a "paralyzing indecision,"[102] a paralysis of action which goes hand in hand with the paralysis of time and history in the proper sense of these terms. Such paralyzed subjects are no longer truly living subjects of freedom, are no longer living incorporations of freedom, but, even though they might seem even the livelier in their own perception, are rather mortified subjects. Indifference generates a relapse into (artificial) nature, and it thereby transforms freedom into something natural, so that, becoming unlimited, it neither limits nor restrains itself, ignoring all commitment and becoming an indeterminate freedom of choice. Indifference thereby generates what Badiou once called a "disaster of unlimitedness."[103] Freedom becomes a natural capacity that wants to be freedom as such, but freedom does not come from a will that decides nothing. This infinity of the non-deciding free will is the correlate of the reified externality characteristic of the artificial state of nature. For "freedom cannot be thought as nature but rather it must be thought within the normativity of the 'concept'"[104]—that is: through determinate decisions.

The (too-) natural state of freedom is freedom as not-deciding, not-resolving indeterminate inner and thus fully externalized freedom of choice: a mortification of freedom that is taken to be (the) life (of freedom); a freedom that is supposed to lie beyond its realization and that therefore is never realized. In this way "numerous clashes have arisen . . . , and the opposition between good and evil has become so weak that in individual instances they appear to turn into one another."[105] The indecisive will collides with itself since it wants everything and anything simultaneously—it wants all possible objects or the possibility of freedom by way of objects—it wants the possibility of freedom by way of the body. This occurs because this will no longer self-determines the form in which it is determined, but rather results from the dependency of objects. Thus each normative determination of good and evil is weakened and vacillates and turns against the individual will that assumes it is infinitely many possibilities of a good and beautiful will but which is ultimately neither, because "[i]n this formal sense of possibility, everything is possible . . . ; the realm of possibility is therefore limitless manifoldness."[106] Hegel's point here is: Freedom in the state of infinite possibility is not freedom. Freedom without restraint, without decision and resolve (*Be-und Entschluss*), without end (*Schluss*) in both senses of the term, is always already lost freedom, and thus it is ultimately another name for unfreedom. There is no possibility of freedom, however limitless and manifold it may seem, without an end of (this) freedom. There is no possibility of freedom without the actualization of freedom, which is to say, the constitution of the possibility of freedom is only brought about through its actualization. Indifference reverses this irrevocable insight. To think freedom in natural and naturalist terms means to conceive of it in terms of freedom of choice; freedom of choice means to conceive of freedom naturalistically. Freedom as given natural possibility is freedom as contradiction. Hegel exposes the truth of this very contradiction.

Modern Indifference: To Will Oneself as Nothing

At this point let us raise a question: Is Hegel's description an account of a transcendental and transhistorical problem of the constitution of spirit or the will, or does (can) the indifference Hegel refers to have a historical index? It is entirely possible to read Hegel such that both are the case. Beyond the structure discussed above in which there is indeterminateness and indecisiveness contained in the will, which is identified with the nature of freedom, there is also a problematic way of dealing with this contradiction, which, in Hegel's conception, is constitutive of modernity. For any will that wills to maintain itself as free from any concrete determinacy is already the result of a determination of the will. In a contradictory way, the determination of freedom as mere possibility already becomes the determination of a realization of freedom inasmuch as realized freedom is construed as the possibility of freedom. Such an understanding produces for Hegel even greater contradictory results. By insisting on the freedom of choice without deciding anything, the free will hypostatizes indeterminacy against all concrete determinations that it perceives as limitations. In this way the will wants to have its cake and eat it too. For, here, freedom is understood only as freedom from determination and identified with indeterminacy, it is identified with the possibility of determinacy without understanding this as a particular determinacy. If one determines freedom as indeterminate (and naturally given freedom of choice), then freedom is not indeterminate but is *determined* as indeterminate. Freedom is *determined* to be indeterminate, yet this determination of freedom claims to be a universal determination of freedom qua freedom at the same time.

By way of this determination, the will that construes striving toward indifferent naturality as its own universal entitlement, indeed as inseparable from its own will, attains a position that is merely particular. This will that holds itself as free is led to the point that, against its will, the identification of freedom with indeterminacy only becomes a particular determination of freedom and is therefore not actual freedom. But precisely because the will that in this state (which is the state of the regression of history to space and of the world to environment) seeks to flee all actual liberating determinations of freedom, it acquires not the form of universality but of mere particularity. Whereas indeterminacy is not a universal concept but rather only the abstract negation of all concrete determination, and is thereby nothing more than a particular side of the distinction between determinacy and indeterminacy, as soon as a concept results solely from the abstract negation of an equally abstract opposite, it is merely a particular concept. In this way one does not attain a universal determination of freedom. In other words: Indifference and its corresponding will that decide nothing, believe that they know what freedom is, yet flee from freedom into unfreedom. In this way, the determination of freedom as indeterminacy—as freedom of choice—reverts against the will of the will and determines the will precisely in the act of fleeing from determination back into indeterminate (not so) innocent nature. The unwilled determination of the will becomes a heteronomous determination of the will; namely, it becomes fabricated, produced, and in this sense becomes second nature. It is heteronomous because it is not posited. As soon as one keeps away from concrete determinations and determinacy, thereby becoming indecisive, non-deciding, and cloistering oneself away, one does violence to oneself, as well as to one's own freedom. The paradigm of this structure is—perhaps paradoxically—what constitutes modernity proper, namely the French Revolution, whose result—as is well known—is the establishment of bourgeois, that is capitalist, society.[107]

Indifference toward one's own freedom is a sign and symptom of a violence of unfreedom that is scarcely visible as such.[108] For I am determined against my will but also determined by a free decision that is imperceptible. In this way I reduce my own claim to freedom to a merely particular claim and the mediation of universality and particularity happens behind my back. A will that abstracts from all concrete determinations and considers itself to be lively and free in indeterminacy is in this way a dead and unfree will. In fact this will is the most unfree when its favorite word is freedom.[109] The mortification of freedom happens if and in such a way that an acting will seeks to abstract from determination and is thus against its will determined heteronomously but is nonetheless the culprit of bringing this heteronomy over itself. This is why it is determined by external things, whose dependency it desires. It acts as if it were free, but this is superstition and arbitrarily posited belief, the superstition of freedom or a myth of freedom. This myth is that of the simple and natural givenness of freedom which leads to the fact that I do not will my own freedom as realized and as real but only as a possible one that appears to me to be already real (and I thereby conflate possibility and actuality). In the indifferent state of nature my free actions are no longer free actions; they are pseudo-actions, thus in proximity to animal consciousness; they are not actions but are rather behavior. Indifference thus always proclaims "that beasts may have the world in empire"[110]—that human beings are those animals who are free by nature since they are the masters of their environment. If there is a peculiar regress to an artificial state of nature that concerns the identification (i.e., determination) of freedom with an indeterminate possibility (of determination)—without determination—we may discern a regress from the human to an artificial animal. In different ways, the Hegelian aftermath will seek to verify this claim.

Conclusion

Toward Another Type of Indifference

Nobody will deny that if the apostles of political indifferentism were to express themselves with such clarity, they would have been sent to the devil a long time ago.

—KARL MARX, "POLITICAL INDIFFERENTISM"

To be politically indifferent means to be politically complacent. A well-fed man is "unconcerned with," "indifferent to," a crust of bread; a hungry man, however, will always take a "partisan" stand on the question of a crust of bread. A person's "equivalence and indifference" with regard to a crust of bread does not mean that he does not need bread, but that . . . he has firmly attached himself to the "party of the well-fed."

—V. I. LENIN, "THE SOCIALIST PARTY AND NON-PARTY REVOLUTIONISM"

At the beginning of modern philosophy, Descartes registered and addressed a peculiar problem. This problem, taking the name of indifference, consists in free beings being able to misunderstand what freedom is. Such a misunderstanding arises from the identification of freedom with a capacity to choose arbitrarily. The identification, here, is problematic because it ascribes to freedom an *actuality prior to its actualization*, and freedom that is not actualized is—of course—not actual freedom. That human beings can misunderstand freedom means that they can also misunderstand themselves, accomplishing the latter misunderstanding in and through the former. If they understand freedom falsely, then they falsely understand what makes free beings into free beings. And this is a misunderstanding that has theoretical and practical consequences since it results in the fact that human beings do not (actually) act

like free beings, but rather act as if they were free even though they don't actualize their freedom. Thus for Descartes they remain at the lowest degree of
freedom. The founding act of modern philosophy with Descartes is thus not
only connected to the insight that freedom—at least gradually—depends on
its actualization, but also that there can be understandings and practical forms
of freedom that lead to problematic reductions of freedom. Such reductions
are problematic because this constellation is not recognized as such at first
sight—or even at second sight. Rather such reductions do seem to spring from
merely individual misunderstandings or misconceptions of freedom—even as,
and at the same time, these misunderstandings can become (socially) predominant, and even gain the status of natural evidences.

Kant took up and modified Descartes's diagnosis. The indifference problem
for him is accompanied by a peculiar and implicit consequence. This can be
articulated as follows: As soon as there is a problematic understanding of freedom, a peculiar regression from truly human action to animal behavior takes
place; with this problematic understanding of the actuality of my freedom I act
as if I were an animal when I act as if I were free, and thereby demonstrate that
I have a problematic understanding of the actuality of my freedom. According to
Kant's diagnosis, such consequences occur when I assume that there can be an
understanding of freedom that would not be rigoristic, that would not be dualist
in general, namely, when I assume that my actions could be neither good nor
evil or if I presume that they could be both at the same time. Indifferentism in
its different forms contends with this position. Indifferentism asserts that actions
from freedom—more precisely: the maxims of actions that are realized in and
through the actions—do not always and not always necessarily have to be good
or evil at all. Orienting itself not only against an adequate understanding of freedom but at the same time also against reason itself, this position effectively puts
into question the—for Kant just commenced—philosophical science that investigates the constitution of reason. Why? Because reason, for this very philosophy,
cannot be indifferent.

How does indifference then arise? For Kant, indifference does not merely
make manifest an epistemological error. An indifferent understanding of
freedom is not generated only by myself and my individual understanding of
freedom. Rather, Kantianism registers, as the discussion on Carl Christian
Erhard Schmid made clear, that there are ideologies of freedom, or, there are
(philosophical-)theoretical positions that approve indifference and give rise to a
problematic propaganda of indifference, through the promotion of misunderstandings of freedom oriented and directed against reason and the reasonable
itself. For Schmid and for Kant, which is to say for the standpoint of rationalist
rigorism, these philosophical positions are a representative symptom, a repre-

sentation of a fundamentally false understanding of freedom on whose basis lie ethically problematic (viz., evil) maxims. They are expressions of an evil maxim because they are directed out of freedom against freedom. Such misrepresentations of freedom are *ideologies* of freedom in the strong sense of the term, because they obscure their inherent falseness in the act of their constitution and their evil nature does not appear as such. Since they don't appear to be particular decisions against freedom and reason, and since they represent themselves as rational options for understanding freedom (viz., as understandings that are allegedly based on the neutral assertion that freedom can have an indifferent and neutral determination), these ideologies are able to develop a peculiar evidential force. Since no ideology announces itself to be a mere ideology, it is this force that initially makes the ideology of freedom into an ideology. The self-obscuring of the decision against freedom which rests at the basis of such an ideology of freedom is what, primarily, then, enables its privative effect.

With regard to its critique of and resistance against indifference and its pseudo-philosophical representatives, Kantian philosophy demonstrated that philosophy must assume the character of an ideology critique in such a way that philosophical rationalism assumes a stance in fundamental opposition to the ideology of freedom, and that this already applies to Descartes. But such a critical and diagnostic opposition to (an) ideology (of freedom) now can be seen to repeat within philosophy. This repetition turns philosophy into a battlefield.[1] However, the Kantian and Schmidian position remained limited—because freedom is an area not of a must but rather of a rational ought—insofar as it can only lead its battle against the ideologies of freedom by claiming that human beings *ought* not to understand themselves as animals. Whether this ought has any practical power at all depends on individual decision, on decisions by individuals, decisions from freedom for or against freedom. Such decisions are not and cannot be influenced by rationalist philosophy. If indifference for Descartes is a question of the epistemology of freedom, even though it produces practical consequences, then for Kant and Schmid it is a moral question. Even though they articulate insights and point to the socio-economico-political dimension of the indifference-problem they are facing, a problem that directly concerns the very existence of philosophy, these accounts remain conceptually still individualistic.

Hegel expanded and recontextualized this discussion. He demonstrated that indifference is not merely external to philosophy (something like the individual free decision against freedom that subsequently finds a representation within philosophy) but that, rather, one must distinguish different types of indifference that are produced from philosophy itself, which relate clearly to the (ideological) atmosphere of the age. On the one hand there is an indifference which is, following the Cartesian model of doubt, liberatory, but on the other hand, there is an indifference that orients itself in philosophy against the very practice of philosophy. The second type of indifference is the indifference toward indifference as liberation that philosophy can produce. This type of ontic indifference is grounded on a conception of freedom which assumes that one possesses freedom as a capacity. But this indifference not only orients itself against an adequate understanding of freedom (that freedom consists in its actualization and not in being assumed as a given), it is also ultimately directed against the liberation from this conception that philosophy for Hegel can generate. It is an indifference toward one's own liberation and from the domination of unactual freedom. For Hegel, then, there exists an understanding of freedom—ontic indifference—that wills to *not* be liberated from false understandings of freedom, which in turn explains the persistence of ideologies of freedom. A freedom directed against the liberation from false freedom. The understanding of freedom on which this indifference is grounded represents "a merely intended freedom,"[2] and this mere intention of freedom, this intended but not thought or practiced freedom, leads to the consequence that human beings—both theoretically and practically—are determined in a heteronomous manner. Freedom, merely intended, leads to unfreedom.

Thus Hegel determines more precisely, first, how it is possible to conceive that human beings in general fall into heteronomous determinacy, and second, the extent to which this leads to the loss of historical consciousness and a peculiar objectification. There is a will against liberation, a will to (ontic) indifference that even directs itself against any attempt to truly (viz., as liberated from the mythical assumption of givenness) think freedom (in and with philosophy). At least in part, this attitude can be identified, as already with Kant and Schmid, as a product of (the problematic form of) philosophy. But (and this is Hegel), it can also be a product of historical changes which become entrenched by philosophy and by ideologues of freedom whose home can also be in philosophy. For Hegel there is not only the declaration of a possibility of indifference in philosophy—as symptom of an evil will—but also a determinate type of philosophy that cannot fail to bring forth indifference. In other words, for Hegel, the critique of ideology, which is a constitutive element of modern rationalism, must also concern philosophy as the thinking of freedom itself. In the sense of its endorsement of the ideology of freedom, even ideology critique can become ideological (or naturalize itself). And this is why philosophy is not a neutral space but rather (still) remains a battlefield—in which one struggles about what it means to struggle; one struggles about struggle itself. In this way Hegel, in showing that there is class struggle in philosophy and this struggle concerns the ontology, the mode of being of freedom, radi-

calizes Kant, who understood his project as the arbitration of the endless conflicts plaguing philosophy.

Where Descartes describes the origin of the identification of freedom with
a capacity as an *epistemological* error, and Kant describes it as a *moral* decision for the immoral which obscures its own decision, thereby characterizing
it as being against the very constitution of reason, Hegel places the focus of
the investigation on the *historically specific* mode of the *ontology and actualization* of the problematic understandings of freedom, describing the backward
and disastrous effects of these understandings such that even philosophy itself
can become the terrain of and therefore also a (reactionary or emancipatory)
weapon within the critique of ideology.[3] The disastrous effects of the ideology
of freedom whose manifestation is indifference not only emerge when there
is a false understanding of autonomy but also when there is a false understanding of the heteronomy from which one can establish what it means to be determined. This leads to a misunderstanding, to the misrepresentation of one's
own nature, the consequences of which are oriented against free human beings,
and, then, practically realize in the form of a peculiar regression of freedom
to heteronomy and compulsion. But the history of the philosophical critique
of the ideology of freedom does not end with Hegel.[4]

After Hegel, Kierkegaard will lament that the entire "external and visible
world . . . is subject to the law of indifference,"[5] that everything belongs to those
who merely own things. It becomes indifferent as to whether these owners realized or have realized—or even whether they work toward—any work, any *oeuvre*. Their material wealth alone makes them owners in the world, even owners
of such freedom that have the (external) capacity to do anything they want.
This problematic indifference continuously emerges and spreads around, but, for
Kierkegaard, the real problem emerges when the owners at the same time ex-
hibit an apparent humility and present their external property as not being the
most valued and valuable thing; they make affirmative references to apparently
more relevant and important things, for example, spiritual riches, inner peace,
the peace of the soul. These claims are problematic, because they remain practically inconsequential: No owner renounces her property or changes his life
and begins with another form of work, since such an owner already feels
humble in and through the mere admission that nothing else counts as much
as the spiritual. Under the condition that one owns sufficient property, according to Kierkegaard, one can be easily satisfied and feel accommodated with and
through the knowledge that there are more important things than property.
More precisely, one feels all the better with what one has, the more one constantly points to what one does not have and by identifying the latter with what
really counts, for instance, another world, of spirit or God.

The knowledge of this other world remains merely abstract knowledge without practical consequences. One claims to know that there is more than just the merely external life oriented around property and enjoys referring to this other life, the more one only leads the former. Ultimately, such "a knowledge . . . presumptuously wants to introduce into the world the same law of indifference under which the external world sighs"[6]—we are supposed to know about another world, about a potential being-other of the world, and we kneel in humility before this other world. But since this knowledge remains empty and does not bring about any practical consequences, it is at the same time indifferent for us. Nothing changes in this world through the empty reference to this other world, apart from the fact that those who refer to it also get to feel even better within this (material) world. In this way Kierkegaard claims that there can be a knowledge that a freedom solely grounded on what one has does not go a long way—yet it is precisely the admission of such a knowledge that enables one to continue to act without changing anything. It is as if one were to say: "I know very well that freedom as a capacity is not truly freedom, but nevertheless I act and think as if it were." Such knowledge is not only indifferent for and to our own practice, but it also makes the sphere of belief into a practically indifferent sphere and leads to a peculiar apologia for the existing circumstances. Thus Kierkegaard formulates a consequence akin to that which Hegel—in a lecture—had already characterized: "a widespread, nearly *universal indifference* toward the doctrines of faith formerly regarded as essential."[7]

After Hegel—*encore*—the great anti-Hegelian Schopenhauer, in an (initially at least) thoroughly Kantian manner, defines the will such that it can under no circumstances be indifferent toward but can only affirm or deny life. In his "Prize Essay on the Freedom of the Will," he attacks and rejects the determination of free will as *liberum arbitrium indifferentiae*, the free will as the freedom to arbitrarily decide in an indifferent manner, as an untenable aspect of metaphysics. This metaphysics of freedom does not, Schopenhauer maintains, simply stand outside of the world on account of it being naturally—viz., spontaneously—given to any human being. There is present, therefore, a spontaneous ideology of freedom which is inscribed in the nature of the human mind; ideology is not an externally imposed form but the very mode in which we (naturally) think: "Anyone's *self-consciousness* proclaims very clearly that he can do what he wills. But since even entirely opposed actions can be thought as *willed* by him, it follows to be sure that he can also do opposed things, *if he wills*."[8] For Schopenhauer this spontaneous ideology of freedom arises from a profound error. Namely, from the assumption of every human being that they possess a freely given and thereby indifferent will. This error thus concerns a confusion of cause and effect, which is so profound an error that it divides philosophy, across its entire history, into two sides. On the one side of this schism there are those who defend the freedom of the will (what Schopenhauer identifies as what I coined the ideology of freedom) and, on the other side, there are the true philosophers who reject this ideology. Philosophy is not only a battlefield now, but its history is a history of struggles for, in, and around freedom.

After Hegel—*encore*—once again—the indifference problem is taken up, this time by perhaps his most influential even though indirect pupil, Karl Marx. It is instructive to conclude, now, by paying some close attention to the Marxist resumption of the problem. Already, the young Marx makes the far-reaching observation that "political economy knows the worker only as a working animal—as a beast reduced to the strictest bodily needs";[9] explicitly taking into consideration the regressive effects a certain understanding of freedom leads to on a practical level. Marx asserts, therefore, that a particular form of social organization, namely capitalism, is organized in such a way that it brings about an extensive and at the same time peculiar *animalization of workers*, which is to say of potentially all members of society. Alain Badiou will later give this thesis a new formulation in arguing that capitalism "is the regime that hypostasizes the idea that the human being is an animal."[10] Capitalism can thus only function as it does because it constantly produces peculiar regressions—and not merely repressions—and it is this insight that Marx's diagnosis pointedly formulates. Capitalism is, relies on, and reproduces an ideology of freedom.[11]

Marx's diagnosis is more complex than it initially seems. For the reduction marked by capitalism is not only regressive (capitalism treats human beings as if they were animals) but also productive. The nature to which the workers are reduced is produced by a reductive and reducing operation, and it does so precisely in the act of reduction. This means that for Marx there are not simply human beings who live in an animal manner merely because they lack the material means to be more dignified, but also it means that there is a specific capitalist animality that is itself the product of the existing relations (of production) and that it is this animality to which human beings in capitalism are reduced. It must itself be understood as an essential part of the abstraction process that makes capitalism into what it is. In other words: Capitalism produces a specific understanding of the human being as an animal to which it then reduces all human beings by way of the (capitalist) organization of society and its procedures.[12] But what it reduces human beings to—in the way that capitalism looks at human beings—is in itself a historical (and in Marx's terms, abstract) product. This is to say, therefore, that capitalism does not imply any evolutionary regression but fundamentally implies and produces forms of regressive production and products.

At the same time it also holds that such a regressive understanding does not remain external, but it becomes part of the self-understanding of human beings (under capitalism). According to Marx's thesis, human beings begin, on the basis of the material conditions in which they live as well as on the basis of the prevailing imaginary representations of these conditions, to identify themselves with a highly abstract entity, namely, to the beast reduced to the strictest bodily needs. This animal to which they are reduced is not merely their (existing) bodily constitution but is rather a product of abstraction processes. It is an abstract, an artificially produced, that is, an unnatural animal. This animal, therefore, becomes the representation of the essence of the human being that is the worker. The human being that is the worker becomes an animal that is merely artificial because for it, according to Marx, nothing else counts but its own body. In this way freedom is converted into a capacity of the body. This type of freedom can be and is then identified as labor power. In sum, Marx's thesis is that the worker *is*, from the standpoint of the economy, nothing more than what the worker *has*, namely the body.[13]

The free being that is supposed to be the human being is, then, constituted through an identity of being and having, and it is precisely this identity that, for Marx, determines the peculiar animal that the human being is supposed to be: The animal "is immediately one with its life activities. It is *them*,"[14] which is why "[i]n the place of *all* physical and mental senses [appears] . . . the sense of *having*."[15] The worker is, essentially, determined through and by what he has. If freedom is supposed to be an essential feature of the worker (qua human being), this peculiar property must also be located in what the worker has (and has as core of her existence). This is to say, in the body. In this way freedom is not only identified with a givenness but also with the givenness of the body and with bodily capacity. However, it must also be taken into account that not only the animal to which the worker is reduced is an abstract product of existing relations, but also that the apparently concrete and individual body is thereby equally a part of this abstract form of production. The body to which bourgeois economy reduces the worker is itself a product of an abstracting reduction—it is a bare, reduced, and (simultaneously in this reduction) produced life. This is the production of an artificial nature, the naturalization of abstract production. Marx articulates this by arguing that there can no longer be a true end in life for the worker, which is also, therefore, to say that potentially there can no longer be a true end in life for anybody living under capitalism. No purpose "exist[s] any longer, and each has ceased to function not only in its human fashion, but in an *inhuman* fashion."[16]

For Marx the worker is an animal deprived of its animality,[17] the consequence of which is that "[w]hat is animal becomes human and what is human becomes animal."[18] The worker feels unfree when she works, but she feels free when she eats, drinks, or copulates during her free time. Within this model of freedom—a freedom that consists of fleeting and indifferent instantiations of bodily functions—the worker gets the feeling and impression that freedom is only actualized in the "now" of his own bodily functions. This implies that, as soon as the "now" (of free time, the weekend, or a longed-for nap, etc.) is past, he ceases to be free (and must continue to work). Since, structurally speaking, each of these now-instances have always already transitioned over to other now-instances, freedom for the worker is always past, and everything exists in the permanently disappearing postponement of taking up labor again. For the worker, then, this labor ultimately only means unfreedom.

In *Capital*, Marx conceives the value that produces labor in its most elementary form (as merely human labor) as "the expenditure of simple labour-power, that is, of the labour power possessed in his bodily organism by every ordinary man, on the average, without being developed in any special way."[19] Political economy assumes that the worker possesses her own bodily functions— which contain her freedom—and these functions can be viewed as the precondition of labor universally—as a form of their actualization. These bodily functions lie in what the worker puts into labor. In this way what is naturalized is the idea that when there is a particular animal function of the body of the worker, the name for the being who has this function is "the worker" such that "worker" is the name for whoever has and can be identified as the owner of these functions, and then the body can (under this idea) be used for anything possible in an indifferent manner. The worker is determined as an animal body in a reductive fashion, and the freedom of the worker becomes a given capacity of that body. It becomes a capacity that can be actualized in an indifferent manner. The truth of the determination of freedom as indifference is revealed by Marx as a naturalizing reduction of the assumed subject of freedom to his body, which at the same time is, in all its determinacy, a reductive product of the abstraction of bourgeois economists, those "scientists" that explain what governs the reality of bourgeois society. The true "downward synthesis"[20] is therefore the effect of the social organization of specific relations of freedom, which are introduced by the bourgeoisie and their capitalist global economy.[21]

It has been necessary to give this immensely abbreviated outline of the Marxian perspective in order that the following wager may now be laid down: that the concept of indifference in modern rationalist philosophy cannot be appropriately registered, diagnosed, and analyzed if one does not see how it is connected to the historically specific, political, and economic organization of modern society in which modern philosophy is embedded. Or, to grasp this

not as a desideratum but positively, one can claim: If modern rationalist philosophy is in at least one of its functions essentially the critique of the ideology
of freedom, then an essential component of philosophy must be to articulate
a critique of capital, a critique of capitalism, and of the specific forms of freedom corresponding to it.[22] However, as Descartes already knew, a merely
critical perspective is insufficient. What is also required is a step away from
the necessary critique and toward the supersession of what is being criticized.
So, how do we proceed with the critique of indifference as the critique of the
ideology of freedom? And what might result from it?

These questions become more urgent when we recall Hegel's remark that
the human being is not merely a bodily but also a spiritual being, and that the
"life of spirit" exists insofar as "[i]t wins its truth only when, in utter dismem-
berment, it finds itself."[23] How, then, is it possible to deal with (umgehen) or to
circumvent (um-gehen) the peculiar effects of the ideology of freedom? To leaving them behind or at least to begin to do so? Marx remarks that the class
which set up society in this way, namely the bourgeoisie, always has an interest in "continually revolutionizing" social relations; that, more precisely, "the
bourgeoisie cannot exist" without this constant revolutionizing. In this way this
class itself seems to play "a revolutionary role of the highest importance,"
namely that of constant modernizing, while all the time and because in melting "[a]ll that is solid . . . into air" they constantly drive a process whose product is a "mass fragmentation"[24] of those who are themselves fragmented. But
even though this seems to concern an incessant *movement* of modernization,
this semblance is deceptive. Which is why it is with this social formation,
namely, with bourgeois-capitalist society, that "[t]he prehistory of human
society . . . closes".[25] That this social formation is a prehistorical social formation shows that—at least for Marx—the step taken by Descartes into
modernity and against the artificially regressive and in that sense premodern
understanding of freedom, the very step Kant tried to repeat, and the preconditions for which step I indicated with Hegel in the last chapter is yet to be
accomplished.

Modernity is in this sense not an unfinished project but is rather a project
that has not yet truly begun. Or more precisely: This means that, as far as the
modernizations with which the bourgeoisie organizes society are concerned,
we are dealing with a peculiar mode of modernization that only appears to
modernize, that is, it is the mere semblance of modernization. This modernization is a semblance because it takes place in bourgeois-capitalist society as
a dissolution and dynamization of all previously held purposes and ends. Yet
this constant change takes place only in order that no effective structural
change will take place. It is a change without change, a transformation that

transforms everything except for what truly enables transformation. It is a change stuck in a particular mode of change and therefore a change that changes nothing; for change that does not alter what change means is no change at all. Thus, constant and generally indifferent change becomes the means through which everything is kept as it ever was.

An additional effect of this is that the prehistory attained in bourgeois-capitalist organizations of society, as well as in the political economy that is its ultimate form of expression, characterizes a society that constantly remains premodern in its mode of modernization—in Descartes's sense.[26] Or, put differently again, with the apparent movement of modernization of bourgeois society, a premodernity—the premodernity inseparable from the mythology of the givenness of freedom—is produced, which is the premodernity upon which bourgeois modernity constitutively relies. And this is why for Marx the following is the case: that prehistorical change is not true change, for true change can only be historical, linked to the advent of history.[27] And true historical movement precludes, as Hegel already indicated, the reduction of the human being to the animal. And so, the step from prehistory to actual history is a step that must necessarily alter the mode of change. Marx's name for such change, at least for a while, was revolution.

Marx characterizes this prehistory as a specific sort of indifferent premodernity as well as of the premodernity of indifference, which is constantly modified and transformed in order to remain the same—and which is already itself a product of (capitalist) modernity or modernization at a formal level. From such a perspective, the answer as to why there is always a relapse into or toward a lingering premodernity, even though modern philosophy already oriented itself or at least tried to orient itself against the premodern understanding of freedom centuries ago, is linked to the existence of the bourgeois-capitalist organization of society.[28] In this way, bourgeois-capitalist political economy and its arrangement of the world is an infinite, manifoldly reductive (as well as peculiarly regressive) and prolifically effective ideology of indifference.[29] But if this then means that modern bourgeois society structurally (re)produces its own (ideological) preconditions (and thereby itself) in premodern form as an effect of its own modernization (because it is prehistorical), how are the conditions for the entry of an actual modernity to be specified? How is it possible to escape this odd "spectral objectivity,"[30] which Marx attributed not only to the elementary form of the political economy of bourgeois society (to the form of the commodity), but also to the constitution of bourgeois society itself, in which one can discern the strange haunting mode of a persistence of an artificially produced premodernity and prehistory at work? How do we escape the spectral objectivity of prehistory and its model of freedom as indifference?

Such descriptions and analyses attain an increasingly drastic explicitness and will go on to do so. Perhaps, then, it is necessary to ask soberly how a way out of this dilemma of freedom is possible, and to direct this question in an equally sober manner to the tradition of modern philosophical rationalism. For modern philosophy since Descartes not only indicates the problem, it also gives an answer, albeit a rather surprising one. This answer will not lead to what one might expect—namely, a revised and direct defense of a positive conception of freedom against the false interpretations as well as the practical effects of freedom as a given capacity—rather, the answer or solution will be framed in such a way that freedom can only be truly thought and created when freedom itself, the givenness of freedom, is put at risk. The only way to rescue freedom is to give up (on) freedom—by traversing what it is to be free. This necessitates a step from ontic to ontological indifference. For only through assuming this shift can it become clear that there is (so far as freedom is concerned) nothing to which one might ever hold fast, nothing to which one ever could refer, and nothing that may ever be our capacity.

Alain Badiou once suggested to supplement Heidegger's analysis of indifference as the symptom and sign of nihilism (viz., of the predominance of technology), mentioned at the beginning of this book, with what he calls a "Marxist concept of indifference,"[31] which takes into account the movement of the universal equivalent, that is, money as form of the expression of value, and the corresponding universal indifference of commodities. Doing so, he not only asserts that there is indifference in our time, but also that it is necessary to split the concept of indifference into two in order to not be held captive, helplessly at the mercy of its movement.[32] *While on the one hand there is an indifference that makes all hierarchies and categories vacillate, and which is thus the symptom of a repeatedly and systematically organized forgetting of difference, there is on the other hand another indifference, that is subtracted from the universal equivalent and its movement, and this is an indifference that persistently evades the distinction between difference and indifference, differentiation and indifferentiation.*[33] The former indifference, which I previously defined as the ideology of freedom, leads to there no longer being a world but rather an all-encompassing environment—"and if there is no world, there is only nature."[34] This also means that it is possible to maintain precisely the "bestial heart," the essential animality of human beings.[35] The latter form of indifference, which I previously referred to as ontological indifference, is related to the study of the concepts of fatalism and the comedy that such study, and indeed fatalism itself, implies. There is thus a way out: the possible-impossible rescue of freedom through abolishing it as a givenness. This, then, is the only way in which this conclusion can close: by indicating the need for a lingering repetition . . . What is needed is the renewed staging of the history of modern philosophical rationalism, which, always orienting and directing itself against any form of freedom which is identified as a given, as a natural capacity, will have prepared a real practical-theoretical orientation. The struggle against the ideology of freedom will have to begin the next round. The struggle begins with abolishing freedom (as capacity).[36]

Translator's Afterword

Heather H. Yeung

The status of the work, at any point in its conception, its variform appearances as lectures or publications, table-talk or workshop fodder, or in its apparently final collecting together, and particularly the status of the work in the context of the c. 21st Academy, is a peculiar one, in which resurges what is considered the apparently original work, oddly revivified and in strange re-versions, by the demand of its differently "fielded," differently affiliated, readers, or by the referential footnote-demand of the continuing work of the (still-living) writer themself. Peculiar, then, is the work of a translator given these conditions of such work. And particularly strange in the case of this work—whose appearance of one part of an habilitation thesis presented in 2017 and subsequent (2018) publication in German as one of two books took on one guise having one particular form of reception, and whose other part was before then published in English in 2016 (of which the German version is subsequent and significantly expanded)—which has up to now had a different reception and readership to its apparent "twin"; this work here presented as a book, which, a number of years since its being originally written, published, and received, now is put out to work again and now also, in a slightly expanded version from its German counterpart, into the English language.

But why must this be a peculiarity of a particular type (after all, we, as impatient readers, are used to navigating the aggravations of the work-not-yet-fully published; the work which is translated piecemeal; the awaiting of the reading matter of a work; and indeed some of these aspects are the foundations upon which are built full exegetic careers)? In part this is because, in the interim, the author of the book out of which the here presented translation, Frank Ruda, has published a number of works written originally *in English not German*, but also many works in German, which extend and make different the ways in which he formulates his approach to the philosophies, philosophers, and indeed to the question of philosophy, of thought, itself, which are brought together here. And he does so, in both languages which he now equally uses but differently, in a manner of form and style which is distinctive, idiomatic, even, in both. And which has (as is the case for any writer) refined and altered itself over time, as the work itself as a whole progresses.

Thus the translator of such a work encounters a primary question: to accede to the style in which the German version of the here-presented work was written (to be dogmatic, orthodox, diplomatic, historicizing) *or* to accede to the style which is taken on in the English version of this work's companion volume (to assume the necessity of a target-language consistency which produces a stylistic mimesis of the "original" source-language "twin" books) *or* to somehow incorporate aspects of the style in which those readers of Ruda's work which is originally written in English takes on with respect to the questions addressed in the here-presented work will be familiar, in particular in relation to the constant refining, in his distinctive idiom, of his positions vis-à-vis Hegel and Marx, which has substantially moved on since the original (German) version of the here-presented work's (original, German) presentation, but of which this (German) work was absolutely formative? In short, given the translator's eternal dilemma of substance versus style, and the various currently fashionable ways of problematizing the visibilization of the inevitable border-crossing issues, literal and academic, of philosophy in particular and the text more generally, how then, given the conditions of the production and publication of this work originally in particular (the book *Indifferenz und Wiederholung*), and the afterlife of the work of this book more generally (the work—or, as Alain Badiou writes in the Foreword of this particular edition—the *oeuvre*—of the thinker of which this is an integral part of this work), to find such a process—now—(re)present this thinker and this work?

These questions have perhaps, on the one hand, found an easier answer than expected, which allow the translation to avoid being plagued by a certain *Sprachskepsis* as well as its symptoms (the most obvious anachronisms)— of becoming a relic for thought (the above option 1), a reliquary for a (possibly crumbled, definitely deformed) relic of thought (the above option 2), and a contemporary revitalization, in a differently written form made galvanically animate, of both reliquary and relic (the abovementioned zombie, or, option 3)— for the translator of the here-presented book was able to work closely, in an almost co-translatorial relationship, with the original author of the German book *Indifferenz und Wiederholung*. The process of translation thus took on a specific mode, in which the author themself was able, not to re-work or re-write the work, but to engage fully with and clarify its English articulation (there are discrete, always very short, passages that are "new" in this book, as well as— mentioned more particularly in the final paragraph below—translations within the translation of works which are quoted from and essential to the progress of the book's thesis but available only in German), and the translator was able, thus, to work with the author as sounding-board for those aspects of translation, essential to the maintenance of argument and style, which can too easily otherwise tip over in bad or meaning-obstructing interpretative choices, even odd parsings. At this, for the most part, we worked facing each other at the same desk, passing paragraphs between sides. The act of translation became a conversation into which the above translation issues were condensed, were a perpetual undercurrent to the (re)formation of the book here presented.

On the other hand, as those readers of and listeners to the presentation of Ruda's work in both German and English will be familiar, Ruda's *style* (too often a dirty word, yet a preconditional presence, in philosophical discourse), and the rhythms in which this style allows for the formation of both commentary and argument within the work, is what may be called without any pejorative resonance idiosyncratic. Idiosyncratic because this is a writer who—unsurprisingly, if one attends to the constellations of thinkers with whom he finds most philosophical resonance—takes form and its tonal articulation seriously. Thus, old yet perennially present figures of rhetoric—punning, parataxis, prosopopoeia, deixis, and so on, as well as the well-worn philosophical tool of the extended speculative simile, or even metaphorical *leap* (hic Rhodus!)—resurge and reform ways in which Ruda writes; against the Aristotle we come to via Kant, perhaps, and with Hegel and Lacan, rather, such a form (or use) of rhetoric is not the antistrophe to dialectic, but instead shapes, undergirds, the full odic (or perhaps more properly, fully dialectic) structure and logical progression of an argument which (here) seeks to expose the danger of vacillation and the illusions and reality of stasis (or epodos), underlining the precision of the comic fatalistic mode ("first time as [. . .] second time as [. . .]"—observed somewhere, oh, and again) necessary in Ruda's formation of a thesis toward philosophy (the traversing of a different form of indifference), here, quite as in the sister-thesis to this one, *Gegen-Freiheit*, or, *Abolishing Freedom*.

One can argue with and must attend to tone and form *as well as* with content; to (have a) *style* is to *take a position*; to fail to see this is to fall into a trap that leads only to odd illusions; to be numb or self-blind to it signals mortal (intellectual) disaffection. Indeed, if we take seriously the subject of this book, which might be said to be the process and ways in which philosophy's unattention to the articulations of form(s of life) has created as its ur-form indifference and its own un-becoming, paying particular attention perhaps to its final chapter, one cannot but so attend. And so, in Ruda, if a passage articulates in a mode, say, reminiscent of Luther (an arbitrary example?) or perhaps of Lenin (perhaps less arbitrary!), it is likely that such a mode is *not* anachronism or metaphysical-apostrophic eruption, rather quite the opposite—a speculative commentary on the commentary itself without the illusions of ahistoricity, an, as it were, stance of demonstration as well as commentary, a sort of *proof* of concept and meaning(making) through tone, through form. If a passage does the same for the dominant discourse style of any given form of philosophy in the contemporary academy (such form that sadly and often hides itself in the assumed cloak of a neutral, easy, personally defensible, (non)position), then it is also likely that the same goes. As Hegel wagers on the radical new puns from a Germanic etymology, we ask you to notice how this work is that of the more-than-singly-grounded. The jokes, here (for there are always, also, jokes), are of course serious ones, and all points are made with a fatal precision (the piqued, more often than not, being both subject and also clumsy or naïve reader). And so, rather pleasurably fencing across the table, we worked to attempt a similar mode of expression *into* and *of* a (nuanced) Englished expression of the (nuanced) thesis of *Indifferenz und Wiederholung*; to make the work—*encore*—the-same-again-and-differently, set out on the adventure of its work.

We will not here enumerate the small shifts that (inevitably) occurred in the passage of the work of *Indifferenz und Wiederholung* into the work of the present book, as this only implies an accession to an odd, dull, self-falsifying, dogmatically comparative hermeticism to which neither translator nor author cleaves; the German book can easily be found and looked at in parallel to the English. But there are some aspects that the more dedicated reader who is, however, only idly or not at all conversant in German (for whom therefore this book is the first encounter with the arguments of the *Indifferenz und Wieder-holung* thesis) may find interesting to note.

— Neither translator nor author chose to re-read the Anglophone version of the sister-thesis to this one (*Abolishing Freedom*), rather, simply worked from the version of the *Indifferenz und Wiederholung* thesis published by Konstanz University Press in 2018, and the author's own notes on that text. Thus, although the original (German) work has a "twin" for formal reasons (the Habilitation-thesis) which elaborates aspects of a larger argument it only alludes to, the relationship between these two works in their English forms, acceding to a time of reception and translation that is variant and across languages, are no more hemiparasitical than may seem any given work of any single author to another of their works to a sensitive reader. This is to write, also, that idiomatic formulations found across both German works will appear differently in each of their English versions. In comparison with its German edition, this book also contains a new preface (by the author, written in English), and a (new) foreword by Alain Badiou (translated from French by the author).

— Readers, however, comparing English and German versions under the auspices of the note above's attention to the importance of form (mediated through, of course, the concept and effects of the speculative sentence on philosophical discourses) will notice immediately changes in the paragraphing, and thus in the apparent rhythmicities, of the work. This is less to do with decisions made about meaning's relation to style in the progress of an argument, and more to do with (and this is really a point only for book historians) the migration away from the formal and material restrictions of the German book-publishing industry, which can determine outside of authorial control paragraph start and cut-off points as it thinks absolutely with the size of the page as its formal predicate.

— One addition to the English version of the work by Ruda in this translation process is the short section regarding aspects of the preface of Hegel's *Phenomenology of Spirit*, concerning the "tramp[ling] underfoot of the roots of humanity" (p. 43), and so on.

— Carl Christian Erhard Schmid (1761–1812), although translated excerpts from his "Lexicon for the Easier Use of the Kantian Writings" (1788) and "Attempt at a Moral Philosophy" (1790) have in the year of this translation's writing been published prominently in Jörg Noller and John Walsh's *Kant's Early Critics on Freedom of the Will* (Cambridge University Press, 2022), have not yet been given much critical attention in the English-speaking world, and there is not yet any comprehensive or full edition available. However, the quite prolific Schmid was the editor of the first Kant dictionary and was also crucial for introducing Kant to thinkers like Schiller. All quotations from Schmid in this book are Ruda's own translations. Similarly throughout the book may be found (as marked appropriately in the notes) the author's own translations into English of still-untranslated texts by other writers.

— Since the question of the philosophical "untranslatable" is currently fashionable and the rare occasion where (academic) linguistic expression evades a direct analogous expression is always interesting as a site where pedantry meets philology and poetics, after some conversation the translator and author, together, here offer: (1) *Gleichgültigkeit,* a rendering of "indifference," which is rendered herein as *indifference* if Latin and/or so indebted, but as *equal-validity, equal valence* if not; (2) the somewhat infamous neuter, "one," in Heidegger is "Man," which is translated as the "they"; (3) where, especially in Hegel, but also in Kant, the German term *Wirklichkeit* is used—a term that has *wirken,* to be effective, to cause or have caused something, as a constituent part—it has been rendered mostly as actuality, sometimes as effectivity and sometimes as reality, dependent upon context, even though the English terms carry quite a different semantic weight.

HY
Dundee, Nov. 2022

Acknowledgments

What one is actually able to think can probably only be determined if one makes the attempt to think what at first does not seem possible. In their very own ways a group of friends, comrades, (co-)thinkers have coerced and forced me to do so—a group to which I therefore owe a debt of gratitude. They are—希蒂—, Alain Badiou, Judith Balso, Ray Brassier, Lorenzo Chiesa, Rebecca Comay, Joan Copjec, Mladen Dolar, Marcus Döller, Alexander García Düttmann, Lorenz Engell, Christopher Fynsk, Agon Hamza, Michael Heinrich, Hugo Heubach, Fredric Jameson, Zdravko Kobe, Thomas Lay, Christoph Menke, Mark Potocnik, Claudia Pozzana, Rado Riha, Gerd and Manuela Ruda, Anneliese Ruda, Alessandro Russo, Eric Santner, Cornelia and Ralf Schmidt, Aaron Schuster, Bernhard Siegert, Jelica Šumič, Christiane Voss, Andreas Ziemann, Slavoj Žižek, Alenka Zupančič.

Notes

Preface to the English Edition: Freedom as Slavery

1. From here one can see why the sexual liberation movement believed in the liberation of that which is considered to be in itself liberating (with regard to work). The problems this movement encountered have been well analyzed and portrayed many times: Its formula could be resumed by claiming that perversion is emancipatory and subversive, which it is only insofar as it never really changes anything in the overall fabric of society or structure, which is why Jacques Lacan indicated that it always presents only a version of the father (authority): a père (father)—version. Cf. Lacan's as to now unpublished seminar XXI, "Les non-dupes errent."

2. Silvia Federici, "Sexuality Is Work," (1975), in *Revolution at Point Zero: Housework, Reproduction, and Feminist Struggle* (New York: PM Press, 2020), 19.

3. Ibid.

4. Ibid.

5. Ibid., 20.

6. Ibid., 22

7. Ibid., 23.

8. Karl Marx / Frederick Engels, *The Communist Manifesto*, in MECW, 6:487.

9. Alain Badiou, *The Pornographic Age* (London: Bloomsbury 2020), 1–20.

10. David Staples, *No Place like Home. Organizing Home-Based Labor in the Era of Structural Adjustment* (New York: Routledge 2007), 4.

11. Peter Linebaugh, *The Magna Carta Manifesto: Liberties and Commons for All* (Berkeley: University of California Press 2008), 244

12. Cf., for example, Karl Marx, "Value, Price and Profit," in: *MECW*, 20, 99–150.

13. Linebaugh, *The Magna Carta Manifesto*, 244.

14. The essence of this labor is therefore for Federici faking that (reproductive) labor, viz., sex, is not work but pleasure. Cf. Federici, "Sexuality Is Work," 23.

15. Silvia Federici, *Caliban and the Witch: Women, the Body and Primitive Accumulation* (London: Penguin 2004), 280.

16. Angela Davis, "The Meaning of Freedom," in *The Meaning of Freedom and Other Difficult Dialogues* (San Francisco: City Light Books, 2012), 63.

17. Ibid., 64.

18. Ibid., 65.

19. Ibid.

20. This is the reason why the subsequent part of the present philosophical project is concerned with the understanding of what it means to abolish.

21. Davis, "The Meaning of Freedom," 65.

22. Ibid.

23. The present book will seek to clarify how we should *not* understand freedom.

24. For this also cf. Angela Davis, *Are Prisons Obsolete?* (New York: Seven Stories Press, 2003).

25. Or if, therefore, slavery is desired as if it were freedom: cf. Fréderic Lordon, *Willing Slaves of Capital: Spinoza and Marx on Desire* (London: Verso, 2014).

26. Davis, "The Meaning of Freedom," 65.

27. Ibid., 68.

28. V. I. Lenin, "Deception of the People with Slogans of Freedom and Equality," in *Collected Works* (Moscow: Progress Publishers, 1972), 29: 333–376.

29. Cf. Frank Ruda, "I, the Revolution, Speak: Lenin's Speculative (Hegelian) Style," in *From Marx to Hegel and Back: Capitalism, Critique, and Utopia*, ed. Victoria Fareld and Hannes Kuch (London: Bloomsbury, 2020), 91–108.

30. Cf. Alain Badiou, *Le Séminaire: s'orienter dans la pensée, s'orienter dans l'existence* (Paris : Fayard, 2022).

31. Cf. Octave Mannoni, *Je sais bien, mais quand-même . . .* (Paris: Seuil, 2022).

32. V. I. Lenin, "Soviet Power and the Status of Women," in Lenin's *Collected Works* (Moscow: Progress Publishers, 1965), 30:120.

33. This is the reason as to why the case of Haiti is an interesting one as for example Slavoj Žižek has repeatedly argued. Cf., for example, Slavoj Žižek, *Incontinence of the Void* (Cambridge: MIT Press, 2017), 125.

34. Marx / Engels, *Manifesto of the Communist Party*, 487.

35. Ibid., 499.

36. Ibid.

37. Jean-Claude Milner, *Le salaire de l'idéal. La théorie des classes et de la culture au XXIème siècle* (Paris: Seuil, 1997).

38. Lenin, "Soviet Power and the Status of Women," 121.

39. Cf. on this Alexandre Kojéve, *Introduction to the Reading of Hegel: Lectures on the "Phenomenology of Spirit"* (Ithaca, NY: Cornell University Press, 1980).

40. Cf. Moishe Postone, *Time, Labor, and Social Domination: A Reinterpretation of Marx's Critical Theory* (Cambridge: Cambridge University Press, 2008). It is important to note here that strangely from a certain point in the development of capitalist economies, something can change, and personal domination can return

(not everywhere but in some pockets, where a new type of "primitive accumulation" has to or will take place). For this, see Rebecca Carson, "Fictitious Capital and the Return of Personal Domination," in: *CT&T* 1, no. 150 (2017): 566–586.

41. On the problems with the form of the bourgeois concept of right, see Christoph Menke, *Critique of Rights* (London: Polity, 2020).

42. Karl Marx, *Capital. A Critique of Political Economy*, vol. 1 (London: Penguin Books, 1982), 280.

43. Theodor W. Adorno, "Culture Industry Reconsidered," in *The Culture Industry: Selected Essays in Mass Culture* (London: Routledge, 2001), 103.

44. For further elaborations on this, see Alenka Zupančič, "Power in the Closet and Its Coming Out," in *Lacan, Psychoanalysis and Comedy*, ed. Patricia Gherovici and Maniya Steinküler (Cambridge: Cambridge University Press, 2016).

45. See Alexander Garcia Düttmann's reading of the queer slogan "we are queer, we are here, get fucking used to it," in Alexander Garcia Düttmann, *Zwischen den Kulturen: Spannungen im Kampf um Anerkennung* (Frankfurt am Main: Suhrkamp, 1997).

46. Alain Badiou has called the assumption that there are only bodies and languages the axiom of democratic materialism; he adds to this the materialist dialectical claim that there are only bodies and languages (of course), except that there are truths—and the latter transform what is by adding new possibilities to both. Cf. Alain Badiou, *Logics of Worlds. Being and Event, 2* (London: Bloomsbury, 2018).

47. Frank Ruda, *Abolishing Freedom. A Plea for a Contemporary Use of Fatalism* (Lincoln: University of Nebraska Press, 2016).

48. See, for example, Angela Davis, Gina Dent, Erica R. Meiners, Beth E. Richie, *Abolition. Feminism. Now.* (London: Penguin Books, 2022).

49. See Georg Lohmann, *Indifferenz und Gesellschaft* (Frankfurt am Main: Suhrkamp, 1991).

50. Marx / Engels, *Manifesto*, 488.

51. For this also see Karl Marx, "Demand," in *MECW*, 6:574–576.

52. It is so internationalist that it can even deal with different forms of nationalism without any problem: one can have a Hungarian nationalism, for example, and an Indian one, and they can tolerate each other as both can function, often even in solidarity, without any issues within a globalized capitalist economy. Capitalism thus allows for an internationalism of nationalisms; this does not (!) mean that it respects local cultures, but that it is so adaptable and flexible that it can tolerate all specific contents as long as they do not change its overall form. Capitalism is capitalism everywhere—this is why its medium is the world market—and it relies on a specific understanding of freedom, which is what the present book examines.

53. Let us not forget that Hegel claimed that the slave who does not desire emancipation from slavery deserves to be a slave—a harsh claim that at the same time is not at all meant as a defense of slavery. What this means for the invisible forms of slavery is at stake in the present book.

54. Samuel Beckett, *The Unnamable* (London: Grove Press, 1978), 103.

Introduction: Indifference and the History of Philosophical Rationalism

1. Martin Heidegger, *Schwarze Hefte (1942–1948)*, in *Gesamtausgabe. IV. Abteilung: Hinweise und Aufzeichnungen*, vol. 97 (Frankfurt am Main: Klostermann, 2015), 260.

2. It is obviously out of the question that Heidegger was, *at the same time*, a Nazi and an important philosopher. It does not seem convincing to me to deduce Heidegger's national-socialist conviction from his philosophy or reduce the latter to the former (both endeavors ultimately will prove untenable).

3. Martin Heidegger, *Plato's Sophist* (Bloomington: Indiana University Press, 1997), 313.

4. Martin Heidegger, *Nietzsche: Nihilism*, Volumes 4 (New York: Harper, 1991), 91–123.

5. Martin Heidegger, *The Question Concerning Technology and Other Essays* (New York: Harper, 1977), 20.

6. Alain Badiou, *Le séminaire: Heidegger. L'être 3—Figure du retrait. 1986–1987* (Paris: Fayard, 2015), 24.

7. Martin Heidegger, *The Fundamental Concepts of Metaphysics: World, Finitude, Solitude* (Bloomington: Indiana University Press, 1995), 356 (translation modified)..

8. Martin Heidegger, *Zu Ernst Jünger*, in *Gesamtausgabe. IV. Abteilung: Hinweise und Aufzeichnungen*, vol. 90 (Frankfurt am Main: Klostermann, 2004), 299. For an instructive problematization of the idea that freedom as (not) being identifiable with the ability to say yes or no, see Christoph Menke, "Ja und Nein," in *Autonomie und Befreiung: Studien zu Hegel* (Berlin: Suhrkamp, 2018), 179–212.

9. Heidegger offers an interpretation of the history of the amalgamation of freedom and indifference in Martin Heidegger, *Basic Concepts of Aristotelian Philosophy* (Bloomington: Indiana University Press, 2009), 93ff.

10. Martin Heidegger, *Schelling's Treatise on the Essence of Human Freedom* (Athens: Ohio University Press, 1985)., 38.

11. Martin Heidegger, *Introduction to Phenomenological Research* (Bloomington: Indiana University Press, 2005), 115.

12. Martin Heidegger, *Seminare Hegel—Schelling in Gesamtausgabe. IV. Abteilung: Hinweise und Aufzeichnungen*, vol. 86 (Frankfurt am Main: Klostermann, 2011), 51. This thesis was subsequently turned into an essential element of the thought of Giorgio Agamben, a pupil of Heidegger's. See Giorgio Agamben, *Remnants of Auschwitz: The Witness and the Archive* (New York: Zone Books, 2002), 41–87.

13. It is important to remember that it is not only relevant to find answers to pertinent questions or solutions to persistent problems, but often the task of the philosopher is to distinguish between the right and the wrong way of framing a question.

14. See Wilfried Sellars, "Empiricism and the Philosophy of Mind," in *Empiricism and the Philosophy of Mind: With an Introduction by Richard Rorty and*

a Study Guide by Robert Brandom, ed. R. Brandom (Cambridge: Cambridge University Press, 1997), 13–25.

15. On the relation between the myth of the given and legal authorization, see Christoph Menke, *Critique of Rights* (London: Polity, 2020).

16. It is crucial to note here that such a determination of modernity does not only emphasize the novelty of modernity against the ancient character of the premodern but rather within the defense of the modernity of modernity an essential feature of the rational critique of mere belief and opinion repeats. This can already be identified in ancient Greece (for example in Plato). However, this does not mean that one defends the novelty of modernity qua novelty, since philosophical rationalism constantly notes that the new is not worth anything because it is just novel (since in that form it can easily be translated into something old, viz., marketable value). The following reflections are, even though they are limited to the realm of modern philosophy, framed such that they allow a more precise determination of the fundamental characteristics of philosophy as a critique of the ideology of freedom, which ought to be related back—at another place—to their early Greek articulation.

17. If one understands philosophy as the critique of the ideology of freedom, then one must pose the question whether this critique—in allusion to Freud—would have to be a terminable or an interminable critique.

18. Among other places, see Louis Althusser, "The Only Materialist Tradition," in *The New Spinoza*, ed. Warren Montag and Ted Stolze (Minneapolis: University of Minnesota Press, 1997), 3–20.

19. The following is helpful for these ideas in Althusser: Warren Montag, *Louis Althusser* (New York: Red Globe Press, 2003).

20. From this perspective, the notorious "end of ideology" that is often associated with the fall of actually existing socialism proves to be the actual ideological discourse on ideology, as ideology of ideology that is at the same time not meta-ideology but rather relies on a problematic and thereby ideological concept of ideology—namely, one which can simply disappear through better insight or historical development.

21. Phrased differently: modern rationalist philosophy does not do this against the abstract past (of antiquity), but against a presently active opponent (whose origin will be more precisely situated by the subsequent investigations). For an account of how to understand the difference constitutive of the modern age, see Alexandre Koyré, *From the Closed World to the Infinite Universe* (Baltimore: Johns Hopkins University Press, 1957).

22. Eckart Förster, *The Twenty-Five Year of Philosophy. A Systematic Reconstruction* (Cambridge, MA: Harvard University Press, 2008).

23. And the title springs from a long conversation with Aaron Schuster in Berlin.

24. Frank Ruda, *Abolishing Freedom: A Plea for a Contemporary Use of Fatalism* (Lincoln: University of Nebraska Press, 2016).

25. This will be achieved in a book on courage, which up to now remains unfinished.

26. Paul-Laurent Assoun, "De Freud à Lacan: le sujet du politique," *Cités*, no. 16 (2003/4): 20. Félicité Robert de Lamennais, *Essai sur l'indifférence en matière de religion*, vol. 1 (Paris: Tournachon-Molin, 1825), 30ff. (All translations from non-English sources are the translator's.)

27. Jacques Lacan, "Science and Truth," in *Écrits. The First Complete English Edition* (New York: W. W. Norton, 2006), 729.

1. Descartes and the Transcendental of All My Future Errors

1. An instructive and extensive overview of the different readings of the animal-man relation, beginning with the pre-Socratics and ending with Derrida, one can find in Élisabeth de Fontenay, *Le silence des bêtes: La philosophie à l'epreuve de l'animalité* (Paris: Fayard, 2015). For a different perspective, cf. Markus Wild, *Die anthropologische Differenz: Der Geist der Tiere in der frühen Neuzeit bei Montaigne, Descartes und Hume* (Berlin: De Gruyter, 2006).

2. Even for Aristotle it is clear that sociality alone does not explain the humanity of human beings, since there are also other social animals (ants, for example). But sociality appears with human beings in a specific form. It is this form that makes the human being human. What is it? The answer is, ultimately, reason. And it is precisely this idea that the anti-Aristotelian Hobbes will disavow. He will attempt to show that the reason of rational animals does not at all make them less animalistic. A reading of the relation between Aristotle, neo-Aristotelianism, and Hobbes can be found in my "Wer denkt asozial? Von Aristoteles zu Hobbes," in: *Das soziale Band*, ed. Thomas Bedorf and Steffen Hermann (Berlin: transcript, 2016), 143–163.

3. Immanuel Kant, *Critique of Judgment* (Oxford: Oxford University Press, 2007), 41. Translation modified, F.R.

4. For a comment on this "Zugleich," see Andrew Benjamin, *Towards a Relational Ontology. Philosophy's Other Possibility* (Albany: SUNY Press, 2015), pp. 167ff.

5. Kant, *Critique of Judgment*, 41.

6. See Hannah Ginsborg, "Interesseloses Wohlgefallen und Allgemeinheit ohne Begriff (§§1–9)," in *Klassiker Auslegen: Immanuel Kant: Kritik der Urteilskraft*, ed. Ottfried Höffe (Berlin: Akademie Verlag, 2008), 59–78.

7. SCF, 182.

8. Ibid., 185.

9. As to why the "yes" and "no" of a decision are located on different logical levels, see Frank Ruda, *For Badiou: Idealism without Idealism* (Evanston, IL: Northwestern University Press, 2015), 48–82.

10. SCF, 186.

11. Ibid., 188.

12. Ibid., 187.

13. Ibid., 191.

14. Sartre: "Freedom is one and indivisible. . . ." Ibid., 180.

15. It needs to be added here that we are dealing with a very specific concept of capacity that differs from the traditional Aristotelian notion. I leave the peculiarities of Sartre's concept of capacity here aside, since my main aim is—albeit via Sartre—Descartes. An instructive rendering of Sartre's theory of freedom can be found in Gavin Rae, *Realizing Freedom: Hegel, Sartre, and the Alienation of Human Being* (London: Palgrave, 2011), 11–110

16. As should be clear already, Descartes does not share this hyper-transcendental account of capacity.

17. It is important to note that it is not only Sartre who is irritated by the seeming inconsistency of Descartes's concept of freedom that is peculiarly linked to the concept of indifference. One of the most prominent readings that points in a similar direction is Etienne Gilson, *La Liberté chez Descartes et la Théologie* (Paris: Vrin, 1913), esp. chaps, 3–7. See also Gary Hatfield, *Descartes and the* Meditations (London: Routledge, 2002), 192ff. The intimate link between freedom and indifference is also briefly examined in Jean-Marie Beyssade, *La philosophie première de Descartes: Les temps et la coherence de la métaphysique* (Paris: Flammarion, 1992), 181–183.

18. Because God is not a fraud (and for Descartes she cannot be one), she cannot "in the strict or positive sense [be] the cause of errors to which we know by experience that we are prone" (DPP, 203). On this see also Ferdinand Alquié, *Lecons sur Descartes: Science et métaphysique chez Descartes* (Paris: Gallimard, 2005), 221–250.

19. That the meditations are linked results inter alia from the fact that Descartes shows in the first meditation that every human being can commit an error in judgment; even though error becomes the link between all human beings, it is decisive *of what* these errors are. Descartes shows that they are errors in relation to what we take to be true. Errors are errors when one assumes something to be true and certain which is neither true nor certain. The media of this sort of misjudgment and deception are multiple. Famously, the overcoming of the possible sources of error motivates Descartes in the three first meditations to doubt everything that might be considered a possible source of error.

20. DMFP, 11. Recall, here, the concise definition of clarity and distinctness that Descartes gives in his *Principles of Philosophy*: "I call a perception 'clear' when it is present and accessible to the attentive mind—just as we say that we see something clearly when it is present to the eye's gaze and stimulates it with a sufficient degree of strength and accessibility. I call a perception 'distinct' if, as well as being clear, it is so sharply separated from all other perceptions that it contains within itself only what is clear" (DPP, 207f.).

21. DMFP, 37.

22. A reading that points in a similar direction is provided in Josef Simon, "Descartes' 'cogito' unter zeichenphilosophischem Aspekt," in *Descartes im Diskurs der Neuzeit*, ed. Wilhelm Friedrich Niebel, Angelica Horn, and Herbert Schnädelbach (Frankfurt am Main: Suhrkamp, 2000), 77–102, esp. 83f.

23. DMFP, 37.

24. Cf. Bernard Williams, *Descartes: The Project of Pure Enquiry* (London: Routledge, 2005), 148–169.

25. DMFP, 38. See also Hans-Heinz Holz, *Descartes* (Frankfurt am Main: Campus, 1994), 117ff.

26. DMFP, 39.

27. An overview of traditional interpretations can be found in Hans Peter Schütt, *Die Adoption des "Vaters der modernen Philosophie": Studien zu einem Gemeinplatz der Ideengeschichte* (Frankfurt am Main: Klostermann, 1998).

28. An instructive study that interprets Descartes extensively in a similar direction is Cecilia Wee, *Material Falsity and Error in Descartes' Meditations* (London, 2006).

29. DMFP, 39.

30. DMFP, 39f. It is this likeness of God through which, as Descartes argues in the third meditation, I recognize myself in God and through which the insights mentioned above have to be conceived of. See Pierre Guenancia, *Lire Descartes* (Paris: Gallimard, 2000), 196–200.

31. DMFP, 40. In a similar vein, Descartes writes later in his life: "Mais je vous avoue qu'en tout ce où il y a occasion de pécher, il y a de l'indifférence" (But I confess to you that where there is an occasion to sin, there is indifférence) and even if God's grace cannot avoid indifference in all cases, "elle nous fait pencher davantage vers un coté que vers l'autre, et ainsi qu'elle l'a [l'indifference, F.R.] diminue, bien qu'elle ne diminue pas la liberté" (it makes us lean more to one side than to the other, and so it [the indifference] diminishes it, even though it does not diminish freedom altogether) (René Descartes, "À un R.P. Jésuite," in *Œuvre de Descartes*, ed. Victor Cousin, vol. 8 (Paris: Levraut, 1825), 169f. Letter to Mesland (1641). Descartes elaborates the concept of the degree of reality as follows: "[A] substance has more reality than an accident or a mode; an infinite substance has more reality than a finite substance" (DMFP, 117).

32. Descartes writes: "Neither divine grace nor natural knowledge ever diminishes freedom; on the contrary, they increase and strengthen it" (DMFP, 40).

33. Rousseau speaks in the *Social Contract* about the fact that the general will of a commonwealth must integrate all individual wills, and "this means nothing else than he shall be forced to be free" (Jean-Jacques Rousseau, *The Social Contract and The First and Second Discourses*, ed. Susan Dunn [New Haven, CT: Yale University Press 1978], 166).

34. DMFP, 40. Adorno will later call this momentum the "addendum" (or the impulse). See Theodor W. Adorno, *Negative Dialectics* (London: Routledge, 1973), 226. This is a momentum that is not derivable from anything that is given, but at the same time decisively inclines us in one and only one direction. An example that Adorno gives concerns the participation in the German resistance against the reign of National Socialism. Adorno writes of a conversation with Schlabrendorff (who was a part of the movement of the 20th July): "I asked him: How was it possible for you and your friends to go ahead with this plot, knowing that you faced not just

death—something that might fit with a so-called heroic attitude—but things that were inconceivably more horrific than death? I told him that I could not imagine people who were able to muster the strength to look all that in the face and to go ahead in spite of it. Herr von Schlabrendorff replied, without much hesitation: 'The fact is I just couldn't put up with things the way they were any longer. And I didn't spend much time brooding about the possible consequences. I just followed the idea that anything would be better than for things to go on as they were'" (Theodor W. Adorno, *History and Freedom: Lectures 1964–1965* [Cambridge: Polity, 2006], 240). For reflections on this notion in the *Negative Dialectics*, see Christoph Menke, "Modell 1: Freiheit. Zur Metakritik der praktischen Vernunft II. Kritik der 'abstrakten Moralität,'" in *Klassiker Auslegen: Theodor W. Adorno, Negative Dialektik*, ed. Axel Honneth and Christoph Menke (Berlin: De Gruyter, 2006), 151–169, esp. 159ff.

35. There are many contributions to the problem of determining "indifference" in Descartes. I will deal with this subsequently in an extensive manner, but want to refer here to one of the most instructive ones: Robert A. Imlay, "Descartes and Indifference," *Studia Leibnitiana* 14, no. 1 (1982): 87–97.

36. It results from a "defect in knowledge [. . .]." See also Tad M. Schmaltz, *Descartes on Causation* (Oxford: Oxford University Press, 2008), 201. In the Latin original Descartes also speaks of a "defectum."

37. The anecdote one can recognize as standing in the background became famous as the one of "Buridan's ass." I will return to this later.

38. DMFP, 40.

39. One can argue that Descartes, as is often the case, here positions himself in opposition to Francisco Suárez, who attempted to mediate between Duns Scotus and Ockham. Suárez himself stands close to Aquinas so that one can assume that the critical volte-face against the concept of indifference is ultimately not only directed against Suárez and Aquinas, but also against all contemporary incorporations of Aristotelianism. On this, see Edward Baert, *Aufstieg und Untergang der Ontologie: Descartes und die nachthomasische Philosophie* (Osnabrück: Rasch, 1997), and Gilles Olivo, "L'efficence en cause: Suárez, Descartes et la question de la causalité," in *Descartes et le Moyen Age*, ed. Joël Biard and Roshdi Rashed (Paris: Vrin, 1997), 91–107. For this also see CDD, 86ff.

40. DMFP, 40.

41. Cf. Wilhelm von Ockham, *Scriptum in Librum Primum Sententiarum Ordinatio*, in *Opera Theologica, Prologus et Distinctio* (New York: Franciscan Institute, 1967), 501. Instructive for this is also Carl Christian Erhard Schmid, *Adiaphora wissenschaftlich und historisch untersucht* (Leipzig: Vogel, 1809). I will return to this work. Extensively on Descartes and the Scholastics: Roger Ariew, *Descartes among the Scholastics* (Leiden: Brill, 2011).

42. It should be clear that here and in the following, I read Descartes in a Hegelian way; I would contend that this is not merely externally hegelianizing. Rather (after Hegel) this will have been internally visible in Descartes.

43. I say "Aristotelianism" because in the following I am not trying to examine if the (implicit and partially explicit) critique of Aristotle is justified. I will rather deal only with the question of what precise problem is, for Descartes, linked to an Aristotelian conception of freedom. The question is thus: What does the name "Aristotle" stand for in Descartes with regard to the concept of freedom? If we were to investigate the cogency of his critique, we would have to take into account how Descartes's criticism of Aristotle's conception of freedom relates to Aristotle's own description of indifference (of equally strong impeti) as inhibiting action. See Aristotle, *On the Heavens* (Cambridge, MA: Harvard University Press, 1932), 295b. Also, Descartes did presumably know Aristotle's work only to a minor degree. Systematic contributions to this question include significantly Vere Chappell, "Descartes's Compatibilism," in *Reason, Will, and Sensation. Studies in Descartes's Metaphysics*, ed. John Cottingham (Oxford: Oxford University Press, 1994), 177–190. For an overview of Descartes's rejection of the contemporary "Aristotelianism" (and of scholasticism) see Frederick Copleston, *A History of Philosophy*, vol. 4: *Descartes to Leibniz* (New York: Paulist Press, 1963), 78ff. A politically colored extensive elaboration can be found in NP, 103–174. It is indisputable that Descartes in his criticism of the mentioned conception of freedom also criticizes Hobbes, but for the argument I unfold here the rejection of Aristotelianism is more relevant.

44. In a rather pragmatic regard, Descartes was confronted from a certain moment on with the problem that in the Netherlands any philosophy except Aristotle's—and thus by implication also his own—was prohibited by the academic senate of Utrecht. See Gustave Cohen, *Ecrivains français en Hollande dans la première moitié du XVII siècle* (Paris: Champion, 1920), 357–602.

45. Some reflections on the relation between Descartes and Aristotle can be found in Murray Miles, *Insight and Inference: Descartes's Founding Principles and Modern Philosophy* (Toronto: De Gruyter, 2012), 11–23, and in Peter R. Anstey, "'De Anima,' and Descartes: Making Up Aristotle's Mind," *History of Philosophy Quarterly* 17, no. 3 (2000): 237–260.

46. Instructive in this context are, inter alia, Schmalz, *Descartes on Causation*, 197–208; Peter A. Schouls, *Descartes and Enlightenment* (Kingston: McGill, 1989), 77–99; and Dorottya Kaposi, "Indifférence et liberté humaine chez Descartes," in *Revue de Métaphysique et de Morale* 1, no. 41 (2004): 73–99.

47. Karl Löwith correctly remarks that "Sartre . . . cannot recognize this debasement of freedom of choice to the lowest degree of freedom." See Karl Löwith, *Gott, Mensch und Welt in der Metaphysik von Descartes bis zu Nietzsche* (Göttingen: Vandenhoeck und Ruprecht, 1967), 63.

48. This also means that it is irrelevant for this critique of freedom if we understand freedom as a kind of meta-capacity of all capacities or if freedom describes the manner and mode in which human beings realize all their capacities. Since, first, Descartes only deals with judgments and actions that are supposed to be called free, and this means, second, that the critique of putting the reality of the possibility of freedom before its realization holds for both understandings—for

freedom as meta-capacity and for freedom as mode of realization of all capacities—as both take freedom to be already real before the realization of freedom. One may therefore be doubtful as to whether this distinction (meta-capacity or mode) has any explanatory value at all. It is also important to remark at this point that to read indifference in terms of indecision is not only one possible interpretation, but can be found directly in Descartes's text itself.

49. Here one can again see an argument that later Hegel will expound in his *Phenomenology of Spirit*.

50. DMFP, 40.

51. "Indifference cripples free agency and condemns the ego to inaction" (Anne Ashley Davenport, *Descartes's Theory of Action* [Leiden: Brill, 2007], 209).

52. This reconstruction makes it possible to give an answer to Sartre's irritation, since the doubt is for Sartre, and justifiably so, a paradigm of the Cartesian concept of freedom. However, Sartre conflates doubt with the possibility of abstaining from judgment and thus with indecision. See SCF.

53. DMFP, 106. Even if things are not clear, the taking and disciplined pursuing of a decision marks a higher grade of freedom than their absence. On this (despite some ambiguities) see Anthony Kenny, "Descartes on the Will," in *Descartes. Oxford Readings in Philosophy*, ed. John Cottingham (Oxford: Oxford University Press 1998), 132–159.

54. It is important to remark that Descartes claims that theoretical indifference must lead to abstention from judgment. The argument, as described by Casey Perin, goes as follows: "Suppose I consider a proposition p and I cannot discern any reason to believe either p or its negation. In this case my will is 'indifferent' (*indifferens*)—I feel no inclination to assent either to p or to its negation. Descartes claims that if by an exercise of will I were to assent either to p or to its negation, I would be at fault. For even if my resulting belief is true, it is true only by accident. More importantly, I have given my assent to a proposition whose truth I did not clearly and distinctly perceive: in Descartes's language, the determination of my will has preceded the perception of my intellect" (Casey Perin, "Descartes and the Legacy of Ancient Skepticism," in: *A Companion to Descartes*, ed. Janet Broughton and John Carriero (Malden: Wiley 2008), 63. In such cases it is therefore theoretically necessary to decide that one cannot decide. But this means that one overcomes indecision. Practically, this must take the form that one takes the absence of good reasons as reason for practical decision.

55. Descartes writes to Mersenne that in a certain sense the whole *Discourse on the Method* is not, as he suggested, to be understood as following in the steps of Francis Bacon, but as practical—in the strong sense—and thus not first and foremost as a theoretical work. This means that what is at stake is what form of practice is necessary in everyday life but also in other practical concerns if or as long as there is theoretical indifference. Descartes: "However, I have not been able to understand your objection to the title; for I have not put *Treatise on the Method* but *Discourse on the Method*, which means *Preface or Notice on the Method*, in order to show that I

do not intend to teach the method but only to discuss it. As can be seen from what I say, it is concerned more with practice than with theory. I call the following treatises *Essays in This Method* because I claim that what they contain could never have been discovered without it, so that they show how much it is worth. I have also inserted a certain amount of metaphysics, physics and medicine in the opening Discourse in order to show that my method extends to topics of all kinds" (René Descartes, "Letters," in *The Philosophical Writings of Descartes III: The Correspondence*, trans. John Cottingham, Robert Stoothoff, Dugald Murdoch, and Anthony Kenny [Cambridge: Cambridge University Press, 1991], 53).

56. DMFP, 40.

57. The stoic-cynic determination of the *adiaphora* is obviously more complex than what I reconstruct here for the present systematic purposes. One can find already in this tradition multiple interpretations of this very term, whose multiplicity resonates in the so-called "Adiaphoristic disputes" that took place in the course of the Reformation (in 1548 to 1560). For some orientation in these complexities, see Johannes Gottschick, "Adiaphora," in *Realencyklopädie für protestantische Theologie und Kirche*, ed. Albert Lauck, vol. 1 (Leipzig: Hauck, 1896), 168–179, and Georg Teichweier, "Adiaphorenstreit," in *Lexikon für Theologie und Kirche*, ed. Josef Höler and Karl Rahner, vol. 1 (Freiburg: Herder, 1957), 145–147.

58. A slightly too one-sided reconstruction of this tradition can be found in Manfred Geier, *Das Glück der Gleichgültigen: Von der stoischen Seelenruhe zur postmodernen Indifferenz* (Hamburg: Rowohlt, 1997). See also Nicholas P. White, "Stoic Values," *The Monist* 73, no. 1 (1990): 42–58.

59. Potentiality means, as indicated, the potentiality of a potential relation to a potential object. I abbreviate this formula when I just refer to potentiality as I did above, but the whole formula should be thought of while reading.

60. DMFP, 40f.

61. In accordance with this idea, Descartes already remarked in his early writing in 1628/29: "If, therefore, someone seriously wishes to investigate the truth of things . . . [h]e should . . . consider simply how to increase the natural light of his reason . . . in order that his intellect should show his will what decision it ought to make in each of life's contingencies" (René Descartes, *Rules for the Direction of the Mind*, in: *The Philosophical Writings of René Descartes*, vol. 1 [Cambridge: Cambridge University Press, 1985], 10).

62. DMFP, 41.

63. This is the structure of what psychoanalysis calls fetishistic disavowal: "I know very well" (that I do not know anything), "but nevertheless" I decide. This is the structure of the will that Descartes discusses.

64. One must add here that this is consistent with Descartes's insistence that the will out of itself cannot generate any error. To will whatever suspends even the distinction of true and false. But if this distinction is suspended—if the will overrides the intellect—this not only generates error, but it also always already relies on the error to assume that the will can defy this distinction at all.

65. As Descartes will later note: "[W]e know that we can withhold our assent when we wish. But if someone's will is indifferent—evenly balanced—between good and evil, that is a fault in it, because it ought to seek the good alone without the 'balance' that is appropriate in non-moral matters" (DCB, 11).

66. This obviously means that the error is ultimately grounded in a failure to recognize error. The whole Cartesian project (of the *Discourse* and the *Meditations*) begins from this point.

67. Here, one might remark that *formally* we still seem to be dealing with decisions, even as this is no longer *materially the* case. For this, see Wee, *Material Falsity.*

68. It is possible to take this to be a definition not of decision but of mere opinion. In this sense such a definition stands at the ground of all relativism. In another direction, see the concept of indifference in Lilli Alanen, "The Metaphysics of Error and Will," in *Klassiker Auslegen: René Descartes, Meditationen über die erste Philosophie*, ed. Andreas Kemmerling (Berlin: Akademie Verlag, 2009), 81–100.

69. Because he conceives of freedom as actualized in a decision for or against X and non-X, Descartes mobilizes that which in a different language is called classicism. For classicism, the principle of the excluded middle and the principle of contradiction holds. This is to say that there is only X and non-X, and one can only choose one of them. One can distinguish from this the intuitionistic logic for which only the principle of the excluded middle is valid, but not the principle of contradiction as well as one can distinguish from both the paraconsistent logic that suspends the principle of contradiction but holds to the principle of the excluded middle. I read Descartes here in such a way that his critique of indifference is a critique of a paraconsistent understanding of freedom and that he claims that the assumption that there could be an intuitionistic logic of freedom is a consequence of this mistake. For this distinction, see Ruda, *For Badiou*, 63–70, and Alain Badiou, "The Three Negations," *Cardozo Law Review* 29, no. 5 (2008): 1877–1883.

70. For these hold: "Free agency thus coincides in practice with the experience of an autonomous overcoming of indecision" (Davenport, *Descartes's Theory of Action*, 207). The emphasis with these decisions lies on practice.

71. DDM, 123. An instructive commentary of this passage is Pierre Macherey, "Marcher en forêt avec Descartes," http://philolarge.hypotheses.org/1720#more-1720.

72. As Descartes states in the *Discourse*: "For it seemed to me that much more truth could be found in the reasonings which a man makes concerning matters that concern him than in those which some scholar makes in his study about speculative matters. For the consequences of the former will soon punish the man if he judges wrongly, whereas the latter have no practical consequences and no importance for the scholar except that perhaps the further they are from common sense the more pride he will take in them, since he will have had to use so much more skill and ingenuity in trying to render them plausible" (DDM, 115). It should be clear that for Descartes truth is not a given, but something produced and generated (which in the last consequence even holds for God who for the first time in the history of philosophy becomes a God that produces truths). For this see, inter alia, Holz, *Descartes*, 50ff.

73. It is important to remark here that for Descartes hesitation is also instructive when things are not clear. But to remain in a state of hesitation easily becomes a practical problem.

74. For how Descartes brings together these decisions of the will against better knowledge with a "conservative and anti-enlightenment wish to persist in one's prejudice" see Johannes Haag, "Descartes über Willen und Willensfreiheit," in *Zeitschrift für philosophische Forschung*, ed. Otfried Höffe with Christoph Rapp, vol. 60 (Frankfurt am Main, 2006), 502. In what follows I will return to this anti-enlightenment tendency of the indifferent will.

75. One has to add here that deferring and hesitating non-decision is different from decided doubting—since the decision to doubt all decisions and judgments is and remains a decision.

76. DMFP, 38.

77. Ibid., 18.

78. Martin Heidegger, *Interpretation of Nietzsche's Second Untimely Meditation* (Bloomington: Indiana University Press, 2016), 213. I leave aside Heidegger's own reading of Descartes here, as I am solely interested in his reading of the concept of privation.

79. DDM, 145.

80. DMFP, 38.

81. Holz elaborates this as follows: "The principle of individuation is as such a principle of privation. Every individual is deprived of a part of the world-potency for it to be able to be within the boundaries of its finitude an individual. If there were no such limitation and everything would be the same and the world would be overall homogenous and indistinguishable" (Holz, *Descartes*, 117). This interpretation presupposes that one can read God's highest grade of reality at the same time as "omni-reality" (ibid., 116). The extent to which my own reading of the Cartesian notion of God differs from this account will in due course become apparent.

82. In this sense, indifference is the lowest degree of reality of freedom of a being that has a lower grade of reality than God. It is constitutively reductive.

83. DMFP, 38. Later one reads in the same meditation: "I have no cause for complaint on the grounds that the power . . . which God gave me is no greater than it is. . . . Indeed, I have reason to give thanks to him who has never owed me anything for the great bounty that he has shown me, rather than thinking myself deprived or robbed of any gifts he did not bestow" (ibid., 42).

84. Ibid., 41. In the background of this reference to free will does not stand the scholastic, previously criticized, understanding, but rather the doctrine of St. Augustine. It is crucial that Descartes is speaking of the use of the will. See Augustine, *On the Free Choice of the Will* (Cambridge: Cambridge University Press, 2010).

85. DMFP, 42.

86. DMFP, 39f. Descartes also speaks—for many interpreters confusingly—in his *Principles* about the fact "that there is nothing we can grasp more evidently or more perfectly" than our "freedom and indifference" (DPP, 206). Cf. Dan Kaufmann,

"Infimus gradus libertatis? Descartes on Indifference and Divine Freedom," *Religious Studies* 39, no. 4 (2003): 391–406. Accordingly, it cannot mean the freedom of choice between two equally valid concrete options, but it must mean another type of choice, namely the choice to determine what we think we mean by freedom. It is precisely in this respect that our freedom is like God's. We are not essentially like God because God creates even the conditions of this freedom, which for Descartes human beings cannot do. But we do create its conditions by creating the ways in which we understand it. One can articulate the difference between infinite-indeterminate freedom in God and infinite-indeterminate freedom in man as follows: God decides in an indifferent way and gives itself reasons which then become necessities. The human being is placed within the frame of this reason's having become necessary. She can only in a limited manner comprehend God's act because she cannot generate necessities herself but only understand them. In contrast, the animal neither knows reasons nor necessities but follows an automatism that appears to it as equally necessary and contingent. But it is important to also add that God's will can never be indifferent about itself. For this also see Andrew Gombray, *Descartes* (Malden: Blackwell, 2007), 127f. and CDD, 86ff.

87. DMFP, 40.

88. Ibid.

89. One can see here again that Descartes takes a counter-position to—at least the early—Sartre, inasmuch as the reduction of freedom to an absolute nothingness, to the lowest degree, is not freedom but rather a freedom that liberates itself of itself. That the counter-move to this absolute reduction is an absolute subtraction—one is the inversion of the other—I have argued in Ruda, *Abolishing Freedom*.

90. DMFP, 38.

91. DPP, 206.

92. Therefore Alexandre Kojève in view of Stoicism—which resonates with many features of the indifference discussed here—mentioned in his reconstruction of Hegel's *Phenomenology of Spirit* the following: "The Stoic ideology was invented to justify the Slave's inaction, his refusal to *fight* to *realize* his libertarian ideals. Thus the ideology prevents Man from acting: it obliges him to be content with *talking*. Now, says Hegel, all discourse that remains discourse ends in *boring* Man" (Alexandre Kojève, *Introduction to the Reading of Hegel: Lectures on the* Phenomenology of Spirit [Ithaca, NY: Cornell University Press, 1969], 53). In this respect, already, Descartes' treatment of the problem of indifference shows that we are here dealing with a problem of ideology.

93. DDM, 123.

94. One can see here how Descartes falls on the side of those who with an expression of Systems Theory one might classify as "traditionally European [*alteuropäisch*]." A different concept of indifference, inspired by Luhmann, is developed in Frithard Scholz, *Freiheit als Indifferenz: Alteuropäische Probleme mit der Systemtheorie Niklas Luhmanns* (Frankfurt am Main: Suhrkamp, 1982). Yet I do indeed try to defend a certain classically European tradition, namely rationalism.

95. Jürgen Habermas, "Ein Pakt für oder gegen Europa?" Lecture on April 6, 2011, http://www.ecfr.eu/page/-/Habermas%20PDF.pdf, 8 (04/2017).

96. This famous formula is found in Louis Althusser, "Ideology and Ideological State Apparatuses," in *On the Reproduction of Capitalism: Ideology and Ideological State Apparatuses* (London: Verso, 2014), 232–272.

97. Antonio Negri interprets Descartes as a philosophical impresario of the ideology of the bourgeois class in formation and then in crisis in a historical-materialist reading. My reading points in the opposite direction. Negri rightly sees that Descartes's project necessarily reflects that "the force of freedom has been hobbled by the aporiae of historically realized freedom" (NP, 144), but he does not see that the historical realization is grounded in a conceptual problem, that is, in a problematic *concept* of freedom and not only in its historically specific realization.

98. DDM, 115.

99. DMFP, 16.

100. Ibid., 15.

101. Descartes's famous formulation is of course: "As I think about this more carefully, I see plainly that there are never any sure signs by means of which being awake can be distinguished from being asleep" (DMFP, 13).

102. Premodern in the sense of the history of philosophy.

103. DDM, 117.

104. DDM, 118.

105. Again, this is a functional analogy, but the body as such is *not* the reason and ground for our errors.

106. This thesis cannot be found explicitly in Descartes. But I do want to argue that it is a consistent consequence of his determination of indifference. In the subsequent chapters this thesis will gain a clearer contour that—I do insist on that—is systematically invested in Descartes.

107. One must clarify here that Descartes assumes human beings can never lose their freedom entirely (as it is their substance), but they can be externally so determined that they make a bad use of it, such a bad use that the elaborated consequences occur.

108. DMFP, 16 (translation altered).

109. But Descartes himself feared that doubt might potentially lead to produce indecision and hesitation everywhere. Cf. CDD, pp. 129–131.

110. Some centuries later, psychoanalysis will rephrase this traversal in terms of "working through" (or as "traversal through the fundamental phantasy") and, under the condition that it works, identify it with the end of analysis. One can say that when the analysis of the phantasy of the givenness of freedom as capacity arrives at its end, this will be the positive concept of freedom. See Sigmund Freud, "Remembering, Repeating, Working Through (Further Recommendations on the Technique of Psycho-Analysis II)," in *SEP*, vol. 12 (New York: Norton, 1963), 145–156. The whole question, then, is whether this end can ever exist and which kind of positive determination can be ascribed to the concept of freedom afterward. For this

question, cf. Ruda, *Abolishing Freedom*, which presents the end of the analysis of problematic conceptions of freedom.

111. DMFP, 15.

112. Descartes's answer—and also that of other post-Cartesian thinkers—will lie in suggesting the self-limitation of the will through the intellect or through reason. Because the will "is not restricted in any way" (DMFP, 39) it is incumbent upon me to set the boundaries by determining it—that is to decide only according to the first and second type of decisions. "[F]or if, whenever I have to make a judgment, I restrain my will so that it extends to what the intellect clearly and distinctly reveals, and no further, then it is quite impossible for me to go wrong" (DMFP, 62). A will without judgments is wrong and it always goes wrong, which is why there must be a will, a freedom within the boundaries of the intellect: Intellect and thought precede the will—this is Descartes's maxim against error.

113. DMFP, 15.

114. HOAD, 41.

2. Kant and the Fall into Natural Necessity

1. KCPR, 99, Avii.

2. Ibid.

3. As Adorno rightly remarks: "For that is precisely what children do when they reply, Yes, but . . . , to every explanation you give, and when they find that they cannot stop asking questions because they do not understand the matter in hand, but instead just keep on asking questions mechanically" (Theodor W. Adorno, *Kant's* Critique of Pure Reason (1959), ed. Rolf Tiedemann, trans. Rodney Livingstone [Stanford, CA: Stanford University Press, 2001], 16).

4. KCPR, 99, Avii, viii.

5. Kant famously calls these "God, freedom, and immortality" (ibid., 139, B7, A3).

6. Ibid., 99, Avii, viii.

7. Ibid.

8. Ibid.

9. An analogous—though at first seemingly different—description of *social* situations is found in Ernesto Laclau and Chantal Mouffe, *Hegemony and Socialist Strategy. Towards a Radical Democratic Politics* (New York: Verso, 1985).

10. A helpful contextualization is found in Rüdiger Bubner, "Metaphysik und Erfahrung," in *Antike Themen und ihre moderne Verwandlung* (Frankfurt am Main, Suhrkamp, 1992), 134–150.

11. Kant takes up the distinction of dogmatists and skeptics (about which I speak in the following) from Wolff. However, Wolff had maintained that all philosophy is either dogmatic or skeptical, either constantly assuming the nature of things or doubting it. A short and helpful presentation of this connection is found in Arsenij Gulyga, *Immanuel Kant: Eine Biographie* (Frankfurt am Main: Suhrkamp, 2004), 117f.

12. KCPR, 117, Bxxx.

13. KAP, 426. Here and in the following, I use Kant's own abbreviated and avowedly political definition as an interpretive foil for the passage under discussion from the *Critique of Pure Reason*.

14. KCPR, 99, Ax.

15. Ibid., 109–110, Bxv.

16. KAP, 426.

17. KCPR, 99, Ax.

18. KAP, 426.

19. KCPR, 109, Bxv. Ferdinand Alquié rightfully remarked that Kant is not concerned with pitting himself against metaphysics, but, on the contrary, "he wants to explain his [metaphysical—F.R.] failure and found his enterprise upon new foundations drawn from the study of reason itself" (Ferdinand Alquié, *La critique kantienne de la métaphysique* [Paris: PUF 1968], 8).

20. As he later remarks, any use of metaphysics "without critique" is dogmatic and "leads to assertions, to which one can oppose equally plausible ones, thus to skepticism" (KCPR, 148, B23–24).

21. Ibid., 99–100, Ax.

22. Ibid.

23. This requires, as Kant says later, "an entirely different birth certificate" (ibid., 221, B119–120, A87).

24. Ibid., 100, Ax.

25. Ibid.

26. Hannah Arendt, *Lectures on Kant's Political Philosophy*, ed. Ronald Beiner (Chicago: University of Chicago Press, 1992), 33.

27. An indication of a link between Kant and Buridan can be found, inter alia, in Thomas Sturm, "Eine Frage des Charakters," in *Kant und die Berliner Aufklärung: Akten des IX. Internationalen Kant-Kongresses, Band IV: Sektionen XI–XIV*, ed. Volker Gerhardt, Rolf-Peter Horstmann, and Ralph Schumacher (Berlin: De Gruyter, 2001), 440–449.

28. KGMM, 59.

29. KCPR, 100, Ax.

30. Therefore, Paul Guyer's account of indifferentism in Kant is too reductive when he writes: "[I]ndifferentism is simply the indifference to philosophical questions that the spectacle of unending dogmatic conflicts can all too easily produce." For Kant, however, indifferentism is at the same time a peculiar progress that hinders itself. See Paul Guyer, *Kant* (London: Routledge, 2006), 9.

31. Immanuel Kant, *Prolegomena to Any Future Metaphysics*, trans. and ed. Gary Hatfield (Cambridge: Cambridge University Press, 2004), 10.

32. Part of the problem is that the previous dogmatic positions never posed the critical question as to "*[h]ow . . . metaphysics as a natural predisposition*" of reason is possible (KCPR, 147, B21–22). Furthermore, "It is already a great and necessary proof of cleverness or insight to know what one should reasonably ask" (ibid., 197, B82–83).

33. Ibid., 100, Ax.

34. Ibid., 100–101, Axi.

35. Ibid., 100, Axii (translation modified).

36. Ibid., 100, Ax–xi.

37. I understand impossibility here in the same way that the early Kant does: "For everything which contradicts itself, that is to say, everything which is thought of as simultaneously being and not being, is called impossible" (Immanuel Kant, "A New Elucidation of the First Principles of Metaphysical Cognition," in *Immanuel Kant. Theoretical Philosophy, 1755–1770*, trans. and ed. David Walford [Cambridge: Cambridge University Press, 1992], 10). Frederick Beiser rightly remarked that "[t]he *Kritik der reinen Vernunft* was born into an indifferent world" (Frederick C. Beiser, *The Fate of Reason. German Philosophy from Kant to Fichte* [Cambridge, MA: Harvard University Press, 1987], 172).

38. KCPR, 113, Bxxii–xxiii.

39. Kant speaks of indifference somewhat less honorably in his later *Lectures on Logic*: "As for what concerns metaphysics, however, it seems as if we had been stopped short in the investigation of metaphysical truths. A kind of *indifferentism* toward this science now appears, since it seems to be taken as an honour to speak of metaphysical investigations contemptuously as mere *caviling*. And yet metaphysics is the real, true philosophy!" (*Immanuel Kant's Logik: Ein Handbuch zu Vorlesungen (A A IX)*, ed. Gottlob Benjamin Jäsche (Königsberg: Nicolovius, 1800), 544).

40. That Kant can arrive at impossibly practical indifference from impossibly theoretical indifference is related to the claim that "theoretical reason cannot be indifferent to practical reason" (Sebastian Gardner, "The Primacy of Practical Reason," in *A Companion to Kant*, ed. Graham Bird [Malden, MA: Wiley Blackwell, 2006], 266).

41. KCPR, 689–690, B858 A830.

42. KRBR, 58.

43. Immanuel Kant, "Idea for a Universal History with a Cosmopolitan Aim," in *Immanuel Kant. Anthropology, History, and Education*, trans. Allen W. Wood (Cambridge: Cambridge University Press, 2007), 117.

44. Immanuel Kant, "Universal Natural History and Theory of the Heavens or Essay on the Constitution and Mechanical Origin of the Whole Universe according to Newtonian Principles," in *The Cambridge Edition of the Works of Immanuel Kant in Translation: Natural Science*, trans. Olaf Reinhardt (Cambridge: Cambridge University Press, 2012), 297.

45. KCPrR, 189.

46. Immanuel Kant, "Conjectural Beginning of Human History," in *The Cambridge Edition of the Works of Immanuel Kant in Translation: Anthropology, History, and Education*, trans. Allen W. Wood (Cambridge: Cambridge University Press, 2007), 168–169. Kant specifies that, furthermore, human history begins with both a transformation of the natural drives (the drives of nourishment and sexual drives) as well as with an insertion into a perspective of the future.

47. KRBR, 57.

48. A helpful interpretation of the *Religion Essay* is found in Peter Fenves, *Late Kant: Towards Another Law of the Earth* (London, Routledge, 2003), 75–91.

49. KRBR, 69.

50. Ibid., 70.

51. Ibid.

52. Ibid.

53. Ibid., 71 (translation modified).

54. Ibid

55. Ibid., 73.

56. Ibid., 71 (translation modified).

57. Carl Christian Erhard Schmid will later write: "If any freedom of human beings ought to be, then it must be *everywhere*. It may never be entirely excluded where human life appears" (SAWH, 224). That freedom must be with human beings everywhere in order to be in general must mean, in a profoundly Kantian manner, that what appears to the human being as his (intelligible) nature (of character) must contain freedom.

58. See the informative commentary in Alenka Zupančič, *Ethics of the Real: Kant and Lacan* (London: Verso, 2000), 35ff.

59. KRBR, 71.

60. Ibid., 85 (translation modified). Kant also describes this such that he speaks of an acquired disposition but "it has not . . . been earned in time"—an acquisition that exists before any time and that one refers to as "natural" because one "cannot derive this disposition from . . . a first act of the power of choice in time" (ibid., 74).

61. Ibid., 71.

62. The following is helpful for the concept of disjunctive judgment: Rudolf Eisler, *Kant-Lexicon. Nachschlagwerk zu Kants sämtlichen Schriften, Briefen und handschriftlichem Nachlaß* (Hildesheim: Olms, 2002), 97f.

63. *Kant-Lexikon*, vol. 3, ed. Marcus Willaschek, Jürgen Stolzenberg, Georg Mohr, and Stefano Bacin (Berlin: D *Companion to Kant* e Gruyter, 2015), 432.

64. KRBR, 71.

65. Ibid., 71–72.

66. SAWH, 253.

67. KRBR, 72.

68. Christoph Coelestin Mrongovius, *Philosophische Abhandlung über Religion und Moral stammend von Immanuel Kant und in die polnische Sprache übersetzt von Christoph Coelestin Mrongovius*, ed. Mirosław Żelazny and Werner Stark (Twarda: Wydawnictwo Naukowe Uniwersytetu Mikołaja Kopernika, 2006), 301.

69. In another remark to the remark under discussion here, Kant tries to show that one must think about a necessary collision of opposed, viz., good and evil, yet equally strong incentives in order to produce a null point and that one cannot assume that there is a fundamental neutrality. As far as the problem of the fundamental nullification is concerned, these reflections do not offer a real solution. See KRBR, 72.

70. Cf. Elisabeth de Fontenay, *Le silence des bêtes. La philosophie à l'epreuve de l'animalité*, 517–526. As Kant remarks at another point in the *Critique of Pure Reason*: "A faculty of choice, that is, is merely *animal* (*arbitrium brutum*) which cannot be determined other than through sensible impulses, i.e., *pathologically*" (KCPR, 675, B831).

71. KAP, 316 (translation modified).

72. Ibid., 317.

73. Ibid.

74. Therefore, Kant also maintains that such an "action" can no longer be attributed to the "subject" of it. "The consequences are not attributed to a deed that is morally indifferent" (Immanuel Kant, *Reflexionen zur Moralphilosophie*, in *Werke*, vol. 19: *Handschriftlicher Nachlaß: Moralphilosophie, Rechtsphilosophie und Religionsphilosophie* [Berlin: De Gruyter, 1934], 159).

75. At least in this case it is thinkable *ex negativo* as that which must be avoided in every respect. Precisely thereby, however, Kant simultaneously goes through the consequences of the case that must be avoided so far as possible. Indifference thus marks the (already transcended) boundary of human practice.

76. Kant famously thinks that animals have no soul, do not think, and are not free, and then human beings, precisely for this reason, have no moral obligations toward them.

77. KRA, 258.

78. Kant himself approaches the concept of regression and reduction when he writes that the human being acts either "according to instinct [*sic*] or principles." "If he acts according to instinct, then he is reduced to animality." Cited in Heiner F. Klemme, "Kants Erörterung der 'libertas indifferentiae' in der Metaphysik der Sitten und ihre philosophische Bedeutung," in *Internationales Jahrbuch des Deutschen Idealismus/International Yearbook of German Idealism* 9 (2011): 29.

79. KRBR, 72.

80. KCPrR, 165.

81. KAP, 355.

82. Ibid.

83. Ibid., 356. Kant says shortly beforehand: "*Whoever* is usually seized by affect like a fit of madness, no matter how benign these emotions might be, nevertheless resembles a deranged person" (ibid., 355).

84. Ibid., 367 (translation modified).

85. Ibid., 368. In this passage Kant makes it clear that only the passionate pursuit of virtue is formally evil because for Kant it is characteristic of virtuous action to have control of oneself.

86. Immanuel Kant, "The Metaphysics of Morals," in *The Cambridge Edition of the Works of Immanuel Kant in Translation: Practical Philosophy*, trans. Mary Gregor (Cambridge: Cambridge University Press, 1996), 536 (translation modified).

87. Ibid.

88. Ibid., 536.

89. See also Gérard Lebrun, *Kant et la fin de la métaphysique* (Paris: Le livre de poche, 1970), 316ff.

90. Kant, "Metaphysics of Morals," 536.

91. Therefore, as Kant wrote in a letter to Plessing in 1784, "he who is indifferent toward his honour deserves all contempt" (Immanuel Kant, "Brief an Friedrich Victor Leberecht Plessing [3. April, 1784]," in *Gesammelte Schriften, Bd. 10: Briefwechsel*, Bd. 1, [Berlin: De Gruyter, 1922], 383).

92. KRA, 258.

93. Ibid., 257.

94. Ibid., 96.

95. Immanuel Kant, *Entwürfe zu dem Colleg—über Anthropologie aus den 70er und 80er Jahren*, in *Gesammelte Schriften, Bd. 15*: Handschriftlicher Nachlaß: Anthropologie (Berlin: De Gruyter, 1923), 729.

96. Ibid.

97. Immanuel Kant, *Zweiter Anhang: Medicin*, in *Gesammelte Schriften*, Bd. 15: Handschriftlicher Nachlaß: Anthropologie (Berlin: De Gruyter, 1923), 952

98. KRA, 259.

99. Kant, *Entwürfe zu dem Colleg*, 746.

100. KRA, 259.

101. HSL, 81.

102. Insofar as philosophy for Kant begins with Kant, as shown in Förster, *The Twenty-Five Years of Philosophy. A Systematic Reconstruction* (Cambridge, MA: Harvard University Press, 2017).

103. KRBR, 72.

104. "Criticism is not opposed to the *dogmatic procedure* of reason in its pure cognition as science (for science must always be dogmatic, i.e., it must prove its conclusions strictly *a priori* from secure principles); rather, it is opposed only to *dogmatism*, i.e., to the presumption of getting on solely with pure cognition from (philosophical) concepts. . . . Dogmatism is therefore the dogmatic procedure of pure reason, *without an antecedent critique of its own capacity*" (KCPR, 119, Bxxxv).

105. For the concept of rigorism see Robert Pippin, "Rigorism and the 'New Kant,'" in *Kant und die Berliner Aufklärung* (Berlin: De Gruyter, 2001), 43–58.

106. Henry E. Allison, "On the Very Idea of a Propensity to Evil," in *Essays on Kant*, (Oxford: Oxford University Press, 2012), 100.

107. As to why indifference stands in antagonism to a strict form of thinking, Kant already established in the *Critique of Pure Reason* at one point as follows: "But if a human being could renounce all interests, and, indifferent to all consequences, consider the assertions of reason merely according to their grounds, then, supposing that he knows no way of escaping from the dilemma except by confessing allegiance to one or the other of the conflicting doctrines, such a person would be in a state of ceaseless vacillation. Today it would strike him as convincing that the human will is *free*; tomorrow . . . he would side with the view that freedom is nothing but self-deception, and that everything is mere *nature*" (KCPR, 503, A475/B503).

108. Informative here is Pierre Jurieu, *La religion du latitudinaire, avec l'apologie pour la Saint Trinité, appellée l'héresie des trois Dieux* (Rotterdam, 1696).

109. Kuno Fischer, *Das Vernunftsystem auf der Grundlage der Vernunftkritik* (Paderborn: Salzwasser Verlag, 2013), 294.

110. KCPR, 100, Ax.

111. These positions from Kant are cited in *Kant Lexicon*, 2765.

112. Immanuel Kant, *Vorlesung zur Moralphilosophie*, ed. Werner Stark (Berlin, 2004), 109f.

113. KGMM, 76.

114. Mrongovius, *Philosophische Abhandlung über Religion und Moral stammend von Immanuel Kant*, 287.

115. Ibid.

116. One can go so far here as to speak of a total and not merely partial error, because it emerges from a "thoroughgoing conflict against the laws of the understanding and reason" (Jäsche, *Immanuel Kants Logik*, 78).

117. Allen W. Wood claims that Kant took up this characterization from J. F. Stapler, *Institutiones theologiae polemicae universae, ordine scientifico dispositae*, 5 vols. (Zürich, 1743–1747). Cf. Allen W. Wood, "Notes to Religion within the Boundaries of Mere Reason," in *Immanuel Kant: Religion and Rational Theology* (Cambridge: Cambridge University Press, 1996), 458.

118. Immanuel Kant, *The Conflict of the Faculties*, in *Immanuel Kant: Religion and Rational Theology*, trans. Mary J. Gregor and Robert Anchor (Cambridge: Cambridge University Press, 1996), 274.

119. At least it is shown here that the indifferent within philosophy, the indifferentists and syncretists, have a certain similarity with the definition which Plato had already given of the sophists. It would be instructive to pursue the interrelationship between indifference and sophism, but this would exceed the scope of this book—for one would have to investigate not only how exactly the problematic of indifference in Descartes, connected with the demands of modern philosophy, are related to the category of adiaphora, but also how the fundamental interrelationship between philosophy and sophistry is related to the self-understanding of philosophy in general. This cannot be accomplished here. (Especially informative for this are the reflections on the syncretic Platonism of Albinus and others in A. H. Armstrong, *The Cambridge History of Later Greek and Early Medieval Philosophy* [Cambridge: Cambridge University Press, 1967], 64ff., 142, 621). Hence, proceeding from the previously explained, it will only be briefly remarked here that one can assert: Indifferentists and syncretists are for Kant modern sophists. Also see SAWH, 549ff.

120. KCPrR, 158.

121. Jäsche, *Immanuel Kants Logik*, 562.

122. Kant, *Entwürfe zu dem Colleg*, 761, 765.

123. KCPrR, 158.

124. Theodor W. Adorno, "Theorie der Halbbildung" (1959), in *Gesammelte Schriften*, vol. 8, ed. Rolf Tiedemann (Frankfurt am Main: Suhrkamp, 1997), 93–121.

125. SAWH, 4.

126. Ibid., 5.

127. Ibid., 6.

128. Ibid., 10.

129. Ibid., 11.

130. Ibid., 12.

131. Schmid uses indifference and *adiaphora* as synonyms throughout.

132. Schmid refers here to both Heraclitus and Anaxagoras as well as Cicero and Voltaire. See ibid., 20ff.

133. Ibid., 39.

134. Ibid., 41. Italics here, and for quotations from Schmid throughout, are as in original. F.R. and Tr.

135. Ibid., 62.

136. Ibid., 87.

137. "[T]he entirety of nature and every part of it" is "to be viewed as—ethical and ascetic—adiaphoron" (ibid., 121).

138. Ibid., 97. To reduce morality to externality, according to the conceptual relation here, or to will to derive morality from it would abolish morality, since it would no longer be related to the free will. Cf. ibid., 115, 16off.

139. Ibid., 98. This thought is explicitly oriented against any form of eudaimonic ethics, as it implies, rather, that, although the human being cannot think God, God is not indifferent toward him, but rather God is absolutely decisive for morality. Cf. ibid., 105.

140. Ibid.

141. Ibid., 118.

142. Ibid., 133.

143. Ibid., 134.

144. Therefore, Schmid can conclude with the following: "If I am a slave of sensibility, then I am not this through the guilt of nature but solely through my guilt" (ibid., 156). Likewise: "The human being, observed as merely a being of nature and separated from all freedom of the will, is what he does and what he has to do, thereby permitting what he can and may refrain from doing" (ibid., 174).

145. Ibid., 138.

146. Ibid., 141. "There is an immediate, ethical self-consciousness" (ibid., 150).

147. This concerns a form of proto-Hegelianism: We already have more (moral) consciousness than we are conscious of, i.e., it is necessary for us to clarify precisely what we already know without knowing it.

148. Cf. ibid., 148.

149. Ibid., 163.

150. Ibid., 157.

151. I will only indicate here that it would be revealing to relate this critical derivation to Kant's concept of "popular philosophy," which is still rarely investigated in the secondary literature—as far as I'm aware. Schmid sees therein

the tendency of a reduction of morality to nature, which is more or less advocated by Grotius, Pufendorf, Hobbes, and other similar theorists of natural right. Cf. ibid., 189ff. I will speak in the next chapter of a comparable category—that of unphilosophy—in Hegel.

152. On the basis of this relation between particular and universal claims, Schmid also maintains that all dogmatic metaphysicians, who advocate merely particular positions, ought "to assert a universal *adiaphorie* of all human actions" (ibid., 185).

153. Ibid., 179.

154. Ibid., 167.

155. Ibid., 205.

156. Ibid., 215.

157. Cf. ibid., 219, 242, 261, 301, 305.

158. In a peculiar anticipation of Heidegger, Schmid writes: "This holds for the annihilation of a human life no less than for the eating of an oyster" (ibid., 276).

159. Ibid., 226.

160. Ibid., 307.

161. Ibid., 315.

162. This is a thought I engage with in another context: Frank Ruda, *For Badiou. Idealism without Idealism* (Evanston, IL: Northwestern University Press, 2015), 132ff.

163. SAWH, 324.

164. I.e., every instance of action can only find application in one way. Cf. ibid., 326ff.

165. Cf. ibid., 338.

166. Ibid., 525.

167. KRA, 453.

168. As I will show in the final chapter, when discussing Marx, the latter will have something to say about this. At the same time, one should maintain here that this does not mean a form of appropriation in the sense given by Bacon and others.

3. Hegel, the Dead Disposition, and the Mortification of Freedom

1. See G. W. F. Hegel, "Habilitationsthesen," in *Werke* (Frankfurt am Main: Suhrkamp 1986), 2:533. See also G. W. F. Hegel, "Habilitation Theses," in *Miscellaneous Writings of G. W. F. Hegel*, ed. Jon Stewart (Evanston, IL: Northwestern University Press 2002), 171. All subsequent quotations of the theses can be found therein, even though I have altered some of the translations (F.R.). For the context also see also Wolfang Neuser, "Schelling und Hegels Habilitationsthesen," *Philosophia Naturalis* 23, no. 2 (1986): 288–292. Just a brief reminder: At that time in Jena the Magister was called doctor and Hegel received his master's degree at the monastery in Tübingen.

2. One must take into account that briefly before Hegel had composed his so-called *Differenzschrift*, in which he positioned—what Schelling called—the

indifference of subject and object against all problematic subjectivist mediation attempts (that is, against Fichte), which remained problematic because they contended—from behind—a precedence of the subject (and turned the mediation of subject and object into a subjective subject-object mediation). Later Hegel will also problematize Schelling's own solution (as an objective subject-object-mediation in indifference of both), for he commits in a certain sense the mirror-mistake of Fichte by defending a precedence of substance—and that is ultimately in Spinozist terms: of nature. This assumption has more of a point, though, because it does not claim to explain the objectivity of subject-object relations dogmatically. But it remains nonetheless problematic because it falls back into a questionable dogmatic metaphysics of substance that is supposed to be neither subjective nor objective but thereby becomes the ultimate—substantialist—ground. See HDFS. Hegel will then in the *Phenomenology*, at the latest, perform the break with Schelling's conception. Later in his life he writes: "The defect of Schelling's philosophy is that the point of indifference of the subjective and the objective is presupposed, not proved" (HLHP III, 263). A detailed account of the transition from Kant—via Fichte and Schelling—to Hegel that focuses on metaphysical subjectivism can be found in Frederick C. Beiser, *German Idealism. The Struggle against Subjectivism, 1781–1801* (Cambridge: Cambridge University Press, 2002). See also Robert B. Pippin, *The Persistence of Subjectivity: On the Kantian Aftermath* (Cambridge: Cambridge University Press, 2005), 37ff. A reading that emphasizes a different kind of continuity can be found in: ZLN, 132–240. I here start with the habilitation theses because, as I will try to show, one can decipher therein a new take on the structure of the Kantian problem of indifference.

3. At least Hegel was, as one can tell from his notes and excerpts, in agreement with Schmid's early essay on empirical psychology. See Martin Bondeli, *Der Kantianismus des jungen Hegel: Die Kant-Aneignung und Kant-Überwindung Hegels auf seinem Weg zum philosophischen System* (Hamburg: Meiner, 1997), 264ff.

4. Wolfgang Wieland, "Bemerkung zum Anfang von Hegels Logik," in *Seminar: Dialektik in der Philosophie Hegels*, ed. Rolf-Peter Horstmann (Frankfurt am Main: Suhrkamp, 1978), 196, and Stefan Schick, *Contradictio Est Regula Veri: Die Grundsätze des Denkens in der formalen, transzendentalen und spekulativen Logik* (Hamburg, 2010), 298–431.

5. One can read this thesis also as an anticipation of Hegel's shortly afterwards given determination of the *Phenomenology of Spirit* as "thoroughgoing skepticism" (HPS, 50).

6. For more on this, see Frank Ruda, *For Badiou: Idealism without Idealism* (Evanston, IL: Northwestern University Press, 2015).

7. This is a formula used by Alain Badiou in his seminar "Comment parvenir à proposer, en temps de désorientation mondiale, une orientation politique, en pensée et en actes, qui ne soit ni interne aux règles dominantes de ce temps, comme le sont les élections par exemple, ni réduite à des actions localisées de type [colère collective]. Une orientation en somme, dont la valeur soit stratégique" (15 May 2023).

8. Gillian Rose, *Hegel contra Sociology* (London: Verso, 1981), 67. This ultimately means that Kant does not only presuppose finitude as a given and derives from it the necessity of assuming the givenness of infinity, too. This also means that he takes their separation as a given, as abstract precondition.

9. More precisely, one could here also state that Hegel takes Kant at his word. Since Kant had rejected all prior attempts in metaphysics as pseudo-philosophical and assumed that only with the critical project a true philosophy as true metaphysics will begin. Hegel's point is that this beginning failed and therefore was not what Kant assumed it was. Hegel's position thus unfolds the truth of this failure.

10. Later Hegel will describe such a—Kantian—position as preconceptual. See G. W. F. Hegel, *Der "Vorbegriff" zur Wissenschaft der Logik in der Enzyklopädie von 1830*, ed. Alfred Denker, Annette Sell, and Holger Zaborowski (Munich, 2010), 26–62.

11. A few years later Hegel notes in this vein: "It is the spirit of Kantian philosophy to have a consciousness of this highest idea but to explicitly extirpate it [the idea]" (HRSP, 269).

12. G. W. F. Hegel, *Lectures on the Philosophy of Religion*, vol. I, Introduction and the *Concept of Religion* (Berkeley: University of California Press, 1984), 377.

13. Hegel will later show the extent to which the antinomies can be grounded upon the limitedness of our cognitive apparatus. The antinomies are not a symptom of the limitedness of our capacity of cognition, but rather the contradictions are constitutive of things-in-themselves.

14. Dieter Henrich, "Historische Voraussetzungen von Hegels System," in *Hegel im Kontext* (Frankfurt am Main: Suhrkamp, 1975), 69.

15. Kant is thus not formal(ist) enough for Hegel. A longer elaboration of this point can be found in Rebecca Comay and Frank Ruda, *The Dash—The Other Side of Absolute Knowing* (Cambridge, MA: MIT Press, 2018).

16. Later Hegel will articulate the critique of Spinoza (in which can be read a critique of Kant) as follows: "What is lacking . . . is the necessity of progression of the absolute to inessentiality; or again, missing are both the becoming of the identity and its determinations" (HSL, 474). This means that Spinoza (as well as Kant) ultimately introduces and postulates an "immediately *given*" (ibid.).

17. As Hegel will later articulate it, Kant had a "fear of the object" (HSL, 30). That is to say, Kant had a fear of thinking and, despite the critical examination of all the fundamental presuppositions of cognition, he preserved himself "from the fall from grace inherent in thinking" because he "lacked the courage to plunge into the fall from grace required by thinking and to follow through with his guilt until a resolution emerged" (G. W. F. Hegel, "Einleitung: Über das Wesen der philosophischen Kritik überhaupt und ihr Verhältnis zum gegenwärtigen Zustand der Philosophie insbesondere," in *Werke*, vol. 2 (Frankfurt am Main: Suhrkamp, 1986), 174.

18. Since "skepticism is more active. It does not remain in the world and disdain its differences, but actively rejects it" (Rose, *Hegel contra Sociology*, 161)—this even holds for the distinction of skepticism and dogmatism.

19. That Kant thus is an incomplete skeptic means also that he finitized the infinity of skeptical doubt, and this is the reason why he regressed to dogmatic metaphysics.

20. HRSP, 313.

21. Ibid., 314.

22. Ibid. Hegel claims in the very same passage that it is exactly the absence of success and acclamation that is a good sign.

23. HRSP, 314.

24. Ibid., 322f.

25. Hegel therefore writes that "[t]here are no better weapons against dogmatism on finite bases" than skeptical weapons (HRSP, 335).

26. That therefore also the meaning of dogmatism must be a different one should be clear. Since for Hegel "[d]ogmatism as a way of thinking, whether in ordinary knowing or in the study of philosophy is nothing else but the opinion that the True consists in a proposition that is a fixed result, or which is immediately known" (HPS, 23). This is the meaning dogmatism has to relinquish.

27. HRSP, 323.

28. One should not forget that the dialogue begins with a critique of Plato's doctrine of the ideas that is put forth by none other than Parmenides, which is then presented as if a series of theories of absolutely incompatible possible worlds. An ingenious reading of this dialogue can be found in Mladen Dolar, "In *Parmenidem Parvii Comentarii*," *HELIOS* 31, no. 1–2 (2004): 63–98.

29. HRSP, 323 (translation modified). It is important to recall at this point what Brady Bowman pointed out, namely that "Hegel himself routinely denies that the authentic skepticism of the ancients, which he takes as the only true and philosophically serious skepticism, is a form of doubt at all. . . . Ancient skepticism does not doubt, but is certain of untruth; it does not wander aimlessly about with thoughts that leave open the possibility that this or that might still be true; rather it proves untruth with certainty. . . . [I]t leaves nothing undecided, but is decidedness in an absolute way, perfectly finished." So for Hegel it does not concern a form of doubt from a secure distance or proceeding from a secure ground. Brady Bowman, *Hegel and the Metaphysics of Absolute Negativity* (Cambridge, Cambridge University Press, 2013), 130.

30. Not much later Hegel will determine the path that his *Phenomenology of Spirit* undertakes "as the pathway of doubt, or more precisely as the way of despair" (HPS, 49). One can see here again in early Hegel an anticipation of the *Phenomenology*. For a reflection on the redoubling of doubt and its twosome nature, see Comay and Ruda, *The Dash*.

31. HRSP, 324.

32. This is a circular self-founding movement that will become prominent in the twentieth century with Jacques Lacan's famous claim that the founding of psychoanalysis by a subject with an unconscious necessitates that one does an analysis of psychoanalysis itself. This immediately and obviously raises the question of how to do this (as there is not a ready-made doctrine of psychoanalysis to rely on).

33. HRSP, 325 (translation altered).

34. "Thoroughgoing skepticism is not a different skepticism, but a skepticism that goes all the way in carrying out its principle." And it is therefore "particularly qualified for providing a beginning to philosophy, because of its presuppositionlessness" (Tanja Staehler, "The Historicity of Philosophy and the Role of Skepticism," in *Hegel's History of Philosophy. New Interpretations*, ed. David A. Duquette (Albany: SUNY Press, 2003), 118.

35. HRSP, 331.

36. Ibid.

37. Ibid., 332 (translation altered).

38. Ibid., 333. This is what Hegel before marked as the positive side of indifference against the necessity of nature.

39. Ibid., 338.

40. Ibid., 337.

41. Ibid.

42. Ibid., 338.

43. HEL1, 141.

44. Tanja Stähler, *Die Unruhe des Anfangs: Hegel und Husserl über den Weg in die Phänomenologie* (Dordrecht: Kluwer Academic, 2003), 148.

45. Pierre Gabriel van Ghert, "Brief an Hegel (22. Juni 1810)," in *Briefe von und an Hegel*, vol. 1 (Hamburg: Meiner, 1969), 317.

46. HDFS, 89. Hegel contends that this need is formed "[w]hen the might of union vanishes from the life of men and the antitheses lose their living connection and reciprocity" (ibid., 91). The problem that emerges with the indifference toward philosophy and freedom is that there seems to be a peculiar might of union which seems to make this need impossible. For a reappraisal of the need of philosophy, see Alain Badiou, *Happiness* (London: Bloomsbury, 2017).

47. On the intricacies of liberation, see Christoph Menke, *Theorie der Befreiung* (Berlin: Suhrkamp, 2022).

48. It is important to remark here that this indifference concerns not only philosophy but also religion. This is why Hegel writes: "One could easily arrive at the view that a widespread, nearly universal indifference toward the doctrines of faith formerly regarded as essential has entered into the general religiousness of the public" (HLPHR I, 156). In indifference toward religion people start believing what they want. I will return to this point.

49. HEL1, 2.

50. HPS, 8

51. Fraud has for Hegel the structure of a positive-infinite judgment and posits the semblance of universality against the truly universal. Fraud is a pretense of universality. See Frank Ruda, *Hegel's Rabble: An Investigation into Hegel's Philosophy of Right* (London: Continuum, 2008), 152ff.

52. This is an implication of what one might call flirting with Lacanian terminology, Hegel's account of the (philosophical) discourse of the university.

53. G. W. F. Hegel, "Rede zum Schulabschlußjahr am 2. September 1811," in *Werke*, 4:344. Instructive for the context of this address: Gerhart Schmidt, *Hegel in Nürnberg: Untersuchungen zum Problem der philosophischen Propädeutik* (Tübingen: Niemeyer Max Verlag, 1960).

54. G. W. F. Hegel, "Brief an Niethammer (7. August 1810)," in *Briefe von und an Hegel*, 1:318.

55. HPS, 317.

56. HPR, 15.

57. Rebecca Comay has remarked that with regard to the business of philosophy there is a twofold danger for Hegel: "Either the work never gets started or the work gets finished all too soon. These are two sides of the same coin, which for Hegel stake out the outer limits of German Idealism—the evil twins, roughly speaking, of Kant and Schelling: the tepid waters of endless critical reflection versus the skyrockets of rapturous revelation; the bad infinite of interminable postponement versus the "bad finite" of instant gratification; delay versus haste" (Rebecca Comay, "Resistance and Repetition: Freud and Hegel," *Research in Phenomenology* 45, no. 2 [2015]: 260). Either all answers are always already given, or one never stops asking the same old question. Both are disappointing and fatiguing.

58. Part of this is that, for example, "the science of logic that makes up metaphysics proper and pure speculative philosophy has to date been much neglected," so one needs "a completely fresh start" (HSL, 9), for "since Aristotle," it "has not undergone change" (ibid., 31). Hegel thus radicalizes Kant, since the latter claimed that progress has not been made since Aristotle because Aristotle said it all, whereas the former sees in it an indication that therefore it is all the more urgently needed (and thus the Habilitations-theses already undertake this very project). Hegel's position contains, therefore, unavoidably a theory of philosophy's being conditioned by extra-philosophical practices (I use the term condition here in the sense of Alain Badiou; see Alain Badiou, *Conditions* (London: Bloomsbury, 2008)). For this see also Frank Ruda, "The Purlieu Letter: Toward a Hegelian Theory of Conditioning," *Problemi International* 58, no. 11–12 (2021): 179–199.

59. Jacques Lacan calls empty speech—of a patient during an analytic session—the kind of speech that constantly says more and more to ultimately say nothing at all. Hegel's punch line here is that this is the kind of discourse of philosophy at his own time. Lacan will draw several conclusions from this diagnosis, and one is to interrupt this speech in a surprising or arbitrary way (and thus develops the idea of flexible session length). Hegel will, as I have shown elsewhere, draw a slightly different conclusion from this, namely a fatalist one. Cf. Frank Ruda, *Abolishing Freedom: A Plea for a Contemporary Use of Fatalism* (Lincoln: University of Nebraska Press, 2016). Also see Jacques Lacan, "The Function and Field of Speech and Language in Psychoanalysis," in *Écrits: The First Complete English Edition* (New York: W. W. Norton, 2006). 97–269.

60. HPCR, 172.

61. HPR, 144.

62. HDFS, 85. Adorno will later emphasize a similar point in a negative manner and state that "[i]ndifference to freedom, to its concept and to the thing itself, is caused by the integration of society, which happens to the subjects as if it were irresistible" (Theodor Adorno, *Negative Dialectics* [London: Routledge, 1973], 216; translation altered).

63. I use the term "saturation" here in line with Sylvain Lazarus. See Sylvain Lazarus, *Anthropology of the Name* (London: Seagull Books, 2015).

64. One should here recall that already the *Critical Journal of Philosophy*, edited by Hegel and Schelling, aimed at establishing a unity of philosophy against all pseudo-philosophical tendencies. Which is why in it one can find very harsh critiques of their contemporaries. This is a trait that Hegel's thought will keep alive throughout.

65. G. W. F. Hegel, "Brief an von Altenstein (6. April 1822)," in *Briefe von und an Hegel*, 2:311.

66. G. W. F. Hegel, "Ankündigung des Journals," in *Werke*, 2:169.

67. One can here see how the freedom (of thought) that is supposed to be an essential part of any philosophical practice is reduced to the arbitrariness of opinions that one simply has; the move from freedom to arbitrariness is also a move into the muddy waters of the natural given capacity. In German "opinion" is "Meinung" and already the word itself that it indicates that what I believe to be true is mine (*mein*). Philosophy as opinion is a peculiar form of *mein-ing* (forgive the pun).

68. HLPHR, 291.

69. Hegel's point is here that any form of belief always implies a belief in belief, so that even the belief to not believe is still a form of belief.

70. G. W. F. Hegel, *Vorlesungen über die Philosophie der Religion II*, in *Werke*, 17:40.

71. HPR, 63.

72. HDFS, 99f.

73. Adorno writes in relation to a similar diagnosis: "The alliance of libertarian doctrine [*Freiheitslehre*] and repressive practice removes philosophy farther and farther from genuine insight into the freedom and unfreedom of the living. Anachronistically, it approximates that jejune edification that Hegel diagnosed as the affliction of philosophy" (Adorno, *Negative Dialectics*, 215).

74. Arsenij Gulyga, *Georg Wilhelm Friedrich Hegel* (Leipzig: Reclam, 1974), 104.

75. HPS, 319. Hegel also calls this a "world of perversion" and of alienated spirit. This will have consequences for the Marxian theory of alienation.

76. It is precisely, therefore, that Marx addresses capitalism as the last stage with which the prehistoric modes of production close. I will present a reading of the intricacies of prehistoric modes of production in another place in the near future.

77. I here note in passing that this comes close to what Hegel discusses as "mechanism" in his *Logic*. I will return to this point at the end of the next chapter. An instructive overview is provided by Nathan Ross, *On Mechanism in Hegel's Social and Political Philosophy* (London: Routledge, 2008).

78. Cf. Alain Badiou, *Logics of Worlds: Being and Event II* (London: Bloomsbury, 2018).

79. HSL, 717.

80. I derive this from the fact that Hegel's *Philosophy of Nature* begins with and in space. For a longer elaboration of Hegel's concept of nature, see Frank Ruda, "Hegel on the Rocks: Remarks on the Concept of Nature," in Slavoj Žižek, Frank Ruda, and Agon Hamza, *Reading Hegel* (Cambridge: Polity, 2022), 101–157.

81. Ludwig Siep, *Der Weg der "Phänomenologie des Geistes": Ein einführender Kommentar zu Hegels "Differenzschrift" und "Phänomenologie des Geistes"* (Frankfurt am Main: Suhrkamp, 2000), 253.

82. G. W. F. Hegel, *Philosophy of Mind* (Clarendon: Oxford University Press. 2010), 181.

83. It might not be overly accidental that a current hugely successful television series is *Succession*, which thematizes some of the intricacies of the necessity, yet impossibility of, succession.

84. Marx will not much later describe bourgeois society as one that creates an atomistic structure of the individuals as the form in which they are bound together in separation.

85. Cf. Peter Sloterdijk, *In the World Interior of Capital: Towards a Philosophical Theory of Globalization* (Malden: Polity, 2013).

86. Michael Baur, "From Kant's Highest Good to Hegel's Absolute Knowing," in *A Companion to Hegel*, ed. Stephen Houlgate and Michael Baur (Malden: Polity, 2011), 457.

87. Cf. Frank Ruda, "Wer denkt asozial? ? Von Aristoteles zu Hobbes," in *Das soziale Band*, ed. Thomas Bedorf and Steffen Hermann (Berlin: transcript, 2016), 143–163.

88. For this distinction see Martin Heidegger, *The Fundamental Concepts of Metaphysics: World, Finitude, Solitude* (Bloomington: Indiana University Press, 1995), 186–273.

89. HPS, 43.

90. Helmut Jendreieck, *Hegel und Jacob Grimm. Ein Beitrag zur Geschichte der Wissenschaftstheorie* (Lengerich: Erich Schmidt Verlag, 1975), 135.

91. HSL, 634.

92. Ibid.

93. For a critique of the contemporary position that goes under the same name see Peter Wolfendale, *Object-Oriented Philosophy: The Noumenon's New Clothes* (Falmouth: Urbanomic, 2014).

94. HPS, 6–7.

95. G. W. F. Hegel, *Vorlesungen über die Geschichte der Philosophie I*, in *Werke*, 18:71.

96. G. W. F. Hegel, *Vorlesungen über die Geschichte der Philosophie III*, in *Werke*, Vol. 20:162.

97. Vance Maxwell, "Affirmative Pathology: Spinoza and Hegel on Illness and Self-Repair," in: *Between Hegel and Spinoza: A Volume of Critical Essays*, ed. von Hasana Sharp and Jason E. Smith (London: Bloomsbury, 2012), 144.

98. HPR, 37.

99. Joachim Ritter, "Auseinandersetzung mit der kantischen Ethik," in: *Metaphysik und Politik: Studien zu Aristoteles und Hegel* (Frankfurt am Main: Suhrkamp, 1977), 305.

100. Hegel, G.W.F. *Vorlesungen über die Philosophie der Religion II*. In *Werke*, vol. 17 (Frankfurt am Main: Suhrkamp, 1986), 144.

101. Ibid., 546.

102. CMS, 105.

103. Alain Badiou, *Can Politics Be Thought?* (Durham, NC: Duke University Press, 2019).

104. Manfred Riedel, *System und Geschichte: Studien zum historischen Standort von Hegels Philosophie* (Frankfurt am Main, Suhrkamp, 1973), 115.

105. HPR, 150.

106. HSL, 479.

107. For an account of this dilemma, see Ruda, "The Purlieu Letter."

108. See Alain Badiou, *The True Life* (London: Polity, 2017).

109. Cf. HPR, 10: "[W]hen its talk is at its driest and most dead [*am totesten*], its favourite words are 'life' and 'enliven.'"

110. William Shakespeare, *The Life of Timon of Athens*, ed. John Jowett (Oxford: Oxford University Press, 2004), 1.14, pp. 392–393.

Conclusion: Toward Another Type of Indifference

1. In a certain respect, what Deleuze once said about Nietzsche also holds for modern philosophical rationalism, namely that "the whole of Nietzsche's philosophy remains abstract and barely comprehensible so long as we don't establish against whom it is directed" (Gilles Deleuze, *Nietzsche and Philosophy*, trans. Hugh Tomlinson [New York: Continuum, 1986], 8, translation modified).

2. G. W. F. Hegel, *Vorlesungen über die Ästhetik I*, in *Werke*, vol. 13, (Frankfurt am Main: Suhrkamp, 1986), 154.

3. Lacan will later argue that there would have to be an analysis of the psychoanalytic community—which leads to the difficulty that this community does not have a pregiven and normative ground, such as a normative ground offered by Freud's teaching. Hegel anticipates precisely this problem.

4. Even though the following thinkers do not seem to belong to a further development in the history of modern philosophical rationalism, they nonetheless maintain a rationality of freedom in different ways, which I take as a starting point for the following brief survey.

5. Søren Kierkegaard, "Fear and Trembling: Dialectical Lyric," in *Fear and Trembling/Repetition. Kierkegaard's Writings*, VI, ed. and trans. Howard V. Hong and Edna H. Hong, (Princeton, NJ: Princeton University Press, 1983), 27.

6. Ibid.

7. G. W. F. Hegel, *Lectures on the Philosophy of Religion*, vol. 1 (Berkeley: University of California Press, 1984),156.

8. Arthur Schopenhauer, "Prize Essay on the Freedom of the Will," in *The Two Fundamental Problems of Ethics*, trans. Christopher Janaway (Cambridge: Cambridge University Press, 2009), 47. Nietzsche will ascribe to this assumption of "believ[ing] in an indifferent subject with freedom of choice" typical of a certain "type of man" the inability to take responsibility for one's own decisions. Friedrich Nietzsche, *On the Genealogy of Morality*, trans. Carol Diethe, ed. Keith Ansell-Pearson (Cambridge: Cambridge University Press, 1997), 27.

9. Karl Marx, *Economic and Philosophical Manuscripts*, in *Early Writings* (London: Penguin Books, 1992), 290. The manuscripts have mainly become famous and influential for Marx's theory of alienation, and he is mostly read as an Aristotelian humanist or a humanist Aristotelian. I contend that it is, systematically, possible to unfold another reading, one that might actually bring Marx closer to Plato than to Aristotle. This comes to the fore when one recalls the theory of "reverse evolution" (Simondon), the first evolutionary theory ever formulated, which can be found in Plato's *Timaeus*. Plato argues that the animal is a logical offspring of man produced by degrading the human of certain of its capacities, for example of reason. The animal is what is produced by depriving man of some of his features. And the early Marx argues in a Platonic vein, but (1) without substantializing the features of the human, and (2) without attempting to give an account of the totality of nature, but rather focalizing on nature in capitalism (viz., a peculiar moment in and of history). Cf. Plato, *Timaeus*, in *Complete Works* (Indianapolis: Hackett, 1997), 1289–1291.

10. Alain Badiou, Frank Ruda, and Jan Völker, "Wir müssen das affirmative Begehren hüten," in Alain Badiou, *Dritter Entwurf eines Manifests für den Affirmationismus* (Berlin: Merve, 2009), 56.

11. The whole setting of Marx's argument resembles in many aspects what Hegel called a "spiritual animal kingdom." For this see HPS, 237–252.

12. I analyze this operation of reduction more thoroughly in Frank Ruda, "Marx in the Cave," in Slavoj Žižek, Frank Ruda, and Agon Hamza, *Reading Marx* (London: Polity, 2018), 62–100.

13. Badiou has also re-actualized this idea when he demonstrated that "[i]n order to validate the equation 'existence = individual = body,' contemporary *doxa* must valiantly reduce humanity to an overstretched vision of animality" (Alain Badiou, *Logics of Worlds* (London: Continuum, 2009), 2. This means that "Man, under the sway of the 'power of life', is an animal convinced that the law of the body harbours the secret of hope" (ibid.)

14. Marx, *Economic and Philosophical Manuscripts*, 276 (translation modified).

15. Ibid., 300. Marx calls this peculiar exchange the production of "absolute poverty."

16. Ibid., 308.

17. This might also be read as a version of an insight that one can also find in Karl Barth, namely that man is distinguished from other animals by the quality of

being able to adapt to whatever extreme situation. See Karl Barth, *Church Dogmatics*, vol. 3: *The Doctrine of Creation* (Edinburg: T. & T. Clark, 1960), 115.

18. Marx, *Economic and Philosophical Manuscripts*, 275.

19. Karl Marx, *Capital: A Critique of Political Economy* (London: Penguin Books, 1993), 135.

20. ZLN, 108.

21. Therefore, the later Marx can claim that when one analyzes money, "it is as if, alongside and external to lions, tigers, rabbits, and all other actual animals, which form when grouped together the various kinds, species, subspecies, families, etc. of the animal kingdom, there existed in addition to the animal, the individual incarnation of the entire animal kingdom" (Karl Marx, *Value: Studies* [London: New Park, 1976], 27).

22. This idea will lead Lenin, inter alia, to reject democracy as a form of government. Even though there is more freedom in democracy than in a monarchy or feudal structures, the problem still emerges in democracy that democratic freedom is simply held to be true and actual freedom—which because of its social and political organization, it is not in bourgeois societies.

23. HPS, 19.

24. All citations here are from Karl Marx and Friedrich Engels, *Manifesto of the Communist Party*, trans. Samuel Moore (Moscow: Progress Publishers, 1969), https://www.marxists.org/archive/marx/works/1848/communist-manifesto/ (translation modified).

25. Karl Marx, *A Contribution to the Critique of Political Economy*, trans. S. W. Ryazanskaya (Moscow: Progress Publishers, 1977), https://www.marxists.org/archive/marx/works/1859/critique-pol-economy/preface.htm.

26. For the idea of historicity qua historicity begins in its full sense with modernity, so that the transition from premodernity to modernity can be more accurately described as the transition from prehistory to history—even though one has to add the retroactive fantasy of there having been a pure premodern moment. Helpful for these dynamics are arguments unfolded in Fredric Jameson, *A Singular Modernity: Essays on the Ontology of the Present* (London: Verso, 2014).

27. See Alain Badiou, *The Rebirth of History: Times of Riots and Uprising* (London: Verso, 2012).

28. From the standpoint of this reading, one must not, as classic and orthodox Marxism has done, construe Descartes's philosophical enterprise as the symptom of the beginning of the bourgeois-capitalist project, but rather one can, as I've tried to show here, establish a line that connects Descartes's critique of indifference to Marx's critique of bourgeois political economy. For an influential and classic reading of this see Franz Borkenau, *Der Übergang vom feudalen zum bürgerlichen Weltbild* (Darmstadt: Wissenschaftliche Buchgesellschaft, 1976), 268ff.

29. This ideology of indifference has been investigated in a social-historical manner with respect to bureaucracy in Michael Herzfeld, *The Production of Indifference: Exploring the Symbolic Roots of Western Bureaucracy* (Chicago: Routledge, 1992).

30. Marx, *Capital*, 128 (translation modified).

31. Alain Badiou, *Le séminaire: Heidegger. L'être 3—Figure du retrait. 1986–1987* (Paris: Fayard, 2015), 61.

32. Ibid., 63f.

33. Ibid., 80f.

34. Alain Badiou, *Le séminaire: Images du temps present, 2001–2004* (Paris: Fayard 2014), 105.

35. Ibid., 107.

36. Frank Ruda, *Abolishing Freedom: A Plea for the Contemporary Use of Fatalism* (Lincoln: University of Nebraska Press, 2016).

Bibliography

Adorno, Theodor W. "Culture Industry Reconsidered." In *The Culture Industry: Selected Essays in Mass Culture*. London: Routledge, 2001.

Adorno, Theodor W. *History and Freedom: Lectures 1964–1965*. Cambridge: Polity, 2006.

Adorno, Theodor W. *Kant's* Critique of Pure Reason *(1959)*. Edited by Rolf Tiedemann. Translated by Rodney Livingstone. Stanford, CA: Stanford University Press, 2001.

Adorno, Theodor W. *Negative Dialectics*. London: Routledge, 1973.

Adorno, Theodor W. "Theorie der Halbbildung." 1959. In *Gesammelte Schriften*, vol. 8, edited by Rolf Tiedemann, 93–121. Frankfurt am Main: Suhrkamp, 1997.

Agamben, Giorgio. *Remnants of Auschwitz: The Witness and the Archive*. New York: Zone Books, 2002.

Alanen, Lilli. "The Metaphysics of Error and Will." In *Klassiker Auslegen: René Descartes, Meditationen über die erste Philosophie*, edited by Andreas Kemmerling, 81–100. Berlin: Akademie Verlag, 2009.

Allison, Henry E. "On the Very Idea of a Propensity to Evil." In *Essays on Kant*. Oxford: Oxford University Press, 2012.

Alquié, Ferdinand. *La critique kantienne de la métaphysique*. Paris: PUF, 1968.

Alquié, Ferdinand. *Leçons sur Descartes: Science et métaphysique chez Descartes*. Paris: Gallimard, 2005.

Althusser, Louis. "Ideology and Ideological State Apparatuses." In *On the Reproduction of Capitalism: Ideology and Ideological State Apparatuses*, 232–272. London: Verso, 2014.

Althusser, Louis. "The Only Materialist Tradition." In *The New Spinoza*, edited by Warren Montag and Ted Stolze, 3–20. Minneapolis: University of Minnesota Press, 1997.

Anstey, Peter R. "*De Anima* and Descartes: Making Up Aristotle's Mind." *History of Philosophy Quarterly* 17, no. 3 (2000): 237–260.

Arendt, Hannah. *Lectures on Kant's Political Philosophy*. Edited by Ronald Beiner. Chicago: University of Chicago Press, 1992.

Ariew, Roger. *Descartes among the Scholastics*. Leiden: Brill, 2011.

Aristotle. *On the Heavens*. Cambridge, MA: Harvard University Press, 1932.

Armstrong, A. H. *The Cambridge History of Later Greek and Early Medieval Philosophy*. Cambridge: Cambridge University Press, 1967.

Assoun, Paul-Laurrent. "De Freud à Lacan: Le sujet du politique." *Cités*, no. 16 (2003/4): 15–24.

Augustine. *On the Free Choice of the Will*. Cambridge: Cambridge University Press, 2010.

Badiou, Alain. *Can Politics Be Thought?* Durham, NC: Duke University Press, 2019.

Badiou, Alain. *Conditions*. London: Bloomsbury, 2008.

Badiou, Alain. *Happiness*. London: Bloomsbury, 2017.

Badiou, Alain. *Le séminaire: Heidegger. L'être 3—Figure du retrait. 1986–1987*. Paris: Fayard, 2015.

Badiou, Alain. *Le séminaire: Images du temps present. 2001–2004*. Paris: Seuil, 2014.

Badiou, Alain. *Le séminaire: S'orienter dans la pensée, s'orienter dans l'existence*. Paris: Fayard, 2022.

Badiou, Alain. *Logics of Worlds: Being and Event II*. London: Bloomsbury, 2018.

Badiou, Alain. *The Pornographic Age*. London: Bloomsbury, 2020.

Badiou, Alain. *The Rebirth of History: Times of Riots and Uprising*. London: Verso, 2012.

Badiou, Alain. "The Three Negations." *Cardozo Law Review* 29, no. 5 (2008): 1877–1883.

Badiou, Alain. *The True Life*. London: Polity, 2017.

Badiou, Alain, Frank Ruda, and Jan Völker. "Wir müssen das affirmative Begehren hüten." In Alain Badiou, *Dritter Entwurf eines Manifests für den Affirmationismus*. Berlin: Merve, 2009.

Baert, Edward. *Aufstieg und Untergang der Ontologie: Descartes und die nachthomasische Philosophie*. Osnabrück: Rasch, 1997.

Barth, Karl. *Church Dogmatics*, vol. 3: *The Doctrine of Creation*. Edinburgh: T. & T. Clark, 1960.

Baur, Michael. "From Kant's Highest Good to Hegel's Absolute Knowing." In A *Companion to Hegel*, edited by Stephen Houlgate and Michael Baur. Malden: Polity 2011.

Beckett, Samuel. *The Unnamable*. London: Grove Press, 1978.

Beiser, Frederick C. *The Fate of Reason. German Philosophy from Kant to Fichte*. Cambridge, MA: Harvard University Press, 1987.

Beiser, Frederick C. *German Idealism. The Struggle Against Subjectivism, 1781–1801*. Cambridge, MA: Harvard University Press, 2002.

Benjamin, Andrew. *Towards a Relational Ontology. Philosophy's Other Possibility*. Albany: State University of New York Press, 2015.

Beyssade, Jean-Marie. *La philosophie première de Descartes: Les temps et la coherence de la métaphysique*. Paris: Flammarion, 1992.

Bondeli, Martin. *Der Kantianismus des jungen Hegel: Die Kant-Aneignung und Kant-Überwindung Hegels auf seinem Weg zum philosophischen System.* Hamburg: Meiner, 1997.

Borkenau, Franz. *Der Übergang vom feudalen zum bürgerlichen Weltbild.* Darmstadt, 1976.

Bowman, Brady. *Hegel and the Metaphysics of Absolute Negativity.* Cambridge: Cambridge University Press, 2013.

Bubner, Rüdiger. "Metaphysik und Erfahrung." In *Antike Themen und ihre moderne Verwandlung,* 134–150. Frankfurt am Main: Suhrkamp, 1992.

Chappell, Vere. "Descartes's Compatibilism." In *Reason, Will, and Sensation. Studies in Descartes's Metaphysics,* edited by John Cottingham, 177–190. Oxford: Oxford University Press, 1994.

Cohen, Gustave. *Écrivains français en Hollande dans la première moitié du XVII siècle.* Paris: Champion, 1920.

Comay, Rebecca. *Mourning Sickness. Hegel and the French Revolution.* Stanford: Stanford University Press, 2011. (CMS)

Comay, Rebecca. "Resistance and Repetition: Freud and Hegel." *Research in Phenomenology* 45, no. 2 (2015): 237–266.

Comay, Rebecca, and Frank Ruda. *The Dash—The Other Side of Absolute Knowing.* Cambridge, MA: MIT Press, 2018.

Copleston, Frederick. *A History of Philosophy,* vol. 4: *Descartes to Leibniz.* New York: Paulist Press, 1963.

Cottingham, John. *A Descartes Dictionary.* Cambridge: Cambridge University Press, 1993, (CDD)

Davenport, Anne Ashley. *Descartes's Theory of Action.* Leiden: Brill, 2007.

Davis, Angela. *Are Prisons Obsolete?* New York: Seven Stories Press, 2003.

Davis, Angela. "The Meaning of Freedom." In *The Meaning of Freedom and Other Difficult Dialogues.* San Francisco: City Light Books, 2012.

Davis, Angela, Gina Dent, Erica R. Meiners, and Beth E. Richie. *Abolition. Feminism. Now.* London: Penguin Books, 2022.

Deleuze, Gilles. *Nietzsche and Philosophy.* Translated by Hugh Tomlinson. New York: Continuum, 1986.

Descartes, René. "À un R. P. Jésuite." In *Œuvre de Descartes,* edited by Victor Cousin, 8:169f. Paris: Levraut, 1825.

Descartes, René. "Au R. P. Mersenne." In *Œuvre de Descartes,* edited by Victor Cousin, 6:138f. Paris: Levraut, 1824.

Descartes, René. "Letters." In *The Philosophical Writings of Descartes III: The Correspondence,* translated by John Cottingham, Robert Stoothoff, Dugald Murdoch, and Anthony Kenny. Cambridge: Cambridge University Press, 1991.

Descartes, René. "Letters." In *The Philosophical Writings of Descartes: The Correspondence,* vol. 3. Translated by John Cottingham. Cambridge: Cambridge University Press, 1991.

Descartes, René. "Meditations on First Philosophy." In *The Philosophical Writings of Descartes*, vol. II. Trans. by John Cottingham (Cambridge: Cambridge University Press, 1984) (DMFP)

Descartes, René. "Principles of Philosophy." In *The Philosophical Writings of Descartes*, vol. 1. Tranlated by John Cottingham. Cambridge: Cambridge University Press, 1985. (DPP)

Descartes, René. *Rules for the Direction of the Mind*. In *The Philosophical Writings of René Descartes*, vol. 1. Cambridge: Cambridge University Press, 1985.

Dolar, Mladen. "In Parmenidem Parvii Comentarii." *HELIOS* 31, no. 1–2 (2004): 63–98.

Düttmann, Alexander García. *Zwischen den Kulturen: Spannungen im Kampf um Anerkennung*. Frankfurt am Main: Suhrkamp, 1997.

Eisler, Rudolf. *Kant-Lexicon: Nachschlagwerk zu Kants sämtlichen Schriften, Briefen und handschriftlichem Nachlaß*. Hildesheim: Weidmannsche Verlagsbuchhandlung, 2002.

Federici, Silvia. *Caliban and the Witch: Women, the Body and Primitive Accumulation*. London: Penguin, 2004.

Federici, Silvia. "Sexuality Is Work." 1975. In *Reproduction at Point Zero: Housework, Reproduction, and Feminist Struggle*. New York: PM Press, 2020.

Fenves, Peter.*Late Kant: Towards Another Law of the Earth*. London: Routledge, 2003.

Fischer, Kuno. *Das Vernunftsystem auf der Grundlage der Vernunftkritik*. Paderborn : Verlag der Wissenschaften, 2013.

Fontenay, Élisabeth de. *Le silence des bêtes: La philosophie à l'epreuve de l'animalité*. Paris: Fayard, 2015.

Förster, Eckart. *The Twenty-Five Years of Philosophy: A Systematic Reconstruction*. Cambridge, MA: Harvard University Press 2008.

Freud, Sigmund. *Inhibitions, Symptoms and Anxiety*. In *The Standard Edition of the Complete Psychological Works of Sigmund Freud (SEP)*, vol. 20. London: Hogarth Press, 1953–66.

Freud, Sigmund. "Remembering, Repeating, Working Through (Further Recommendations on the Technique of Psycho-Analysis II)." In *SEP*, 12:145–146. New York: Norton & Norton, 1963.

Gardner, Sebastian. "The Primacy of Practical Reason." In *A Companion to Kant*, edited by Graham Bird, 259–274. Malden, MA: Blackwell, 2006.

Geier, Manfred. *Das Glück der Gleichgültigen: Von der stoischen Seelenruhe zur postmodernen Indifferenz*. Hamburg: Rowohlt, 1997.

Gilson, Etienne. *La Liberté chez Descartes et la Théologie*. Paris: Vrin, 1913.

Ginsborg, Hannah. "Interesseloses Wohlgefallen und Allgemeinheit ohne Begriff (§§1–9)," In *Klassiker Auslegen: Immanuel Kant. Kritik der Urteilskraft*, edited by Ottfried Höffe, 59–78. Berlin: Akademie Verlag 2008.

Gombray, Andrew. *Descartes*. Malden, MA: Blackwell, 2007.

Gottschick, Johannes. "Adiaphora." In *Realencyklopädie für protestantische Theologie und Kirche*, edited by Albert Lauck, 1:168–179. Leipzig: Hauck, 1896.

Guenancia, Pierre. *Lire Descartes*. Paris: Gallimard, 2000.

Gulyga, Arsenij. *Georg Wilhelm Friedrich Hegel*. Leipzig: Reclam, 1974.

Gulyga, Arsenij. *Immanuel Kant: Eine Biographie.* Frankfurt am Main: Suhrkamp, 2004.

Guyer, Paul. *Kant.* London: Routledge, 2006.

Haag, Johannes. "Descartes über Willen und Willensfreiheit." In *Zeitschrift für philosophische Forschung*, edited by Otfried Höffe, with Christoph Rapp, 60:483–503. Frankfurt am Main: Suhrkamp, 2006.

Habermas, Jürgen."Ein Pakt für oder gegen Europa?" Lecture on 6 April 2011. http://www.ecfr.eu/page/-/Habermas%20PDF.pdf.

Hatfield, Gary. *Descartes and the* Meditations. London: Routledge, 2002.

Hegel, G. W. F. "Brief an Niethammer (7 August 1810)." In *Briefe von und an Hegel*, 1:318. Hamburg: Meiner, 2015.

Hegel, G. W. F. *Der "Vorbegriff" zur Wissenschaft der Logik in der Enzyklopädie von 1830*, edited by Alfred Denker, Annette Sell, and Holger Zaborowski, 26–62. Munich: Meiner, 2010.

Hegel, G. W. F. *The Difference between Fichte's and Schelling's System of Philosophy.* Translated by H. S. Harris and Walter Cerf. Albany: SUNY Press 1977. (HDFS)

Hegel, G. W. F. "Einleitung: Über das Wesen der philosophischen Kritik überhaupt und ihr Verhältnis zum gegenwärtigen Zustand der Philosophie insbesondere." In *Werke*, vol. 2. Frankfurt am Main: Suhrkamp, 1986.

Hegel, G. W. F. *The Encyclopedia Logic: Part I of the* Encyclopedia of the Philosophical Sciences *with the Zusätze.* Translated by T. F. Geraets, W. A. Suchting, and H. S. Harris. Indianapolis: Hackett, 1991. (HEL1)

Hegel, G. W. F. "Habilitationsthesen." In *Werke*, 2:533. Frankfurt am Main: Suhrkamp, 1985.

Hegel, G. W. F. "Habilitation Theses." In *Miscellaneous Writings of G. W. F. Hegel*, edited by Jon Stewart, 17. Evanston, IL: Northwestern University Press, 2002.

Hegel, G. W. F. *Lectures on the Philosophy of Religion*, vol. 1: *Introduction and the Concept of Religion*. Berkeley: University of California Press, 1984.

Hegel, G. W. F. *Miscellaneous Writings of G. W. F. Hegel*. Edited by Jon Stewart. Evanston, IL: Northwestern University Press, 2002.

Hegel, G. W. F. "On the Relationship of Skepticism to Philosophy, Exposition of its Different Modifications and Comparison of the Latest Form with the Ancient One." In *Between Kant and Hegel: Texts in the Development of Post-Kantian Idealism*, translated by H. S. Harris, 311–362. Indianapolis: Hackett, 2000. (HRSP)

Hegel, G. W. F. *Phenomenology of Spirit*. Translated by A. V. Miller. Oxford: Oxford University Press, 1977. (HPS)

Hegel, G. W. F. *Philosophy of Mind*. Clarendon: Oxford University Press, 2010.

Hegel, G. W. F. "Rede zum Schulabschlußjahr am 2. September 1811." In *Werke*, vol. 4. Frankfurt am Main: Suhrkamp, 1986.

Hegel, G. W. F. *The Science of Logic*. Translated by George di Giovanni. Cambridge: Cambridge University Press, 2010.

Hegel, G. W. F. "Über die Bekehrten (von Ernst Raupach)." 1826. In *Werke*, 11:72–82. Frankfurt am Main: Suhrkamp, 1986.

Hegel, G. W. F. *Vorlesungen über die Ästhetik I*. In *Werke*, vol. 13. Frankfurt am Main: Suhrkamp, 1986.

Hegel, G. W. F. *Vorlesungen über die Ästhetik III.* In *Werke*, Bd. 15. Frankfurt am Main: Suhrkamp, 1986.

Hegel, G. W. F. *Vorlesungen über die Geschichte der Philosophie I.* In *Werke*, vol. 18.

Hegel, G. W. F. *Vorlesungen über die Geschichte der Philosophie III.* In *Werke*, vol. 20.

Hegel, G. W. F. *Vorlesungen über die Philosophie der Religion II.* In *Werke*, vol. 17. Frankfurt am Main: Suhrkamp, 1986).

Heidegger, Martin. *Basic Concepts of Aristotelian Philosophy.* Bloomington: Indiana University Press, 2009.

Heidegger, Martin. *The Fundamental Concepts of Metaphysics: World, Finitude, Solitude.* Bloomington: Indiana University Press, 1995.

Heidegger, Martin. *Interpretation of Nietzsche's Second Untimely Meditation.* Bloomington: Indiana University Press 2016.

Heidegger, Martin. *Introduction to Phenomenological Research.* Bloomington: Indiana University Press, 2005.

Heidegger, Martin. *Nietzsche: Nihilism*, vol. 4. New York: Harper, 1991.

Heidegger, Martin. *Plato's Sophist.* Bloomington: Indiana University Press, 1997.

Heidegger, Martin. *Ponderings VII–XI: Black Notebooks, 1938–1939.* Bloomington: Indiana University Press, 2017.

Heidegger, Martin. *The Question Concerning Technology and Other Essays.* New York: Harper, 1977.

Heidegger, Martin. *Schelling's Treatise on the Essence of Human Freedom.* Athens: Ohio University Press, 1985.

Heidegger, Martin. *Schwarze Hefte (1942–1948).* In *Gesamtausgabe. IV. Abteilung: Hinweise und Aufzeichnungen*, vol. 97. Frankfurt am Main: Klostermann, 2015.

Heidegger, Martin. *Seminare Hegel—Schelling in Gesamtausgabe. IV. Abteilung: Hinweise und Aufzeichnungen*, vol. 86. Frankfurt am Main: Klostermann, 2011.

Heidegger, Martin. *Zu Ernst Jünger.* In *Gesamtausgabe. IV. Abteilung: Hinweise und Aufzeichnungen*, vol. 90. Frankfurt am Main: Klostermann, 2004.

Henrich, Dieter. "Historische Voraussetzungen von Hegels System." In *Hegel im Kontext*, 41–73. Frankfurt am Main: Suhrkamp, 1975.

Herzfeld, Michael. *The Production of Indifference. Exploring the Symbolic Roots of Western Bureaucracy.* Chicago: University of Chicago Press, 1992.

Holz, Hans-Heinz. *Descartes.* Frankfurt am Main: Campus, 1994.

Imlay, Robert A. "Descartes and Indifference." *Studia Leibnitiana* 14, no. 1 (1982): 87–97.

Jameson, Fredric. *A Singular Modernity: Essays on the Ontology of the Present.* London: Verso, 2014.

Jäsche, Gottlob Benjamin. *Immanuel Kants Logik: Ein Handbuch zu Vorlesungen* Königsberg, 1800.

Jendreieck, Helmut. *Hegel und Jacob Grimm: Ein Beitrag zur Geschichte der Wissenschaftstheorie.* Lengerich: Erich Schmidt Verlag, 1975.

Jurieu, Pierre. *La religion du latitudinaire, avec l'apologie pour la Saint Trinité, appelée l'hérésie des trois Dieux.* Rotterdam, 1696.

Kant, Immanuel. "Anthropology from a Pragmatic Point of View." 1798. In *The Cambridge Edition of the Works of Immanuel Kant: Anthropology, History, and*

Education, translated by Robert B.Louden, 227–429. Cambridge: Cambridge University Press, 2007.

Kant, Immanuel. "Brief an Friedrich Victor Leberecht Plessing (3 April, 1784)." In *Gesammelte Schriften, Bd. 10: Briefwechsel*, Bd. 1. Berlin, 1922.

Kant, Immanuel. *The Conflict of the Faculties*. In *Immanuel Kant: Religion and Rational Theology*, translated by Mary J. Gregor and Robert Anchor Cambridge: Cambridge University Press, 1996.

Kant, Immanuel. "Conjectural Beginning of Human History." In *The Cambridge Edition of the Works of Immanuel Kant in Translation: Anthropology, History, and Education*, translated by Allen W. Wood. Cambridge: Cambridge University Press, 2007.

Kant, Immanuel. *Critique of Judgment*. Oxford: Oxford University Press, 2007.

Kant, Immanuel. *Critique of Practical Reason*. 1788. In *The Cambridge Edition of the Works of Immanuel Kant: Practical Philosophy*, translated by Mary J. Gregor. Cambridge: Cambridge University Press, 1996. (KPCpR)

Kant, Immanuel. *Critique of Pure Reason*. Translated by Paul Guyer and Allen W. Wood. Cambridge: Cambridge University Press, 1998. (KCPR)

Kant, Immanuel. *Entwürfe zu dem Colleg—über Anthropologie aus den 70er und 80er Jahren*. In *Gesammelte Schriften, Bd. 15: Handschriftlicher Nachlaß: Anthropologie*. Berlin: De Gruyter, 1923.

Kant, Immanuel. "Groundwork of the Metaphysics of Morals." 1785. In *The Cambridge Edition of the Works of Immanuel Kant: Practical Philosophy*, translated by Mary J. Gregor, 37–108. Cambridge: Cambridge University Press, 1996. (KGMM)

Kant, Immanuel. "Idea for a Universal History with a Cosmopolitan Aim." In *Immanuel Kant: Anthropology, History, and Education*, translated by Allen W. Wood. Cambridge: Cambridge University Press, 2007.

Kant, Immanuel. "The Jäsche Logic." In *Immanuel Kant. Lectures on Logic*, translated and edited by J. Michael Young. Cambridge: Cambridge University Press, 1992.

Kant, Immanuel. *Menschenkunde oder philosophische Anthropologie: Nach handschriftlichen Vorlesungen*. Edited by Friedrich Christian Starke. Leipzig, 1831.

Kant, Immanuel. "The Metaphysics of Morals." In *The Cambridge Edition of the Works of Immanuel Kant in Translation: Practical Philosophy*, translated by Mary Gregor. Cambridge: Cambridge University Press, 1996.

Kant, Immanuel. "A New Elucidation of the First Principles of Metaphysical Cognition." In *Immanuel Kant: Theoretical Philosophy, 1755–1770*, translated and edited by David Walford. Cambridge: Cambridge University Press, 1992.

Kant, Immanuel. *Prolegomena to Any Future Metaphysics*. Translated and edited by Gary Hatfield. Cambridge: Cambridge University Press, 2004.

Kant, Immanuel. *Reflexionen zur Moralphilosophie*. In *Werke*, vol. 19: *Handschriftlicher Nachlaß: Moralphilosophie, Rechtsphilosophie und Religionsphilosophie*. Berlin: De Gruyter, 1934.

Kant, Immanuel. "Religion within the Boundaries of Mere Reason." In *The Cambridge Edition of the Works of Immanuel Kant: Religion and Rational Theology*, translated by George di Giovanni, 39–216. Cambridge: Cambridge University Press, 1996. (KRBR)

Kant, Immanuel. "Universal Natural History and Theory of the Heavens or Essay on the Constitution and Mechanical Origin of the Whole Universe According to Newtonian Principles." In *The Cambridge Edition of the Works of Immanuel Kant in Translation: Natural Science*, translated by Olaf Reinhardt. Cambridge: Cambridge University Press, 2012.

Kant, Immanuel. *Vorlesung zur Moralphilosophie*. Edited by Werner Stark. Berlin: De Gruyter, 2004.

Kant, Immanuel. *Zweiter Anhang. Medicin*. In *Gesammelte Schriften, Bd. 15: Handschriftlicher Nachlaß: Anthropologie*. Berlin: De Gruyter, 1923.

Kaposi, Dorottya. "Indifference et liberté humaine chez Descartes." *Revue de Métaphysique et de Morale* 1, no. 41 (2004): 73–99.

Kaufmann, Dan. "Infimus gradus libertatis? Descartes on Indifference and Divine Freedom." *Religious Studies* 39, no. 4 (2003): 391–406.

Kenny, Anthony. "Descartes on the Will." In *Descartes: Oxford Readings in Philosophy*, edited by John Cottingham. Oxford: Oxford University Press, 1998.

Kierkegaard, Søren. "Fear and Trembling: Dialectical Lyric." In *Fear and Trembling/Repetition: Kierkegaard's Writings, VI*, edited and translated by Howard V. Hong and Edna H. Hong. Princeton, NJ: Princeton University Press, 1983.

Klemme, Heiner F. "Kants Erörterung der 'libertas indifferentiae' in der Metaphysik der Sitten und ihre philosophische Bedeutung." *Internationales Jahrbuch des Deutschen Idealismus/International Yearbook of German Idealism* 9 (2011).

Kojève, Alexandre. *From the Closed World to the Infinite Universe*. Baltimore: John Hopkins University Press, 1957.

Kojève, Alexandre. *Introduction to the Reading of Hegel: Lectures on the* Phenomenology of Spirit. Ithaca, NY: Cornell University Press, 1969.

Lacan, Jacques. "The Function and Field of Speech and Language in Psychoanalysis." In *Écrits: The First Complete English Edition*, 97–269. New York: W. W. Norton, 2006.

Lacan, Jacques. "Science and Truth." In *Écrits: The First Complete English Edition*, 726–746. New York: W. W. Norton, 2006.

Laclau, Ernesto, and Chantal Mouffe. *Hegemony and Socialist Strategy: Towards a Radical Democratic Politics*. New York: Verso, 1985.

Lamennais, Félicité Robert de. *Essai sur l'indifférence en matière de religion*, vol. 1. Paris: Tournachon-Molin, 1825.

Lazarus, Sylvain. *Anthropology of the Name*. London: Seagull Books, 2015.

Lebrun, Gérard. *Kant et la fin de la métaphysique*. Paris: References, 1970.

Lenin, V. I. "Deception of the People with Slogans of Freedom and Equality." In *Collected Works*, 2:333–376. Moscow: Progress Publishers, 1972.

Lenin, V. I. "Seventh All-Russia Congress of Soviets." In *Collected Works*, vol. 30. Moscow: Progress Publishers, 1965.

Lenin, V. I. "The Socialist Party and Non-Party Revolutionism." In *V. I. Lenin: Collected Works*, vol. 10: November 1905–June 1906, translated by Andrew Rothstein. Moscow: Progress Publishers, 1962.

Linebaugh, Peter. *The Magna Carta Manifesto: Liberties and Commons for All*.
    Berkeley: University of California Press, 2008.
Lohmann, Georg. *Indifferenz und Gesellschaft*. Frankfurt am Main: Suhrkamp, 1991.
Lordon, Fréderic. *Willing Slaves of Capital: Spinoza and Marx on Desire*. London:
    Verso, 2014.
Löwith, Karl. *Gott, Mensch und Welt in der Metaphysik von Descartes bis zu
    Nietzsche*. Göttingen: Vandenhoeck und Ruprecht, 1967.
Macherey, Pierre. "Marcher en forêt avec Descartes." http://philolarge.hypotheses
    .org/1720#more-1720.
Mannoni, Octave. *Je sais bien, mais quand-meme . . .* Paris; Seuil, 2020.
Marx, Karl. *Capital. A Critique of Political Economy*. London: Penguin Books, 1993.
Marx, Karl. *A Contribution to the Critique of Political Economy*. Translated by S. W.
    Ryazanskaya. Moscow: Progress Publishers, 1977. https://www.marxists.org
    /archive/marx/works/1859/critique-pol-economy/preface.htm.
Marx, Karl. "Demand." In Karl Marx and Friedrich Engels, *Collected Works*,
    6:574–576. London: Lawrence and Wishart, 1980.
Marx, Karl. *Economic and Philosophical Manuscripts*. In *Early Writings*. London:
    Penguin Books, 1992.
Marx, Karl. "Political Indifferentism." https://www.marxists.org/archive/marx/works
    /1873/01/indifferentism.htm.
Marx, Karl. *Value: Studies*. London: New Park, 1976.
Marx, Karl. "Value, Price and Profit." In Karl Marx and Friedrich Engels, *Collected
    Works*, 20:99–150. London: Lawrence and Wishart, 1980.
Marx, Karl, and Friedrich Engels. *Manifesto of the Communist Party*. Translated by
    Samuel Moore. Moscow: Progress Publishers, 1969. https://www.marxists.org
    /archive/marx/works/1848/communist-manifesto/.
Marx, Karl, and Frederick Engels. *Manifesto of the Communist Party*. In Karl Marx and
    Friedrich Engels, *Collected Works*, vol. 6. London: Lawrence and Wishart, 1980.
Maxwell, Vance. "Affirmative Pathology: Spinoza and Hegel on Illness and
    Self-Repair." In *Between Hegel and Spinoza: A Volume of Critical Essays*, edited
    by Hasana Sharp and Jason E. Smith (London: Bloomsbury, 2012.
Menke, Christoph. *Critique of Rights*. London: Polity, 2020.
Menke, Christoph. "Ja und Nein." In *Autonomie und Befreiung: Studien zu Hegel*,
    179–212. Berlin: Suhrkamp, 2018.
Menke, Christoph. "Modell 1: Freiheit. Zur Metakritik der praktischen Vernunft II.
    Kritik der 'abstrakten Moralität.'" In *Klassiker Auslegen: Theodor W. Adorno,
    Negative Dialektik*, edited by Axel Honneth and Christoph Menke, 51–169. Berlin:
    De Gruyter, 2006..
Menke, Christoph. *Theorie der Befreiung*. Berlin: Suhrkamp, 2022.
Miles, Murray. *Insight and Inference: Descartes's Founding Principles and Modern
    Philosophy*. Toronto: De Gruyter 2012.
Milner, Jean-Claude. *Le salaire de l'idéal: La théorie des classes et de la culture au
    XXIème siècle*. Paris: Seuil, 1997.

Montag, Warren. *Louis Althusser.* New York: Red Globe Press, 2003.

Mrongovius, Christoph Coelestin. *Philosophische Abhandlung über Religion und Moral stammend von Immanuel Kant und in die polnische Sprache übersetzt von Christoph Coelestin Mrongovius.* Edited by Mirosław Żelazny and Werner Stark. Twarda: Wydawnictwo Naukowe Uniwersytetu Mikołaja Kopernika, 2006.

Negri, Antonio. *Political Descartes: Reason, Ideology, and the Bourgeois Project.* London: Verso, 2007. (NP)

Neuser, Wolfgang. "Schelling und Hegels Habilitationsthesen", in: *Philosophia Naturalis* 23 (2), 1986, pp. 288–292.

Nietzsche, Friedrich. *On the Genealogy of Morality.* Translated by Carol Diethe and edited by Keith Ansell-Pearson. Cambridge: Cambridge University Press, 1997.

Ockham, Wilhelm von.*Scriptum in Librum Primum Sententiarum Ordinatio.* In *Opera Theologica, Prologus et Distinctio.* New York: Franciscan Institute, 1967.

Olivo, Gilles. "L'efficence en cause: Suárez, Descartes et la question de la causalité." In *Descartes et le Moyen Age,* edited by Joël Biard and Roshdi Rashed, 91–107. Paris: Vrin, 1997.

Ovid. *Metamorphoses.* New York: W. W. Norton, 2004.

Paulus, Caroline. "Brief an Hegel vom 18. 12. 1810." In *Briefe von und an Hegel,* 342. Hamburg: Meiner, 2015.

Perin, Casey. "Descartes and the Legacy of Ancient Skepticism." In *A Companion to Descartes,* edited by Janet Broughton and John Carriero. Malden, MA: Wiley, 2008.

Pippin, Robert B. *The Persistence of Subjectivity: On the Kantian Aftermath.* Cambridge: Cambridge University Press, 2005.

Pippin, Robert. "Rigorism and the 'New Kant.'" In *Kant und die Berliner Aufklärung,* 43–58. Berlin: De Gruyter, 2001.

Plato. *Timaeus.* In *Complete Works,* 1289–1291. Indianapolis: Hackett,1 997.

Postone, Moishe. *Time, Labor, and Social Domination: A Reinterpretation of Marx's Critical Theory.* Cambridge: Cambridge University Press, 2008.

Riedel, Manfred. *System und Geschichte: Studien zum historischen Standort von Hegels Philosophie.* Frankfurt am Main: Suhrkamp, 1973.

Ritter, Joachim. "Auseinandersetzung mit der kantischen Ethik." In *Metaphysik und Politik: Studien zu Aristoteles und Hegel.* Frankfurt am Main: Suhrkamp, 1977.

Rose, Gillian. *Hegel Contra Sociology.* London: Verso, 1981.

Ross, Nathan. *On Mechanism in Hegel's Social and Political Philosophy.* London: Routledge, 2008.

Rousseau, Jean-Jacques. *The Social Contract and The First and Second Discourses.* Edited by Susan Dunn. New Haven, CT: Yale University Press, 1978.

Ruda, Frank. *Abolishing Freedom: A Plea for a Contemporary Use of Fatalism.* Lincoln: University of Nebraska Press, 2016.

Ruda, Frank. *For Badiou: Idealism without Idealism.* Evanston, IL: Northwestern University Press, 2015.

Ruda, Frank. "Hegel on the Rocks: Remarks on the Concept of Nature." In *Reading Hegel,* by Slavoj Žižek, Frank Ruda, and Agon Hamza, 101–157. London: Polity, 2022.

Ruda, Frank. *Hegel's Rabble: An Investigation into Hegel's Philosophy of Right*. London: Continuum, 2008.

Ruda, Frank. "I, the Revolution, Speak: Lenin's Speculative (Hegelian) Style." In *From Marx to Hegel and Back: Capitalism, Critique, and Utopia*, edited by Victoria Fareld and Hannes Kuch, 91–108. London: Bloomsbury, 2020. Ruda, Frank. "Marx in the Cave." In *Reading Marx*, by Slavoj Žižek, Frank Ruda, and Agon Hamza, 62–100. London: Polity, 2018.

Ruda, Frank. "The Purlieu Letter: Toward a Hegelian Theory of Conditioning." *Problemi International* 58, no. 11–12 (2021): 179–199.

Ruda, Frank. "Wer denkt asozial? Von Aristoteles zu Hobbes." In *Das soziale Band*, edited by Thomas Bedorf and Steffen Hermann, 143–163. Berlin: transcript, 2016.

Sartre, Jean-Paul. "Cartesian Freedom." In *Literary and Philosophical Essays*. Vancouver: Collier, 1967. (SCF)

Schick, Stefan. *Contradictio Est Regula Veri: Die Grundsätze des Denkens in der formalen, transzendentalen und spekulativen Logik*. Hamburg: Meiner, 2010.

Schmaltz, Tad M. *Descartes on Causation*. Oxford: Oxford University Press, 2008.

Schmid, Carl Christian Erhard. *Adiaphora wissenschaftlich und historisch untersucht*. Leipzig: Vogel, 1809.

Schmidt, Gerhart. *Hegel in Nürnberg: Untersuchungen zum Problem der philosophischen Propädeutik*. Tübingen: Niemeyer Max Verlag, 1960.

Scholz, Frithard. *Freiheit als Indifferenz: Alteuropäische Probleme mit der Systemtheorie Niklas Luhmanns*. Frankfurt am Main: Suhrkamp, 1982.

Schopenhauer, Arthur. *Prize Essay on the Freedom of the Will*. In *The Two Fundamental Problems of Ethics*. Cambridge: Cambridge University Press, 2009.

Schouls, Peter A. *Descartes and Enlightenment*. Kingston: McGill, 1989.

Schütt, Hans Peter. *Die Adoption des "Vaters der modernen Philosophie": Studien zu einem Gemeinplatz der Ideengeschichte*. Frankfurt am Main: Klostermann, 1998.

Sellars, Wilfrid. "Empiricism and the Philosophy of Mind." In *Empiricism and the Philosophy of Mind: With an Introduction by Richard Rorty and a Study Guide by Robert Brandom*, edited by R. Brandom, 13–25. Cambridge: Cambridge University Press, 1997.

Shakespeare, William. *The Life of Timon of Athens*. Edited by John Jowett. Oxford: Oxford University Press, 2004.

Siep, Ludwig. *Der Weg der "Phänomenologie des Geistes": Ein einführender Kommentar zu Hegels "Differenzschrift" und "Phänomenologie des Geistes."* Frankfurt am Main: Suhrkamp, 2000.

Simon, Simon. "Descartes' 'cogito' unter zeichenphilosophischem Aspekt." In *Descartes im Diskurs der Neuzeit*, edited by Wilhelm Friedrich Niebel, Angelica Horn, and Herbert Schnädelbach, 77–102. Frankfurt am Main: Suhrkamp, 2000.

Sloterdijk, Peter. *In the World Interior of Capital: Towards a Philosophical Theory of Globalization*. Malden, MA: Polity, 2013.

Stähler, Tanja. *Die Unruhe des Anfangs: Hegel und Husserl über den Weg in die Phänomenologie* (Dodrecht: Kluwer Academic, 2003.

Stähler, Tanja. "The Historicity of Philosophy and the Role of Skepticism." In *Hegel's History of Philosophy: New Interpretations*, edited by David A. Duquette. Albany: SUNY Press, 2003.

Stapler, J. F. *Institutiones theologiae polemicae universae, ordine scientifico dispositae*, 5 vols. Zürich, 1743–1747.

Staples, David. *No Place Like Home: Organizing Home-Based Labor in the Era of Structural Adjustment*. New York: Routledge, 2007.

Sturm, Thomas. "Eine Frage des Charakters." In *Kant und die Berliner Aufklärung. Akten des IX. Internationalen Kant-Kongresses, Band IV: Sektionen XI–XIV*, edited by Volker Gerhardt, Rolf-Peter Horstmann, and Ralph Schumacher, 440–449. Berlin, 2001.

Teichweier, Georg. "Adiaphorenstreit." In *Lexikon für Theologie und Kirche*, edited by Josef Höler and Karl Rahner, 1:145–147. Freiburg: Herder, 1957).

van Ghert, Pierre Gabriel. "Brief an Hegel (22 June 1810)." In *Briefe von und an Hegel*, vol. 1. Hamburg: Meiner, 1969.

Wee, Cecilia. *Material Falsity and Error in Descartes' Meditations*. London: Routledge, 2006.

White, Nicholas P. "Stoic Values." *The Monist* 73, no. 1 (1990): 42–58.

Wild, Markus. *Die anthropologische Differenz: Der Geist der Tiere in der frühen Neuzeit bei Montaigne, Descartes und Hume*. Berlin: De Gruyter, 2006.

Wieland, Wolfgang. "Bemerkung zum Anfang von Hegels Logik." In *Seminar: Dialektik in der Philosophie Hegels*, edited by Rolf-Peter Horstmann. Frankfurt am Main: Suhrkamp, 1978.

Willaschek, Marcus, Jürgen Stolzenberg, Georg Mohr, and Stefano Bacin, eds. *Kant-Lexicon*, vol. 3. Berlin: De Gruyter, 2015.

Williams, Bernard. *Descartes: The Project of Pure Enquiry* (London: Routledge 2005.

Wolfendale, Peter. *Object-Oriented Philosophy: The Noumenon's New Clothes*. Falmouth: Urbanomic, 2014.

Wood, Allen W. "Notes to Religion within the Boundaries of Mere Reason." In *Immanuel Kant: Religion and Rational Theology*. Cambridge: Cambridge University Press, 1996.

Žižek, Slavoj. *Less Than Nothing: Hegel and the Shadow of Dialectical Materialism*. London: Verso, 2012. (ZLN)

Zupančič, Alenka. *Ethics of the Real: Kant and Lacan*. London: Verso, 2000.

Zupančič, Alenka. "Power in the Closet (and Its Coming Out)." In *Lacan, Psycho-analysis, and Comedy*, edited by Patricia Gherovici and Manya Steinkoler. New York. Cambridge University Press, 2016.

Index

abstraction, 119–121
adiaphora, 29–30, 60–1, 65, 68, 71, 74–6, 79, 143, 146, 157–9
Adorno, Theodor W., xvii, xix, 73, 137, 142, 143, 151, 157, 165
Agamben, Giorgio, 138
Althusser, Louis, 8, 9, 139, 150
animal, 5–7, 13–6, 22 44, 47, 56–7, 60, 62–4, 79–81, 102–3, 106, 112, 114–5, 119–121, 123–4, 140, 149, 155, 168–9
Aristotle, Aristotelian, Aristotelianism, 14, 26, 83, 92, 129, 138, 140, 141, 143, 144, 164, 166, 167, 168

Badiou, Alain, vii–x, 109, 119, 124, 128, 131, 133, 135–8, 140, 147, 159, 160, 163–4, 166–70
Barth, Karl, 168–9
beauty, 14–5, 56
Beckett, Samuel, xxiii
Beiser, Frederick, 153

capacity, xix–xx, xxii, 4–8, 11, 19–20. 26–31, 33, 37, 39–40, 44–5, 47–8, 53, 63, 66, 69, 79–80, 93, 109, 113, 116–8, 120–1, 124–5, 141, 144–5, 150, 156, 161, 165
capitalism, capitalist, xiv–xvi, xx–xxii, 119–120, 122, 137, 150, 165, 168
choice, xii, 4–8, 19–20, 22–30, 34, 38–9, 43, 47, 51, 53, 58–9, 61, 65, 75–6, 86–92, 109–11, 144, 148–9, 154–5, 168
Comay, Rebecca, 133, 161, 162, 164

contradiction, 77, 83–5, 89, 91–2, 99, 102–3, 106–8, 110, 147
contingency, contingent, 26, 34–5, 44, 146, 149

Davis, Angela, xiv, xv, xx, xxiii, 136
dogmatism, dogmatic, 49–54, 58, 68–9, 71, 81, 85–94, 97–100, 128, 130, 151–2, 156, 159–62
Dolar, Mladen, 162

education, 76, 153; "Half-Education" (Theodor W. Adorno), 74
environment, 103, 106–7, 111–2, 124

fatalism, xx, 11, 124, 137, 139, 164, 170
Federici, Sylvia, xi–xiii, xv, xxii, 135
forgetting, 3, 5–6, 36, 90, 124
free time, xii–xiii, 121
free will, xix, 18, 24, 34, 37–9, 43, 64, 76, 79, 109–11, 118, 148, 158,
Freud, Sigmund, 13, 105, 139, 149, 164, 167

Habermas, Jürgen, 41
Heidegger, Martin, 1–7, 11–12, 36–9, 124, 132, 138, 148, 159, 166
Hobbes, Thomas, 14, 105, 140, 144, 159, 166
Horkheimer, Max, 46
humanity, 2, 5, 7, 74, 106, 131, 140, 168

Jameson, Fredric, 169

FRANK RUDA is Professor of Modern and Contemporary Philosophy at the University of Dundee, Scotland. His most recent books are *Reading Hegel* (with Agon Hamza and Slavoj Žižek); *The Dash—The Other Side of Absolute Knowing* (with Rebecca Comay); and *Abolishing Freedom: A Plea for a Contemporary Use of Fatalism*.

ALAIN BADIOU is former chair of the École Normale Supérieure in Paris, France, and, with Gilles Deleuze, Michel Foucault, and Jean-François Lyotard, founder of the faculty of Philosophy at the University of Paris VIII.

HEATHER H. YEUNG is Reader in Literature (Poetry and Poetics) at the University of Dundee.

www.ingramcontent.com/pod-product-compliance
Lightning Source LLC
Chambersburg PA
CBHW020540030426
42337CB00013B/920